Beyond Economics

BEYOND ECONOMICS

Essays on Society, Religion, and Ethics

KENNETH E. BOULDING

Ann Arbor: The University of Michigan Press

Preface

The papers in this volume have been written at many different times and for many different occasions. Inevitably, therefore, the reader will find some repetitions and some gaps. The papers were designed to stand alone, and they may, indeed, be read in virtually any order. Nevertheless, there is a certain coherence among them, and taken together they reflect the process of transition from being a fairly pure economist to being a rather impure social philosopher. The first paper, indeed, "Is Economics Necessary?" which was given at the centennial celebration of the American Association for the Advancement of Science in 1948, catches me, as it were, in the moment of transition, defending both the purity of economics as a discipline and the necessity for moving forward into a more general social science. In a sense, all these essays represent rather errant missiles blasting off from the launching pad of economics in the general direction of a more unified social science. Whether they reach any destination is for the reader to decide.

I have divided the papers into four groups; within each, the articles are arranged chronologically. The first group is concerned essentially with the defense of economics and the economist's way of looking at things. The articles point out the importance of the evaluation process and of the economist's contribution to the theory of decision-making. They point out the importance of scarcity and the importance both of "natural liberty," in the sense of Adam Smith, and the need for a certain amount of artificial liberty in the shape of employment policy. They point both to the importance of the price mechanism and to the necessity for supplementing this with a proper matrix of government policy and integrative institutions. Thus, I see the contribution of economics as two-fold: first, the classical and neoclassical economics, which points out that the structure of relative values in society which determines the structure of terms of trade, that is, how much people get for what they give, is not arbitrary, but has a "normal" pattern in any given society which is closely related to the pattern of rates of substitution and production. This does not mean, of course, that the normal pattern is sacred, or that it cannot be interfered with. If it is interfered with, however, there will be certain real costs which must be justified by returns expressed in wider social objectives.

The second contribution of economics is macroeconomics, a heroically simplified model of the *total* economy which has transformed economic policies of governments the world over.

The second group of papers revolves around general systems and the applications of system concepts to society. The first three of these papers emerged mainly as a result of an interdisciplinary faculty seminar which I conducted at the University of Michigan entitled "Problems in the Integration of the Social Sciences" in the years from 1950–56. To the colleagues who participated in this seminar I owe a great debt, and much of my subsequent work has come out of it. The seminar was in itself a modest enterprise. Each year we took up a subject which was of interest to a number of different disciplines. I rounded up a few faculty members from different disciplines who were interested in the subject; we tried to teach each other something of what we knew, and to learn from each other, and out of this came the conviction in my own mind that something like general systems was possible, not so much in the sense of a single unified theory of the world but in the sense of a point of view and of a spectrum of theoretical systems spreading over related fields.

I have no pretensions to any special competence in the fields of natural and biological sciences and once the principle of general systems has been established it was reasonable to concentrate on their application in the area of social systems with which I was most familiar. The next three papers, therefore, represent applications of the general systems approach in various fields of social systems. The paper with the macabre title, "A Pure Theory of Death," is really an application to the international system; the paper on "The Relations of Economic, Political, and Social Systems" is an attempt at a fundamental taxonomy of genetic processes in social systems, and the paper on "Some Questions on the Measurement and Evaluation of Organization" is perhaps an overly ambitious attempt to interpret social evolution.

Out of these strivings towards a more general theory of social dynamics emerged a conviction that the key to the dynamic process in social evolution, and indeed in all evolution, was the concept of learning and the process of the increase of knowledge in the broadest possible sense of the word. The last three papers in this section therefore refer to the knowledge process as the crucial element in the dynamics of society.

The next group of papers on religion and ethics takes off in a somewhat different direction and reflect perhaps the impact of a more personal interest. I was brought up in the Methodist Church in England, I became a member of the Society of Friends when I was a student, and I have continued in active membership in that body ever since, what is now close to forty years. Religion, therefore, has been an important part of my personal life, and it would be surprising if this did not spill over into my professional interests. Ethics and religion are not, of course, universal partners, for each can exist without the other. Nevertheless, in the form of religion which I have practiced, they are very closely connected. Hence my interest in the ethical problems of economic life is closely related to my religious interests. It is perhaps this complex interaction between religion and ethics which leads to a certain paradox which may be detected in this aspect of my life, that I am both sectarian and ecumenical; religiously somewhat sectarian, enjoying the close fellowship of a small religious society, and being conscious of some separation from the world even of other churches, and at the same time participating in ecumenical activities in, for instance, the Department of Church and Economic Life of the National Council of Churches, of which I was a member for many years, and even in wider ecumenical outreach to communists and secularists. These papers represent the ecumenical aspect of my activity in that they concern themselves with the relationship of the disciplines of social science and the disciplines of religion.

The last group of papers I have headed with some hesitation "Towards Politics" as they represent in a sense a movement from economics through ethics towards a political philosophy. The three major dimensions of a political philosophy seem to me to be justice, freedom, and progress, and the first three essays in this section deal with these three concepts, though the title of the third essay may seem to disguise the fact. The political philosophy which underlies all these essays is nowhere, I think, clearly stated. It is a gap which perhaps the reader will have to close for himself and which I have by no means closed in my own mind. It is a philosophy which stresses the learning process as the essence of political development as well as of all other development, and it stresses the learning of community as perhaps the great moral arrow which gives meaning and direction to human history. It looks upon threats and coercion as a half-way house which may hopefully be left behind, and it looks forward shamelessly to a world in which war has been abolished, in which a realistic sense of community covers all of mankind, and in which the learning process that leads to the good life is open to all.

The last paper is a single representative of a considerable volume of my writing which deals with conflict, international systems, and peace research. This will perhaps some day merit a volume of its own. In the meantime, this final article in a sense sums up a good deal of my thinking of the last ten years, which has been inspired by the work of the Center for Research on Conflict Resolution.

As I look back over the past eighteen years I am enormously grateful to the University of Michigan for the encouragement which it provided and for the unusual group of people which it has gathered together on its faculty. It is now time to take stock and perhaps go in new directions; these essays reveal that these eighteen years have been something of a piece. To the people, both faculty members and students and friends too numerous to name, who have contributed to my learning processes I am grateful beyond what conventional words can say, and to my wife and my children, who have taught me more than anyone else, this volume is affectionately dedicated.

KENNETH E. BOULDING

Ann Arbor, Michigan

Contents

Part IV: Towards Politics 239

Economics

Is Economics Necessary?*

Being an economist, I can hardly be expected to answer "No" to the question that forms the title of this paper. My thesis is, however, that economics is necessary, not merely for the support of economists, but for the development and perhaps even for the survival of science in general and the civilization that supports it. I propose to consider particularly what justification there is for a separate discipline of economics, and what contribution this discipline makes to the general advancement of knowledge.

The social sciences are reputed, at least in popular imagination, to be less "successful" than the physical sciences. The "success" of a science is judged mainly by its ability to predict or to control future events in its field. For the common man, as for the operational philosopher, knowledge is identified with power, and knowing with know-how. By this standard even economics, which has a certain reputation as the most successful of the social sciences, makes a poor showing compared with the prediction of eclipses, the certainties of chemistry, and the miracles of genetics. This, we hasten to explain, is a result of the difficulties of the science, not of the inadequacies of the scientist. We sympathize with the wayward universe of the meteorologist even as we chafe at the waywardness of his predictions, and, if the predictions of the economist are even more wayward, it is because of the complex and unstable nature of the universe with which he deals. Moreover, the social scientist faces a problem which normally does not bother the nonsocial scientist, in that he is himself part of the field of his investigation. If the heavenly bodies were themselves moved by astronomers, or even if they were moved by temperamental angels who guided their behavior by the astronomers' predictions, the astronomers would find themselves in just as bad a fix as the economists. The bacteriologist who must stain his bacteria in order to see them would

* The Scientific Monthly 68, 4 (April 1949): 235–40.

This paper was presented at a symposium on "Sciences of Society" at the Centennial Celebration of the American Association for the Advancement of Science in Washington, D.C. in September 1948.

be in even worse trouble if his bacteria blushed when they were observed. Of course not even the astronomer seems to be exempt from observer trouble in these days of relativity, but in the case of the social sciences the trouble develops long before we approach the speed of light. Nowhere is the positivistic fiction of a dispassionate, objective observer wholly removed from the field of his observation more absurd than in the social sciences. The difference between the social and the other sciences, however, is merely one of degree, and as the nonsocial sciences run increasingly into observer trouble it may be that not merely the results but the methods also of the social sciences may be of interest to other scientists.

Economics has a certain reputation—not, I think, wholly undeserved—for being the most scientific of the social sciences. It does possess, I think, a larger body of analytical propositions that are widely accepted by competent persons than either sociology or political science. It also exhibits the marks of the history of a true science, in that it exhibits an orderly development toward greater and greater generality. The older theories—i.e., of the classical economists—can easily be formulated as special cases of the more general modern theory. This very internal consistency and success, however, has developed in some economists a certain spiritual pride which has injured the development of social science as a whole, and I think the profession is coming to realize more and more the necessity for trade among the various disciplines if further specialization is to be fruitful. We are reaching out on all sides today toward a unified social science—a regional federation, as it were, which must be accomplished before we can proceed to that great federation of all knowledge that is the ultimate task of the inquiring spirit. All the social sciences have much to learn from one another, and the same might be said of sciences of any kind.

I

Economics, like any other science, has two closely related parts— the pure science and the empirical science. Pure economics is a branch of logic or of mathematics (in these days there does not seem to be much distinction between them). It attempts to construct systems of hypothetical propositions, mainly of a qualitative nature (if A rises, B falls) relating certain "economic quantities" such as prices, wages, outputs, interest rates, etc. Such a system is called a "model," and the construction of such models is, of course, the characteristic activity of the "pure" part of any science. The nature of the models themselves, however, is determined mainly by the empirical content of the subject matter of the science. Thus, even though the model is an abstraction, not depending on any correspondence with empirical reality for its self-consistency, yet the act of model-building—except perhaps in pure mathematics—is not unrelated to the empirical interests of the model builder, and the usefulness of a model depends on the degree to which it helps in interpreting the complexities of the empirical world. The Keplerian theory of a single planet revolving around a sun is a good example of an "astronomical" model. It has no exact counterpart in reality, at least in our solar system, yet it derives interest and significance from the fact that it helps to interpret (by being capable of extension and generalization) the movements of the actual solar system. Similarly in economics the marginal analysis of the individual economic unit (planet!) or the Walrasian system of equations of general equilibrium of the price system under perfect markets (which corresponds somewhat to the Laplacian system in astronomy) is a "model" which derives interest from the light it throws on the workings of the intolerable complex of social relationships. Models which do not apparently abstract from an empirical universe may be called "non-Euclidian" models from the analogy with non-Euclidian geometry. Thus it would no doubt be possible to construct models of planetary systems assuming different laws of gravitational attraction, of momentum, etc. than those which seem to prevail in our system; indeed, I have no doubt this has been done. Nor are these non-Euclidian models mere idle exercises of an overactive mind; they may turn out to have more than an aesthetic value, as witness the significance of non-Euclidian geometries in modern physics. In economics also there is something to be said for model-building for its own sake, and there is no need whatever to stick to the assumptions of the elementary textbook. Economics is in no way bound to such assumptions as profit maximization; there never has been an economic man even in economics, except as a very first approximation, and by means of the indifference curve analysis economics has increasingly liberated itself from any narrowness of assumption. The *methods* of economic analysis would apply just as well to a Franciscan economy as to a Benthamite! Nevertheless, the *interests* of the model builder are likely to be determined to a considerable extent by the empirical world in which he lives, and even by the practical problems he faces. It is no accident, for instance, that the depression of the thirties was the scene of a great deal of theoretical activity centering around the problem of unemployment. Similarly, in the elementary theory of the firm, the assumption is made that the firm selects that position of the variables under its control which results in the maximization of some measure of money profits. As a first approximation, this assumption yields useful results. But it is quite possible, and indeed necessary, to go beyond it, and to take account of more complex motivations, such as the desire to be important, or to be well regarded, or to obey the dictates of conscience, or even to be liquid.

It is not generally realized, I think, how far economics has gone in the direction of becoming a generalized theory of choice. Economics begins as an attempt to explain the magnitudes and movements of certain quantities, such as prices, wages, outputs, sales, and so on. Very early in its development it became clear that these quantities cannot be treated as an independent world of their own, for they are thrown up as a result of the whole complex of human choices operating within the strait jacket of a niggardly natural environment. Thus even in Adam Smith we find the explanation of wage differences in terms of what might be called the nonmonetary advantages of the various occupations; and little more than a hundred years later we find Wicksteed illustrating the principles of value theory with reference to the problem of how high a cliff one would dive off to save a mother-in-law, or how much family prayers should be shortened to speed a parting guest to the train—problems that are a long way from what is usually thought of as economic. Nevertheless, it is an inevitable logic that has turned the study of prices into a theory of value, for the price system is simply one reflection of the general problem of "scarcity," and the choice between nuts and apples differs only in its simplicity from the choice between income and leisure, between freedom and security, between love and power, between color and form, or between better and worse. Value, in the sense of what we have to give up of one thing in order to get a unit of another—i.e., as a "transformation ratio"—is a phenomenon we meet in every conceivable branch of human activity, for wherever there is limitation, wherever there is choice, wherever we cannot have our cake and eat it, there the value phenomenon pops up. The novelist balancing up his chapters, the painter balancing his picture, the general apportioning his troops, the preacher arranging his service, the professor preparing his course, the cook planning a menu, the government formulating a policy, are all of them facing essentially the same "economic" problem as in the apportionment of time or the spending of money. Wherever resources are limited, choice is necessary and value raises its earthy head. It may be, as Wordsworth says, that "High Heaven rejects the lore of nicely calculated less or more" (i.e., economics), but, even if this is the case (and Wordsworth's authority is by no means unimpeachable), it is merely because High Heaven is presumably possessed of unlimited resources. In some fields the "less or more" may be less nicely calculated than in the market place, though one sometimes wonders after studying the exotic behavior of banks, corporations, and labor unions whether these phenomena could not be profitably studied with the techniques of the cultural anthropologist. Custom, habit, tradition, and ritual play an important part in the day-to-day activity of the most solemnly economic and ostensibly money-making institution. On the other hand, the balancing of advantage against disadvantage which is the mark of the "economizing" process is found among the most primitive tribes, the most careless bohemians, and the most other-worldly saints. Indeed, it may well be that the saint—who knows what spiritual goods he wants and who goes after them regardless of how many norms of conventional behavior he shatters—is closer to the pattern of economic man than is the frock-coated banker whose watchword is respectability (a thoroughly primitive, anthropological concept) and whose walk of life is hedged about with innumerable barriers of established custom.

Economics is significant, then, not merely because it investigates an important slice of life in the market place, but because the phenomena which emerge in a relatively clear and quantitative form in the market place are also found in virtually all other human activities. Hence, economic life itself, in the narrow sense of that part of human activity that is concerned with buying, selling, producing, and consuming, is a "model" of the whole vast complex of human activity and experience, and the principles which are discovered in a clear and quantitative form in the market may be applied to the understanding of apparently quite unrelated phenomena in biology, art, religion, morals, politics, and the whole complex structure of human relationships. I do not mean, of course, that economic principles are *sufficient* to the understanding of the complex universe of reality; but they are, I believe, a necessary implement in the inquirer's tool chest.

It is also true, of course, that principles which come to the clearest expression in the study of other subject matters are of great importance in the interpretation of so-called "economic" phenomena. The concept of an ecological system, which was developed first in the biological sciences—i.e., of a system of populations of various things, in which the equilibrium size and the movement of each population are dependent on the size of other populations—is an interpretive principle of the utmost value in the social sciences. Just as a pond develops an equilibrium population of frogs, fishes, bacteria, algae, and the like, all in subtle competitive and cooperative relationships with one another, so society is a great pond, developing equilibrium populations of Baptist churches, post offices, gas stations, families, counties, states, wheat farmers, chickens, and so on, which also exhibit complex co-operative and competitive relations one with another. The concept of mechanical equilibrium, both static and dynamic, has also had an immense impact—indeed, too great an impact—on the social sciences. Wherever we find a potential difference producing a current or flow by overcoming a resistance, we find something like Ohm's law, exhibited in its purest form in the study of electricity, but valuable as an interpretive principle when we study the flow of goods or of resources in response to price differences (economic potential) against the resistance imposed by costs of transport. In the theory of electrical circuits we may find clues to some baffling phenomena connected with the circuit flow of money.

Within the social sciences themselves, concepts which have been developed in anthropology, such as systems of ritualistic and customary behavior, and concepts which have been developed in sociology and social psychology, such as the crisis-adjustment patterns in family relationships, are all applicable to the subject matter of economics.

Indeed, I see the great empire of human knowledge, not as a conglomeration of independent and perhaps even warring kingdoms, each cultivating its own little field of subject matter by its own methods and each living wholly on its own produce, but as a great Republic of the mind, comprised, it is true, of subdivisions such as Physics, Chemistry, Economics, Botany, and the like, the boundaries of which are, like the boundaries of political states, partly the result of historic accident and partly the result of the lay of the land, but all uniting and cooperating in a common task of producing and exchanging the most precious of all commodities, and, indeed, exchanging not only the results of their labors, but exchanging also the tools which the special requirements of each field have perfected.

II

I propose to devote the remainder of this article, therefore, to a brief discussion of the contribution which the methods of economics may be able to make to other fields.

Recent developments in economics in the theory of oligopoly have an important bearing on problems of political science. It is perhaps significant that there was no representative from political science in this symposium. In a day when civilization itself is threatened by our inability to solve an essentially political problem (the abolition of war), it is tragic that so little fundamental thinking is being done in political science. Even the World Federalists—the only group who seem to be intellectually active in this field at all—seem to have got little further than the eighteenth century. It may well be that a significant revival in political thought will come out of the economics of oligopoly, where we are concerned essentially with problems of *strategy*—i.e., situations in which the choices of each person or organization involved depend upon their expectations regarding the choices of the others. It may be that the present bankruptcy of the national state, which can provide us with neither security, justice, peace, nor honor, is closely associated with the duopolistic character of international rivalry. There are marked similarities between the power struggles of oligopolistic firms and the power struggles of states: price wars and sales wars exhibit in a simplified form many of the essential problems of that most destestable of sciences, military science. There is no more striking contrast than between the resourcefulness and inventiveness which is shown in dealing with the "war" problem in the business world, with its multitudinous forms of agreement and federation, and the sterility and ritualistic rigidity of the political world.

Economics can also make an important contribution to those sciences in which general equilibria or a great multiplicity of interconnected relationships are characteristic of the subject matter. In economics, as in astronomy, the experimental method is almost impossible. We cannot simplify our universe, as the chemist or the physicist does, by the artificial creation of conditions in which virtually all factors but the ones we are investigating are excluded. We cannot take a businessman or a household and expose them first to one set of prices and then to another set to see what happens. Our subject matter is presented to us in a manner that is for the most part not within our control; there is no recipe for unscrambling in fact the magnificent omelette of social experience. We are always faced with an overwhelming and baffling multiplicity, and because of the very dominance of the problem we have been forced to devise methods for handling it.

These methods fall into three groups. There is first the *ceteris paribus* approach, identified mainly with the name of Marshall, which is in a sense a method of intellectual experiment, involving the isolation of a single problem by the assumption that all variables other than those investigated are held constant. This method has yielded valuable results in a limited sphere, and is a necessary prerequisite to the solution of more difficult problems. Nevertheless, it also has its dangers, especially the danger of overgeneralization from the particular to the general case. Thus the fact that a fall in the wages of carpenters is

likely to lead to a rise in the amount of employment offered to them
by no means implies that the remedy for general unemployment is
general wage reduction. It is easy to fall into fallacies of composition
when using this method, but in spite of its dangers it remains a necessary implement in the economist's, and indeed in any scientist's,
tool bag.

The second method is one that is familiar in the physical sciences,
the method of simultaneous equations. In economics this is associated
chiefly with the name of Leon Walras and the Lausanne school. It is
based on the proposition that any system of n variables, each of which
can be written as a function of all the others, yields n of these equations which may be capable of solution to yield values of the variables
each of which is consistent with every other. The difficulty of the
method is that unless we know a good deal about the form of the
assumed functional relationships we cannot be positive that the system
has a "real" solution, or that it does not have many real solutions. It
may even have solutions that are mathematically correct but economically meaningless, such as negative prices. Consequently, if we
except the pioneering work of Leontieff at Harvard, the method has
not been particularly fruitful of results in economics, in spite of its
superior elegance and generality.

The third method is that associated with the name of Keynes, now
frequently called that of "macroeconomics." This consists essentially
in using large aggregates of economic variables as the basic parameters
of simplified models, the exact properties of which can be fairly easily
determined. In a sense this combines the simplicity and fruitfulness
of the Marshallian approach with the generality of the Walrasian.
Marshall's method is admirable in discussing the forces that determine
the price and output of, say, limburger cheese, but it cannot deal with
the problems of the system as a whole. Walras deals with the system
as a whole, but at such a level of generality and abstraction that
practically nothing can be said about it except that it exists. Keynes,
by taking the system as a whole, but ruthlessly lumping it into large
aggregates, the relationships of which he explores, affects in a sense a
combination of the virtues of both the other methods. The macroeconomic models are simple enough to be handled, and yet cover the
whole system. Not that the macroeconomic method is without its own
dangers. Aggregates like "the national income," or "the level of employment," or "the price level" are all heterogeneous conglomerations,
and there is danger, particularly for the more mathematical and less
philosophical users of the technique, of neglecting the *structure* of
these aggregates. It is fatally easy to write "Let the National Income

be Y and the Price Level be P" and straightway to get so deliciously involved in the manipulation of our Y's and P's that we forget that they are not simple aggregates but have a complex structure which may well be relevant to the problem in hand. This "fallacy of aggregation" is a common one; it is at the root of most of the fallacies of Marxism, with its assumption of homogeneous classes; of Nationalism, with its assumption of homogeneous nations; and it even accounts for the spectacular lack of prophetic success among the brighter young economists. Nevertheless, for all its dangers, the macroeconomic method has led to a revolution in economic thought, the end of which is by no means visible, and it creates a discipline and habit of mind which might easily create revolutions in other sciences as well. I suspect that the natural scientists are also subject to both the fallacy of composition and the fallacy of aggregation; that they are much too uncritical of their basic taxonomic systems, much too prone to generalize on the basis of particular experience, and too little sensitive to the abominable interrelatedness of things! It would be a valuable experience for any scientist to familiarize himself thoroughly with what may be called the "macroeconomic paradoxes"—the propositions which are true in individual experience but which are quite untrue for society as a whole. Thus an individual can increase his money stock by "hoarding"—i.e., spending less money than he receives: but the attempt on the part of all individuals to hoard does not result in general "hoarding;" it merely decreases the total volume of money payments. An individual can get rid of money by spending it: a society cannot. For an individual, expenditure and receipts are two very different things: for society they are exactly the same thing, every expenditure being another person's receipt. An individual can "save"— i.e., increase his net worth—by not consuming as much as his income. If everyone tries to do this the result may not be an increase in society's capital but a decline in income and employment. In distribution these paradoxes abound. A trade union may raise the wages of its members: it is very doubtful whether trade unions as a whole can raise wages as a share of the total income. Profits are determined by the level of investment, not by the wage bargain; the more business distributes in dividends, the greater will be the profits out of which dividends can be paid. The macroeconomic world is a Wonderland full of widow's cruses and Danaïd jars, where nothing is what it seems, where things do not add up, where the collective result of individual decisions is something totally different from the sum of these decisions. Moreover, this is the real world: yet it cannot be understood by any generalization from individual experience; it can only be understood through the kind of intellectual discipline which economics provides. Moreover, it is not only in economics that this topsy-turviness prevails. In politics prohibiton leads to drunkenness, the quest for national security leads to national destruction, the more literate we make people the less educated they become, and the conquest of nature by the physical sciences leads to ever-increasing misery, fear, and degradation.

III

I have not attempted in this paper to defend economics by reference to the importance of its subject matter, as that can hardly be a matter of question. Was Marx right in supposing that capitalism has an inherent contradiction in it? What is the necessary minimum of governmental intervention into economic life? Can inflations and depressions be remedied? How far can the distribution of income be equalized without destroying the roots of economic progress? These and like questions cannot possibly be answered without serious study, and the name of this serious study is economics. One needs no more reminder of its necessity. It is trite, but frighteningly true, to say that the survival of this present civilization depends, not on the further development of natural science, but on the solution of certain serious intellectual problems in the social sciences.

In conclusion, I should like to urge the necessity for the study of economics not only for its conclusions and methods, but also for the state of mind it produces. In the old Cambridge tripos, economics—or, to give it its grander title, political economy—was listed as a Moral Science. For all the attempts of our positivists to dehumanize the sciences of man, a moral science it remains. Its central problem is the problem of value: and value is but a step from virtue. Every science, like every craft, imposes certain of its marks on its practitioners. I would hesitate to suggest, especially to members of the AAAS, that geologists grow like their rocks, chemists like their smells, or even astronomers like their heavens. I cannot forbear, however, from quoting from Professor Robbins, of the London School of Economics: "It is not an exaggeration to say that, at the present day, one of the main dangers to civilisation arises from the inability of minds trained in the natural sciences to perceive the difference between the economic and the technical." In the lurid twilight of science in which we live, when it has gained the whole world and lost its own soul, when it is everywhere prostituted to special interests, whether of the dairy farmers, the steel industry, or the national state, when the search for truth is subordinated to the lust for power, it is not altogether an accident that it is in the social science departments that the occasional voice crying in the wilderness is most likely to be heard. In a world of technicians, it is the economist who raises the cry that the technically most efficient is not necessarily, or even usually, the socially most efficient; that the best cow is not the one that gives the most milk; the best business is not the one that makes the most profits; the best army is not the one that creates the most havoc; and, above all, that the best training is not the best education. In a day when self-interest, nationalism, totalitarianism, militarism, and a dreadful pride threaten our very existence, economics points always toward the general interest, looks toward a free-trading world society, claims that the business of living even in a complex society can be accomplished with a small minimum of police coercion, urges that plenty is the source of power and war the greatest enemy of plenty, and by its very failures induces that humility for lack of which we perish.

An Economist's View of the Manpower Concept*

When one has to raise a lonely voice in denunciation of a respected object one has the choice of two methods. One can keep the bad news till the last and then make an exit before the tomatoes begin to fly, or one can apply the shock technique and stun the audience into insensibility by letting the cat out of the bag at the beginning. It is the second of these alternatives which I propose to follow. Let me begin then by saying that I find the whole manpower concept repulsive, disgusting, dangerous, fascistic, communistic, incompatible with the ideals of liberal democracy, and unsuitable company for the minds of the young. This at least gives me something to defend.

The manpower concept is basically, I suspect, an engineering concept, and one of the main problems of society is to keep engineers in a decently subordinate position. It contemplates society as having a single well defined end which is to be pursued with *efficiency*. Society is conceived as a great machine, feeding Manpower in at one end and grinding out maximum quantities of the Single Well Defined End, which I propose to call the SWED, at the other. The manpower problem is, then, that of getting as much SWED per unit of Manpower as possible. The efficiency of the society is measured by the SWED/Manpower ratio, and, of course, we want to maximize this. I suspect, however, that the ardent proponents of Manpower want to do much more than maximize Efficiency. They actually want to maximize not merely Efficiency, but the Output of SWED. SWED is the thing, not men, and the more SWED the better. Rout people out of their beds, abolish arm chairs and hammocks, away with lolling on the beach

* *Proceedings of the Conference on the Utilization of Scientific and Professional Manpower* (New York: Columbia University Press, 1954), pp. 11–26.

This paper was presented at a conference on The Utilization of Scientific and Professional Manpower at Arden House, The Harriman Campus, Columbia University, October 7–11, 1953.

or anywhere else, down with unused resources, with the vacant gaze and the cowlike meditation—to work, to arms, to something, increase Manpower, get out the SWED.

All this is fine and rousing. The only trouble with SWED is that it does not exist. There is no Single Well Defined End of Society, measured in bushels or gollops or even dollars. There are a great many different ends of a great many different people, some of which are competitive, some complementary, and some independent. Moreover, there is no such thing as manpower, save as a hot abstraction to be handled with long tongs. Not Manpower, but Men—with this cry I propose to arouse the populace to the threat which menaces them. I repeat, not manpower, but men: men in their infinite variety and sacredness, in their complex personalities and unfolding desires. Man as Manpower is all very well for a slave society, where man is a domestic animal, to be used for ends which are alien to him. But in a free society man is not manpower; he is not a donkey chained to a great churn for the production of SWED. He is a free being, the lord of society and not its slave, the creator of demand as well as of supply. In these days we are all in danger of being overcome by the great Feudal myth of Society, a frowning overlord to whom we are all too subservient, even if he has the impressive title of Lord National Interest or even Lord Social Interest.

I am sure that I cannot go on ranting in this vein for long without being called an anarchist, a rank, selfish individualist, or even perhaps an economist. I must confess that I like the anarchists and find them much more sympathetic than the socialists, but I must confess also that I have never quite been able to make the grade as an anarchist. There do seem to be, I regretfully conclude whenever I think about it, certain minimum functions of those attempted monopolies of coercion which arrogate to themselves the name of "governments." It will be useful, however, to start with a model of society which is as close to anarchy as we can get, to see what the "manpower" problem looks like under these conditions. Then we may be able to detect certain defects in the model which will lead to clarification of the nature of the minimum functions of government.

Let us suppose then a society in which the functions of government are confined to the definition and protection of private property. What does the "manpower" problem mean under these circumstances? It is a purely theoretical problem, of course, as nobody proposes to do anything about it. Nevertheless there is a theoretical problem, and it is an interesting one. It consists of two questions. The first is what determines the distribution of the population both geographically and between occupational groups—that is, what determines the number of doctors, dentists, shoemakers, and so on, in the various geographical divisions in which the society may be divided. The second is in a sense contained in the first, but is worth stating separately, and it is, what determines how great a proportion of its resources the society devotes to investment in human capital—i.e., to education and training.

The answer to these questions was really stated by Adam Smith, in two famous chapters of his *Wealth of Nations* which are almost the only part of that great work to remain almost completely un- scathed and unmodified by the criticisms and discoveries of a hundred and seventy-seven years. If a people are free to move, either geo- graphically or between occupations, then they will move if the gains from moving outweigh the cost. The gains from moving are the *total* differential advantages of the alternative places or occupations. In the case of movements which involve little or no investment and in which the returns are immediate, a simple balance of gain over loss is all that is required. The gains and losses here, it must be emphasized, are *total* gains and losses, not merely monetary or even those which may be measured in terms of money. Thus, a man might reasonably feel that he would not want to move to a situation or occupation with a larger *money* income than the one he now enjoys, because of the differences in the non-monetary advantages of the various occupations —prestige, pleasantness of work, burden of responsibility, non- marketable goods such as climate and scenery, and so on.

We would then say that the *total* advantages of the two situations or occupations were equal. It is clear that if there were no difficul- ties or costs of movement of any kind between occupations or locations, that the population would tend to distribute itself in such a way as to make the total advantages of all occupations and situations equal. This is the principle which has been christened the "principle of equal advantage." It must be observed, of course, that when the total advantages of all occupations and locations are equal, the monetary advantages are likely to be very different. The total advantage of any situation is the sum of the monetary and the non-monetary advan- tages. If the total advantages of all situations are equal, then we would expect to find that the monetary advantages—wages or real incomes— would be high where the net non-monetary advantage is low, and low where the net non-monetary advantage is high. Thus, other things being equal (and I shall add later that they seldom are), we would expect pleasant, honorable, and decent occupations to be rather poorly paid, and unpleasant, dishonorable, and indecent occupations to be rather well paid. In the interests of charity, prudence, and friendship, I refrain from giving examples.

The principle of equal advantage must, of course, be modified when there are obstacles, natural or artificial, to the movement of people between occupations or locations. Differences in total advantage may be thought of as different levels of potential, like the level of water in different tanks. Potential differences tend to be eliminated by movement, but if the movement is impeded by resistances then the potential differences can persist for long periods or even indefinitely. The "costs" of movement should not perhaps be thought of as resistances, but as subtractions from the total advantages of the various occupations. Nevertheless, there are real resistances to movement which establish permanent differences even in the total advantages of different occupations and locations.

There are, for instance, certain occupations which require very scarce natural abilities. These abilities represent, as it were, a fence around the occupation preventing all but the most agile from getting into it. Under such circumstances the number inside the fence will be small enough to make the total advantages, on anybody's scale of preferences, high compared to the advantages of outside occupations. Yet, because of the natural scarcity of the peculiar abilities required, there is no net movement into the occupation sufficient to equalize the advantages. There may also be "artificial" barriers to entry into certain occupations or locations, in the form of high professional entrance requirements, high trade union initiation fees, "caste" relationships whereby only those connected by family with the existing tenants of the occupations are allowed to enter it, immigration restrictions into favored countries, and so on. Any of these restrictions on entry will prevent equilibrating movements in the form of *transfers* of individuals from locations or occupations of low total advantage to those of high total advantage.

Here, however, it may be well to notice a certain qualification introduced by the fact that people are born and die. We must not think of the distribution of the human population as consisting of apportioning a fixed population of unchanging individuals among various categories. The proportion and the absolute numbers of people in different occupations or locations change not merely because individuals *change* their situation, but because there are various rates of exit by death and entry by birth or by training. It is instructive in this connection to consider the theory of a pure caste society in which every occupation is a caste recruited only by birth and vacated only by death, and in which no individual can move from the occupation into which he is born. It might be thought that in such a society there is absolutely no principle regulating the proportion of people in different occupations. Such, however, is not the case. We can still appeal to the famous subsistence theory, and suppose that in each caste the population will increase by natural increase as long as the returns to the occupation permit it, but that in each caste also, as the numbers increase the returns will tend to diminish, and, when returns have diminished to the point where the population within the caste no longer grows, equilibrium has been reached. In such a society, then, the average income of each caste in equilibrium will be that at which it will just reproduce itself. If the only checks on the increase of population in any caste are starvation and misery, as in the classical Malthusian model, then the population will grow until it is sufficiently starved and miserable to prevent continuing growth. If, however, economic or other considerations can prevent the increase in population before the physical subsistence level is reached, then, of course, by voluntarily restricting its population a caste in such a society could maintain high levels of income indefinitely.

Most actual societies lie somewhere between the "pure caste" society and the absolutely "free" society. The "defense" of any group which maintains advantages higher than other groups then consists partly in the restriction of their natural increase, partly in the encouragement of emigration from the group (consider, for instance, the importance of younger sons in the establishment of colonial empires), and partly in the discouragement of immigration into the group. In addition, there may also be efforts directed toward increasing the demand for the product of the group, which would permit any given size of group to obtain higher advantages.

The principle of equal advantage, suitably modified by considerations of immobility, is sufficient to determine the distribution of real income among the different groups of society. It is not in itself sufficient to determine the number or the proportion of the population in each group. Such can very easily be determined, however, if we introduce a function for each group relating the total number of people in the group with the total real income of the group. This function, it should be observed, is then sufficient to determine both the average and the marginal real income of the group. If, for instance, we know that for a certain group 100 members would receive a total income of $500,000 and 101 members would receive a total income of $503,000, we can readily calculate the average income and also the marginal income for each size of group: a group of 100 would have an average income of $5,000, and the income of the 101st member would be $3,000. Suppose we call this function the "total real income function" for each group.

If the equilibrium of the distribution of the population is to be stable, the marginal income function must be a decreasing function—that is to say, the increase in the numbers in each group must result in a decline in the marginal income of the group. Otherwise, the movement of population between groups, whether by natural increase or decrease or by immigration and emigration, will have perverse effects on the potential differences which gave rise to it. Thus, suppose we have two groups, one of which enjoys a larger marginal total advantage than the other. We should expect a shift in the distribution of population so that the more advantaged group will grow relative to the less advantaged group. If this movement, however, results in the richer group getting still richer as it grows larger, and the poorer group getting still poorer as it grows smaller, obviously the movement is carrying us away from equilibrium, and the movement in response to the gap between the prosperity of the two groups is actually widening the gap rather than lowering it. Only if the transfer of relative numbers makes the rich poorer and the poor richer will it work toward a stable equilibrium. This does not mean, as we have seen, that in equilibrium all groups are in fact equally rich, only that the differences among them are not sufficient to overcome the resistances to change.

Let us inquire further, then, into the nature and determinants of the total income function for each group. Let us assume first, what is not actually quite true, that the marginal non-monetary advantages for each group are independent of the numbers in the group. Then the marginal total advantage depends only on the marginal real income. This in turn depends on two other factors: the productivity or efficiency of the group in producing its own product, and the "terms of trade" of the group—that is, the rate of exchange between its own product (which it sells) and other products which it buys. Thus, the total real income of the group is the *product* of its own output and the "price" or purchasing power of its output in terms of other things. If we take money as representing the "other things," it is clear that the income of a group is equal to the physical output of its product multiplied by the price of that product, and that the group's income can rise either because its physical output increases or because the price (i.e. the purchasing power per unit) of its product increases.

Why, then, should the marginal income of a group decline as its size increases? The answer must be found either in a decline in physical productivity, in the sense that successive additions to the population of the group result in successively smaller additions to physical product, or it must be found in a decline in the price or (marginal) purchasing power of the product as the amount which has to be sold increases. Both these things are likely to happen when the size of the group increases beyond a certain critical point. When the group is very small the movements may be reversed. That is to say, the growth of very small groups may actually result in an increase in their marginal physical productivity as an increase in numbers permits better organization, greater internal division of labor, and so on. It is even possible that at small volumes of sales, increased sales result in better terms of trade, again largely because of the greater specialization, or, perhaps, because of dynamic influences such as the growth of habits of consumption, and the reinforcement of demand by experience. Nevertheless, these upward movements cannot persist indefinitely. A point must come eventually when "diminishing returns" set in, both in the form of decreasing marginal physical productivity as the group grows large, and worsening terms of trade as its sales grow larger.

Suppose, then, for each group we know how much product will be produced at each level of population of the group. Suppose, also, that we know at what price each quantity of produce can be sold, so that we know also what will be the *value* in dollars or some other measure of each quantity of product. Then we know for each group what will be its total income at each level of population, and by comparing the total income at two adjacent levels of population we can find the *marginal* income at each level of population. Now, given the total population of the society, we can find how it must be distributed among the various groups so that the marginal incomes in each group are *equal*. This might be described as the first approximation to equilibrium. We can then approach a second approximation by showing how some groups maintain higher marginal incomes than others by being able to restrict their populations, either by natural or by artificial means.

A meaningful *equilibrium* distribution of the population among various groups is possible even if there is no single end of society, simply through the ecological interaction of the innumerable desires of innumerable people. What I have been describing is, of course, the famous "invisible hand" of Adam Smith—this extraordinary process in the operation of a market society whereby resources are in fact apportioned in what seems to be a fairly reasonable way, not by planning from above, not by the government telling anybody what he has to do or how he has to do it, but by the persistent pressure of the principle of equal advantage whereby if anybody knows of a better hole he goes to it if he can. This is the great principle which Adam Smith calls "natural liberty."

If now we are to justify governmental intervention in the allocation of human resources we must show in what regard either the equilibrium, or the process of moving toward the equilibrium of "natural liberty" is undesirable according to fairly well defined standards of judgment. That is, we must justify divergences from the state of splendid anarchy. Some divergences are, of course, fairly easy to justify in principle, though the question of *how much* divergence is desirable is always a matter of dispute. Not even the most anarchistic of liberal economists would deny the existence of certain "collective wants" which the mere apparatus of the market does not, and cannot, provide. There are certain "overheads" of society which are difficult to charge for on the basis of service rendered to individuals, mainly because of the cost of collection, as in the case of roads, or because of certain undesirable sociological relations which would be introduced by too strict adherence to the principles of the market, as in the case of police and justice, or because there are certain economies of monopoly, as in the case of the post office and certain public utilities. The case for the market, or at least for the abolition of state monopolies, is stronger in some of these instances than is generally imagined, but I am not disposed to argue these cases at the moment.

It should be observed, however, that the provision of these collective wants is generally accomplished through the system of public *finance*, not by any system of forced labor. That is to say, the state distorts the "natural" system of distribution of the labor force by providing a monetary demand for certain products and services. If inflation is to be avoided, of course, this monetary demand on the part of the state must be offset by a contraction of monetary demand on the part of private persons and institutions, a contraction which is generally accomplished through taxation. What we have here is the state nosing its way into the general system of equilibrium, attracting resources to itself, but not essentially destroying the operation of the principle of equal advantage. Men go into occupations which they would not otherwise have done because it has been made advantageous for them to do so through the financial power of the state, not because they have been forced unwillingly into these occupations by the threat of the police power.

We can see the distinction clearly if we contrast the feudal method of road building through the corvée—i.e., forced labor on the roads— with the modern method of road building through finance, i.e., through finding money to hire people to work on the roads. In both cases road building requires the withdrawal of resources from other uses. In the case of the corvée, this withdrawal is accomplished directly by the whip. In modern states the withdrawal is accomplished indirectly, either because the consumption of the mass of the people is restricted in some degree by taking money away from them through taxes or loans, or because it is restricted through inflation.

On the whole, the movement of the past few hundred years has been away from the "manpower" concept of directed or forced allocation of human resources toward the "financial" concept of the organization of human resources through the market. Slavery has been abolished. Serfdom has been largely abolished, corvées and press gangs have vanished. Only in one conspicuous area of life has this process been reversed. The last great stronghold of the manpower concept is, of course, in the armed forces. The growth of conscription represents a striking reversal of the movement toward a society of natural liberty, and it is a reversal which unfortunately seems to be gathering momentum. Conscription, like the corvée, is an attempt to satisfy a collective want by the exercise of the police power (the threat of legal penalties, prison, etc.) rather than by the financial power. The status of the conscript is technically similar to that of a temporary serf—he cannot leave his unchosen occupation before his time is up; he is outside the regular law and is rather at the mercy of his feudal superiors in the officer class. The conscript is "exploited" in the sense that because of the exercise of the police power it is possible to employ him at a much lower wage than would be necessary to attract him to his occupation in a free society. It is a device for forcing a major part of the economic burden of national defense on the unexempted young, and as such inevitably results in gross anomalies and inequalities. It is unquestionably the most disastrous social invention of the past two hundred years, and I find it difficult to forgive the French for inventing it. They have, however, had their reward. Where it has been long practiced, it results in an almost universal corruption of society, a decline in its morals and in its morale, a decay of that unfeigned and unforced love of country which is the only sure foundation even of military success, and the weakening of that exercise of free choice and the voluntary spirit which is the prerequisite of a healthy democracy.

Let me now try to apply some of these principles to the problem of the education and training of the professional classes. Suppose we return for a moment to the model of natural liberty, and see how a professional class arises and how its numbers are determined, in case we might be under the illusion that if government did not intervene there would be no doctors to cure us or parsons to bury us. Clearly, given a demand on the part of existing groups for professional services, then, if the numbers in the professions are "too small," there will be high remuneration for professional people and their numbers will grow until the net advantages of the professions are low enough to prevent any addition to their population. If there are so many professional people that their marginal remuneration is too small to make it worth their while entering the professions, recruitment will drop off, some will transfer themselves bodily to more advantageous occupations, and the numbers will decline. There seems to be nothing here which would lead to a breakdown of the principle of equal advantage.

There are, however, some complications. Entering the professions requires *investment* in education. The equilibrium value of professional incomes is that in which the excess over non-professional incomes is just sufficient to attract enough recruits in over the "wall" of the long and expensive education. We can calculate the rate of return on investment in education roughly—indeed, it has frequently been done. The greater the excess of professional incomes over non-professional, and the less the cost of education, the greater the rate of return. If the rate of return is "too great," many people will be induced to invest in professional education, and the numbers in the professions will increase and the differential advantage of the professions will fall. Here, again, it seems as if the introduction of the investment concept really makes no difference to the general principle: so far there seems to be no reason for regarding the professions as a "problem" requiring active intervention of government.

Now, however, I feel myself pursued by a host of indignant voices. What—am I arguing against education, that most sacred of all cows! Would I indeed leave education to private enterprise, to be enjoyed only by those whose parents can afford to pay! Do I believe in aristocracy, in a class society, in the perpetuation of privilege, in the shocking waste of talent and ability which goes on, even in our society, among the poor? If I can make my voice heard above the cries of indignation, I hasten to say Nay, indeed Nay! I would be indeed ungrateful if I spurned the very educational ladder up which I myself, by dint of being good at passing examinations, have scrambled. I have been making an extreme case, because it is comforting, to me at any rate, to realize that in spite of all the clamors that Something should be Done about Everything, if Nothing is Done about Anything at least the world will not come to an end, and, indeed, might have a better fighting chance of survival than it has now.

Let us then consider exactly *why* Something should be Done, which is the same question as why the equilibrium of natural liberty is not the *best* position possible. There are several good reasons why a position of natural liberty might not be optimal. In the first place, there may be a divergence between perceived private advantage and actual social advantage. In the market economy it is perceived private advantage which is the motive force, the potential difference which orders the distribution of resources. Perceived private advantage may differ from some reasonable if vague concept of social advantage for several reasons. There may be ignorance—i.e., a divergence between perceived and actual private advantage. There are situations in which ignorance is bliss, but this is probably not one of them. What we mean by ignorance in this situation is that there are people who do not now think it worth while to change their jobs or to undertake investment in education, but who, if they did these things, would finally be glad they had done them. If people are ignorant of their ignorance, there clearly cannot be any demand on their part for knowledge, and there is a clear case here for an omniscient government to undertake the provision of occupational and educational information, and a good case even for real governments doing so.

In the second place, there may be private monopoly, in which differential advantages are perceived but in which the organization of the professional group is designed to limit numbers and so perpetuate the differential advantages. Most of the professions are highly suspect in this regard, especially the medical profession, where monopolistic restriction of entry under the guise of high professional standards has been so great that it has resulted in the development of a number of sub-professions ranging from the osteopath to the Christian Science Practitioner who undercut the regular medicos in the sickness market. The most foolish and public spirited of all professions in this regard is, of course, my own. The teaching profession not merely fails to restrict its numbers, except perhaps through the relatively trivial device of the Ph.D., but actually encourages young people to enter it by the provision of scholarships and financial assistance of all kinds. Where these private professional monopolies exist, there is a clear case for undermining them by government action.

The third reason for a possible divergence between natural liberty and public interest is the existence of non-appropriable or unidentifiable benefits or misfortunes. This is the problem which is generally discussed in economics under the name of "external economies," positive or negative. What this means is that there are certain costs and returns which do not get into the private accounting system but which nevertheless must be included in any public appraisal of the contribution of any group or occupation. The man who beautifies his garden improves the value of his neighbors' property, but there is generally no way in which he can collect from the neighbors. The cost of collection from the enjoyers of some benefit or the perpetrators of some evil may be too great to make the attempt worth while, if the benefits and evils are very diffuse. This argument is particularly strong in the case of investment in education, where the benefits are great and yet are much too diffuse to be appropriated. This, perhaps, is the strongest reason for supposing that the mechanism of the market cannot be relied upon to yield an optimum position.

The fourth reason is that there may be inadequate arrangements in some fields, notably education, for the *finance* of investment. Investment in professional education is usually extremely profitable. One would think, therefore, that the impecunious but able student should be able to finance his education by means of loans, for, if rates of interest are moderate, the rate of return on his investment in education will be so large that he will still be much better off even after repaying the loan. Here, however, what might be called social risk and individual risk differ, and an investment which is clearly profitable for society is risky and difficult for the private supplier of funds, because of the difficulty of knowing just who, in advance, are the people who will justify the investment. I confess that I do not see any fundamental reason why specialized lending institutions in the finance of education should not have developed; the lack of such institutions, however, clearly indicates that there may be good reasons for their non-existence.

I seem to have argued myself out of my most extreme positions. There is, of course, a strong case for state support and intervention in professional training. But still a word of warning should be issued. The effect of the subsidization of *entry* into the professions, through the diminution of the private cost of education to the individual who gets its, inevitably results in a diminution of the different *returns* to education. This is not to be complained of; it is, indeed, one of the fundamental objects of such subsidization. We must distinguish the effect of this *cheapening* of professional services, which is a movement on the "supply side" from an increase in the quantity of professional services which comes from changes on the "demand side." The problem is complicated by a degree of interrelation between supply and demand, in that part of the demand for professional people arises from the necessity of passing on the skills to the next generation. Indeed, in the obscurer arts and sciences this constitutes almost the sole demand. These complications aside, however, the question of whether it is cheaper for society to subsidize demand or to subsidize supply is a very interesting and difficult one, and unfortunately is beyond the scope of this paper. There is a certain presumption, I think, in favor of subsidizing supply; the case, however, is not a clear one, especially if the subsidization of one part of the supply results in a decline in some other part of the supply. We might find, for instance, that extensive subsidization of professional training so lowered the returns to such training that no private capital went into it, and the state would find itself taking over the whole burden of the investment. On the other hand, if both supply and demand are rather elastic, a subsidization of demand (e.g., by providing public health service in the case of the doctors) might bring about a considerable expansion of the profession at rather small cost to the state.

The problem which the Ford Foundation faced in its attempt to expand the "behavioral sciences" is an interesting case in point: should the Foundation offer scholarships and bursaries to make it easy for young men to become "behavioral scientists," or should it subsidize the "demand" for behavioral scientists by "buying" research, etc.? This is not, of course, an either/or proposition—a little of both is usually indicated—but how much of one or the other gives the best results is a hard question to decide.

I suppose what I am ultimately protesting about in the manpower concept is its delusive simplicity. There has grown up in recent years a wave of protest against the use of financial standards and criteria and methods, some of which is perhaps justified. It is true, of course, that finance is a "veil" which hides the physical realities of the economic system, and that money is merely a symbol for men and things. It is tempting, therefore, to draw up "manpower budgets" in terms of "needs and requirements," to say that we "need" so many doctors or dentists or economists (?) per head of the population, and that if by these standards there is a deficiency of doctors in Dahomey or economists in Ethiopia, the answer is simply for somebody to send them there. This approach to the problem unfortunately neglects the no doubt deplorable multidimensionality of life and society and the immense variety of men, things, places, and cultures. For purposes of thought and decision it is true, we do have to force this multidimensionality into some kind of simple linear indices. We find it easy to perceive that one line is longer than another or that one number is larger than another. It is very hard to perceive immediately whether one great multidimensional splodge is larger or smaller, better or worse, than another great multidimensional splodge. Yet, reality is always a splodge; the lines and the numbers are always abstractions.

What I have been arguing is that the "manpower" abstraction is appallingly crude, and that the attempt to think of the problem of allocation as if it were simply a matter of counting noses not only misses most of the realities of the case, but leads inevitably to a *solution* in terms of a monolithic, military, communistic type of society in which allocation is made by threat of violence imposed by superior members of a hierarchy. The financial abstraction is still, of course, a crude abstraction from reality, and it is only a place to start from, not a place to rest in. But it does lead to the notion of a "multilithic" society, not dominated by any single will but guided by the interaction of the wills of all its members. Granted that the financial mechanism should not remain unmodified. But it should be modified, not destroyed.

Economics: The Taming of Mammon[*]

It is not the noisy revolutions of politics but the silent revolutions of skill that change the course of man's destiny. The rudder and the horse collar were mightier than Caesar, and the turnip and steam between them changed the face of the earth more than Napoleon. When historians of the future turn back to the twentieth century, it will not be the public turmoil and wars which will attract their main attention. Hitler and Stalin will be seen as disturbances, mere pimples on the changing countenance of time. The great movement of this century will be seen as a continuation of that fabulous increase in human skill which constitutes the scientific and technological revolution, a continuation furthermore not only toward new material skills, as in the atomic revolution, but toward new skills of organization and of society.

The economist is participating fully in this revolutionary increase of skill. The skill of the economist is not so spectacular as that of the physicist or the engineer. Here again, however, it is the silent revolution which may echo longest. There has been a Great Change in economics, a mutation which took place almost entirely in the period between the two World Wars. And this Great Change may have much more effect on the future history of man than the wars which serve to date it. Evidence for this change is found not only in the text book and the lecture room: it is written in the contrasting histories of the postwar periods. World War I was followed by a deep, though short, depression in 1919–20, a period of unsteady prosperity in the United States, catastrophic inflation in Germany, and a long depression in England even before the collapse of 1929–32. After the much worse catastrophe of World War II there was no postwar depression, no German inflation—indeed, a spectacular economic recovery of devastated Europe—no depression in England, and to date, ten years of postwar full employment in the United States. If we get through

* In: *Frontiers of Knowledge in the Study of Man*, Lynn White, Jr., ed. (New York: Harper and Brothers, 1956), pp. 132–49. Copyright © by Harper & Row, Publishers Inc. Reprinted by permission of the publisher.

This paper was commissioned by Dr. Lynn White, Jr. for the volume in which it appears.

the next ten years without war and without serious depression we may confidently proclaim a New Era. Until then, those who remember the collapse of an earlier New Era in 1929 may be excused a little skepticism. It may be claimed also with some justification that the economic success of the past ten years has not been the result of wise and conscious economic policy but has been largely an accident—due, among other things, to the cold war and the high level of armaments.

Nevertheless, a professional economist cannot doubt the Great Change in economics. It has three aspects, all closely related. It is a change in theory, a change in information, and a change in policy. The change in theory is associated above all with the name of the late Lord Keynes. The change in information concerns the development of adequate statistics of national income and its components. The change in policy consists of the acceptance of responsibility by governments for the maintenance of full employment and economic stability.

I shall never forget the excitement, as an undergraduate, of reading Keynes' *Treatise on Money* in 1931. It is a clumsy, hastily written book and much of its theoretical apparatus has now been discarded. But to its youthful readers it was a peak in Darien, opening up vistas of uncharted seas—"Great was it in that dawn to be alive, and to be young was very heaven!" Imagine, therefore, the expectancy with which the *General Theory of Employment, Interest, and Money* was received in 1936—an expectancy baffled at first by the obscurity of much of the writing, gradually yielding to the realization that a great step forward had been made as the obscurities were resolved, the inconsistencies cleared up, and the meaning made clear by successive commentators.

To understand the nature of this advance it is necessary to take a look at the state of economics in, say, the 1920's.

On the practical side there was an obsession with the problems of international trade almost to the exclusion of domestic economic problems, and a striking lack of concern for the problems either of unemployment or of inflation. The restoration of the Gold Standard and "back to normalcy" represent the peak of practical economic wisdom.

On the theoretical side the basic model was that of a price-profit equilibrium: given resources are supposed to be divided among different industries and occupations in such a way that profits and wages in all industries tend to equality, subject to adjustments for nonmonetary rewards and immobility. Market prices are those which "clear the market," that is, which do not leave any unsatisfied buyers or sellers.

Market prices determine the actual rewards accruing to resources in different industries, and hence always tend to move toward "equilibrium"—a set of "normal" values at which no further transfer of resources between occupations takes place. Unemployment is regarded as an essentially temporary disequilibrium, soon to be remedied by appropriate adjustments of prices and wages. Saving and investment are brought into equilibrium by the rate of interest—"too much saving" immediately results in a fall in interest rates, which stimulates investment and discourages savings.

This is an ingenious and admirable system, and was first stated essentially by Adam Smith in 1776. It throws a lot of light on the major forces that determine the system of relative prices. If, for instance, a pound of butter usually costs four or five times as much as a pound of bread, the reason is that if it were not so, the "natural" forces of self-interest and mobility would soon change the situation. If a pound of butter was worth ten pounds of bread, butter production would be profitable, bread production not so profitable by comparison, butter production would increase, bread production diminish, and this would lower the price of butter and raise the price of bread until the "normal" ratio was restored. What the system does *not* do is to give an adequate account of what determines the over-all or aggregate output, price, income, or employment levels of the system. It became frighteningly clear in the 20's, and especially in the 30's, that unemployment could not be regarded as a "temporary disequilibrium" but was a deplorably stable element of the system. The great achievement of the Keynesian economics was to show that simple theoretical models could be constructed which dealt with the *whole* economic system in terms of a few large aggregated quantities—total output, total consumption, total investment—and that this theoretical model under certain circumstances could show an *underemployment equilibrium.* Unemployment was then seen not as a temporary divergence from equilibrium to be dealt with by patiently waiting for the economy to turn a corner, but as a deep-seated equilibrium property of the system which could only be dealt with by deliberate government policy.

The basic notions of the Keynesian theory are so simple that once they are grasped it is difficult to realize the desperate intellectual struggle by which they were evolved. The basic concept is that of the Gross National Product—the total value, measured in constant prices, of all goods and services produced. The basic idea is that the national product must be "disposed of" in some way. Four broad ways of disposal may be distinguished. The product can be taken by households (consumption). It can be taken by government. It can be shipped abroad (the foreign balance). What is not used up by these three methods must still be around somewhere in the hands of businesses. What is "still around somewhere" is the addition to the real capital of businesses, and is called "investment" or "accumulation." Just to simplify the argument, let us suppose that we lump the first three items together under the head of "consumption," and suppose further that total consumption *depends* on the national product itself—that is, for each value of the national product there is a given value of consumption habits, assuming that institutions, policies, etc., are held constant. Then for each possible level of the national product there is only one possible level of *actual* accumulation.

To take an example: suppose consumption were always 80 per cent of aggregate production. Then if production were 300, consumption would be 240, and aggregate accumulation would have to be 60. Now suppose that people are not willing to add 60 to their holdings of goods. Actual accumulation is greater than desired. Stockpiles of all sorts of things would then be piling up at a rate faster than their owners wanted. Two things might happen. People might try to get rid of their stockpiles of goods by offering to sell them at lower prices, and prices might fall until people became willing to buy the existing stocks. Or the producers of goods would simply cut back production, thus creating unemployment, hoping that excessive stocks would thereby be reduced. Under a "sticky" price and wage system the latter is more likely to happen. Unemployment is thus seen as a result of a deficiency in "aggregate demand"—that is, an inability or unwillingness of people to consume and accumulate as much as they can produce at full capacity. If such is the case, and if the society is operating at full capacity, there will be unwanted accumulations. The attempt to get rid of these reduces output and employment down to the point where accumulation is small enough to be absorbed voluntarily. Especially in a rich society the decline in output and employment may have to go a long way before accumulation is sufficiently reduced, because each reduction in output also reduces consumption; output chases consumption, trying to reduce the distance between them (accumulation), but consumption flees as output pursues; only as output finally succeeds in gaining on consumption does accumulation decline.

It is not necessary to go into the details of the Keynesian system. It is, of course, an oversimplified theory. It is bulldozer economics, designed to push large problems around, not scalpel economics designed for fine operations. There are still important theoretical problems unresolved, especially in the area of time lags between causes and effects. Nevertheless this system, simple as it is, makes the difference between being hopelessly at sea when faced with the problem of unemployment and having a faint light by which to steer. We know now what we did not know clearly in 1929, that a developed market economy is subject to the possibility of serious and meaningless fluctuations in aggregate output and in the level of employment, and that in order to prevent ups and downs positive action must sometimes be taken by government. We know moreover the direction that these actions should take. We know at least that when faced with unemployment we should *not* raise taxes, balance the budget, and stiffen interest rates. We know that when faced with inflation we should *not* lower taxes, increase the budget deficit, or lower interest rates.

This change in theoretical viewpoint, which it is not unfair to call the Keynesian Revolution, has been paralleled and supported by an important development in economic information in the form of the collection of National Income statistics. This revolution in the collection and presentation of economic information has had an impact on economic thought and knowledge at least comparable with that of the revolution in theory. It dates essentially from 1929, when the U. S. Department of Commerce first began to issue annual estimates of aggregate income, output, consumption, investment, and government purchases for the United States. Estimates are available back to 1919, but they are not reliable. For more than twenty-five years now, however, we have records of the major aggregate magnitudes of the American and of several other important national economic systems.

This information, covering as it does by now a major cycle in economic activity and a World War, has had a profound effect on economic thought. The late Professor Schumpeter of Harvard, one of the wisest and most learned economists of the last generation, once said in a jocular vein "How nice economics was before anybody knew anything!"—meaning that the steady growth of information about the real world is constantly limiting the free play of the economist's speculative imagination. There are still great gaps in the economic information system. We know little about the composition and distribution of assets—stocks of goods, money, and securities—though this gap is closing. We know still less about the more stable psychological factors which affect economic life—people's hopes and fears and expectations, though this gap, too, is beginning to be filled. Compared with the pre-1929 economist, however, the economist of today moves in a world in which all the larger outlines of the economic landscape are visible. We know from quarter to quarter not only the over-all size of national income, but its components (consumption, investment, government purchases, foreign balance) and its distribution as between wages, profits, interest, rents. By contrast the pre-1929 economist operated in a dense fog in which only scattered lights and noises, like price data and foreign trade statistics, gave much indication of what lay about him.

The revolution both in the theoretical position of the economist and in the information available to him has had a profound effect on the political attitudes and policy recommendations of economists. This change has taken place so slowly and subtly that it has not received much attention, but it may easily be the most significant result of the movement in economics of the past twenty-five years. In the old days economists could be classified easily along the radical-conservative or socialist-liberal spectrum. There were Marxists at one end, social-democrats in the middle, and laissez-faire economists at the other end. Now all this is changed, and it has become hard to tell a liberal from a conservative. One can regard the "new economics" as in some sense a Hegelian synthesis of the old quarrel between the two apparent extremes of socialism and capitalism, making that dispute curiously obsolete and irrelevant. The orthodox Marxist and the orthodox laissez-faire man are today stranded on their little self-contained islands while the great commerce of discourse has swept to other shores. Keynes has drawn the sting of the Marxist scorpion by showing that the instability of capitalism—its tendency to intermittent periods of underemployment—is a real defect which is capable of remedy by fairly simple means. The position of the conservatives who maintain that there is no defect in an unregulated market economy was made untenable by the Great Depression.

Thus we emerge with a genuine Political Economy. Government has certain economic functions and responsibilities which it cannot dismiss. Its main function is not to "take over" the operation of the economic system, but to act as a "governor"—to throw forces into the system which will counteract the tendency of unregulated systems of private enterprise and free markets to spiral into unnecessary depressions or inflations. Just as the governor of an engine speeds it up when it is going too slow or slows it down when it is going too fast, or a thermostat turns on the heat when the house is too cold and turns it off when the house is too hot, so government must be inflationary when the private economy is deflating and deflationary when the private economy is inflating.

There is almost universal agreement also among economists that by far the most powerful instrument of government stabilization is the system of public finance, and especially the tax system. Banking policy and other indirect controls have their place, but it is a secondary one. The shift from regarding the tax system simply as a method for raising money for government to spend to the view of taxes as an instrument of stabilizing the whole economy is perhaps the most fundamental change in policy outlook of this period.

This rather optimistic picture is not, of course, the whole story and it is time for a few academic hems and haws. It is still a moot question, for instance, whether a vigorous full employment policy does not land us in a long-run rise in the general level of money prices. If government overdoes its counterbalancing role, and especially if it displays too much inflationary ardor in a time of threatened depression, remitting too many taxes, running too large a deficit, making borrowing too easy, the result will be an aggregate demand in excess of what can be satisfied at current prices even at full employment, and prices will rise. Once they have risen it may be hard to get them down again, for whereas an overdose of inflationary government action will raise prices, deflationary government action may merely create unemployment if prices are "sticky." Hence we get what has been called a "ratchet effect," and what goes up doesn't come down as much as it went up. It may be, of course, that the thing to do with long-run inflation is to learn to live with it, and there are many signs that we are adjusting our institutions in this direction—for example, pension plans based on stocks rather than bonds, or with cost of living adjustments in them, and so on. On the other hand, the example of countries which have had a long inflation, like Brazil, is not wholly encouraging, and there may be long-run problems in this connection which will only emerge over the decades.

Another problem of great importance which is yet unsolved is that of the distribution of income and wealth. We have moved noticeably in the direction of greater equality of incomes in the past fifty years, mainly through the instrument of the graduated income tax. Nothing like clarity and unity has emerged in the field of distribution, however, either in theory or in policy, by comparison with the field of stabilization. There is still much dispute even about what ultimately determines the distributional shares, especially as between wages and profits. One fact of importance emerges from the national income figures—that the rise of the labor movement has been much less important in affecting the over-all distributional shares than is popularly supposed. Indeed, the percentage of national income going to wages actually *fell* from 74 per cent in 1933 to 62 per cent in 1942, at a time when trade union membership was rising from under four million to about fifteen million—the effects of full employment and inflation effectively masked small influences such as the Wagner Act and the rise of the C.I.O.! Even our economic information in this crucial area is incomplete: we do not know for sure, for instance, whether rent control made incomes more or less equal. Furthermore, many of our policies which are ostensibly directed towards removing inequalities or injustices actually have the reverse effect. Much of American agricultural policy, for instance, probably benefits rich farmers much more than it does poor ones.

Another area with many unsolved problems is that of economic progress (more fashionably called "development," "progress" being a word of deplorably nineteenth-century connotations). Here is a field where, oddly enough, the classical economists from Adam Smith to J. S. Mill still have important things to say, and where no modern economist has arisen to weld the insights of the classics into a coherent system. The difficulty here may lie in the limitations of the economist's abstractions—economic development is merely one aspect of the larger problem of cultural change. Economic progress is something which we take almost for granted in our own society. The study of other societies, however, indicates that there is no necessity about progress, and that it has roots deep in the religious, domestic, educational, and political institutions of society as well as in economic life.

Thus many periods of economic development are associated with profound changes in religious outlook—for instance, the rise of the monastic movement in early medieval times had something to do with the economic developments of the tenth and eleventh centuries, the rise of Islam certainly had something to do with the amazing development of Arab civilization, and the Protestant and Evangelical reformations are intimately connected with the so-called Industrial Revolution. Sometimes political revolutions have set off economic growth, as in modern Turkey or nineteenth-century Japan. The land grant college had a profound effect on American economic life through its impact on agriculture. There is much work to be done here: the Keynesian economics throws a lot of light on the forces which sometimes make for stagnation, but not much on those which make for growth.

Although the Keynesian Revolution is unquestionably the Great Change in economics, it must not be thought that it is the only change. The interwar period also saw important developments in price theory, in "welfare economics," and in the theory of economic behavior. These, too, have had important consequences for economic policy. In price

theory we have seen the development of a theory of "imperfect competition." Before 1930 economists generally worked with two models:
a theory of perfect competition on the one hand, and a theory of
monopoly on the other. Competition was "good," monopoly "bad,"
and if monopoly threatened to raise its head, the thing to do was to
restore competition by breaking the monopolistic firm into competing
parts. This is, rather crudely, the philosophy of the Sherman Anti-Trust
act of 1888.

Criticism was raised from many quarters at the end of the last
century that this view of affairs did not correspond very well to reality.
It was not, however, until the 1930's that a theory of imperfect competition was developed which explicitly recognized that the great bulk
of the economic system operated neither under perfect competition
nor under monopoly but under various intermediate forms of market
behavior and interaction. It cannot be claimed that at the present time
this part of economics is in good shape, and in regard, for instance,
to antimonopoly policy it may be that the new theoretical developments have merely confused the issues. The anti-trust division of the
Department of Justice sometimes reminds one of the knight who
jumped on his great white horse and rode off in all directions. It can
at least be said, however, that much of the unreality which flavored
the old theory based on perfect competition has gone, and that economics can today take account of a wide variety of market conditions.

Another important, though again rather frustrating, development
in economics goes under the name of "welfare economics." The name
is apt to give the layman a false impression, as welfare economics has
nothing to do with social work or welfare agencies, but is an abstract
mathematical discipline which has attempted to answer the question,
"When is one set of conditions or circumstances economically 'better'
than another?" The conclusion seems to be finally that we can never
be sure that one set of economic conditions is better than another
unless we have some way of ordering the various possibilities on a
scale of "better or worse," and this ordering cannot be found within
the formal framework of economics itself. In spite of this rather negative ultimate conclusion, however, the struggle to make clear what we
mean when we say that one set of conditions is "economically" better
than another has been a valuable one. It at least saves us from the
error of invoking scientific authority to support our personal preferences—an error to which other social scientists, and especially the
psychologists, are unusually prone. It has done more than this, however; it has led to a clarification of some *objectives* of economic policy,

its influence can be traced in some actual policies, and it has made an important contribution to the controversy about socialism.

An attempt was made, for instance, to erect guides for economic policy on the theory that we could be sure that a policy was good if it made some people better off and nobody worse off. This led to the "compensation principle"—that a change was worth making if the people who benefited from it could compensate the people who were injured by it, and still leave themselves better off than before. Another important conclusion is that people will be better off if they are allowed to trade freely than if they are not. None of these conclusions can be maintained absolutely, for reasonable exceptions can be envisaged. Rascals, for instance, should presumably not be compensated for their rascality, nor should vested interests be vested for ever. Nevertheless, it is not a bad thing to suggest that sometimes things can be done which make everybody better off, even at the cost of buying off a few rascals. The consequences of these developments for economic policy have been to develop a greater respect for individual freedom of choice, even among socialists and planners. An example of a wartime policy which would almost certainly not have developed without the influence of the economists is "point" rationing. Instead of trying to allot scarce goods to people according to their supposed "needs," a "price system" in terms of ration points was developed which would permit a certain amount of individual choice. The scarcer items were given higher "point prices," which meant that only the people who wanted these things very badly would sacrifice their ration points for them. Thus there was some tendency for scarce items to go to people who wanted them the most, instead of being distributed according to some administrator's fancy.

Closely related to the above developments is the rapidly expanding field of "decision theory," or the theory of "rational behavior," or "economic behavior." The problem here is akin to that of welfare economics. When we think of "rational" behavior—as opposed, perhaps, to instinctive, compulsive, or purely mechanical or habitual behavior—we envisage a situation in which the actor confronts a number of possible choices and selects one of them. This implies knowledge of the alternatives which are open to the actor, an ability to rank these alternatives on a scale of "better or worse," and the further ability to detect which alternative stands highest on the scale. The selection of the "highest" or "best" alternative is known as "maximization"—hence this type of behavior is known as "maximizing behavior." An elaborate and rather beautiful theory has been worked out around this notion, especially in the simple case of the business firm, which, it is supposed, maximizes "profit." That is, it selects those prices, selling activities, outputs, and other quantities under its control which will yield it the highest profit.

The practical impact of this theory on business has not been great except perhaps in the direction of arousing the interest of accountants in what they call "incremental" and what economists call "marginal" cost—the *addition* to cost produced by a unit *addition* to output, a figure which must be known if profits are to be maximized. There has also been a good deal of criticism of the theory from economists themselves—not all of it well considered, but having in the mass a certain force. It is argued, for instance, that people simply do not behave in the way supposed—that their behavior is influenced by all sorts of irrational, impulsive, or compulsive considerations and that we do not usually calmly survey the field of choice and pick out the finest plum on the tree. The criticism is not without point, and yet it can be argued in defense of rational behavior that these irrational elements can be regarded as chance disturbances, that people do not consistently choose the worse rather than the better alternative, and that almost all behavior, even at animal levels, involves some kind of selective process out of a field of alternative choices. There is important support for this view coming out of recent biological and psychological theories —the view, for instance, that even in simple perception we perceive the world the way we do because it "pays" us to see it that way!

A more important criticism of simple maximization theory which has led to an extensive new theoretical development, is that it does not take into account the fact that information about possible alternatives is limited and uncertain. What do we mean by "rational" behavior when we do not know, or at least know only very imperfectly, the consequences of our acts and therefore the real nature of the choice we are making? Practically all choices are actually made under conditions of ignorance and uncertainty. We invest, we buy a car, we marry, we take a job, we build a factory, or we go into a war in desperate ignorance of the consequences. Investments go bad, cars turn out to be lemons, marriages break up, jobs and factories alike turn out badly, wars are lost, yet everyone goes into these enterprises in hope of gain. It is hope and faith that guide poor old economic man, and maybe charity that helps him to bear the constant weight of disappointment. But what becomes of "rationality" when hope and faith rule the field of choice?

One answer to this question has been sought in the "Theory of Games"—a relatively new development dating only from 1947. This seeks to answer two questions: what is rational behavior for a single person operating under uncertainty as to the consequences of his decisions, and can there be a *coordinated* and consistent system of rational behavior for a number of persons when the decisions of each one affect the *consequences* of the decisions of the others? A number of "rational" persons interacting according to definite rules is what the mathematicians mean by a "game," which may, of course, be a game of cards, a war, or economic competition. One interesting rule emerges from this highly abstract mathematical theory—act so that you will make the best of it if the worst happens. Every action is thought of as having not a single consequence but a range of possible consequences: spread out in your mind the worst of these, and pick the best of this bunch, rather than thinking only of the most favorable possibilities. Marry the girl who will be a good wife even in adversity, not one who will be wonderful but only if things go smoothly.

Another important recent development arises out of the reflection that decisions are generally made by organizations rather than by individuals, and that even the individual himself is a kind of internal committee. Interesting work is under way on the problem of how organizations should be structured, and especially how information should be gathered and circulated, in order to give the best chance of the right decisions. This recognizes that all decisions are a result of a political process of compromise, and at this point economics finds itself veering toward a union with political science and sociology.

It is in this area of decision-making that we may perhaps look for the most important developments of the next few years—developments which may have great importance for the practical conduct of affairs as well as for pure theory. Up to now the decision-making process, in government, in war, in business, in marriage, in the conduct of a household, in fact in all human affairs, has been a matter of "feel" —an almost subconscious weighing of alternatives in the dim light of uncertain information and a decision formed we know not how. It is as unlikely as it would be undesirable that we will eliminate this element of subconscious "judgment" and have all our decisions made for us by electronic calculators. We are facing an age, however, in which minor decisions will become more and more a matter of conscious calculation, and the area of subconscious judgment will be pushed back to more fundamental and momentous decisions. A fascinating possibility is emerging, for instance, that we will begin to know something about the circumstances under which ignorance is bliss—one can have too much, as well as too little information for successful decision-making, and we see in the making today a much more self-conscious control of their own information systems on the part of the decision-makers. This has frightening as well as desirable aspects—the "Brave New World" of endless manipulation and machination in the interest of nothing much in particular is too close around the corner for comfort.

Looking towards the next twenty-five years in economics, it may perhaps be doubted whether they will be quite as exciting as the past twenty-five. As far as the Keynesian economics is concerned we appear at the moment to be in the time of the disciples, not of the master— a period of clarification and consolidation rather than of great new ideas. To be sure, a new genius may appear next month. But genius apart, within the present boundaries of economics there are still important problems which demand attention. We have already noticed the unsatisfactory state of the theory of monopoly and competition, of the theory of distribution and income, and of the theory of economic development. There are great opportunities here for the pioneers.

It also seems probable, however, that the next period will be one in which economics will grow towards many other disciplines, and in which the most exciting areas of advance will be those which lie somewhere between the regularly established disciplines. Even in the present generation, for instance, there has been an enormous increase in the use of sophisticated mathematics in economics. The amount of formal mathematical training used by economists has been steadily increasing, from zero at the time of the classical economists, to simple geometry, algebra, and calculus by 1900, to matrix algebra, set theory, symbolic logic, and the theory of games at the present day. This is not to say that economists *must* be familiar with these more erudite branches of communication. There are still many economists who plod along usefully with simple apparatus, and there is still and always will be a great deal of "not-mathematics"—good judgment, sensitivity to empirical reality, knowledge of affairs, and so on—necessary in the skill of the economist. The sharper the tools the easier it is to cut oneself with them, and there have been sad cases of mathematical economists grinding out nonsense because it happened to come out of their equations. Nevertheless, as the economist ventures into the handling of more and more variables, both in theory and in empirical work, more and more powerful mathematical tools have to be devised to deal with the complexities involved. Mathematics is a set of tools, and just because tools may be misused or used for improper purposes does not mean that they should be thrown away. At the frontiers of economics today therefore will be found many able young men working away at complex problems with complex equipment, and if no great simplicities have emerged as yet from all this complexity, bases are being established from which any further advance must set forth.

It may be objected that mathematical economics is not really an "interdisciplinary" development, mathematics being a language or a tool rather than a "science." However that may be, there are many signs that economics is stretching out towards other sciences. There are signs, for instance, of what is perhaps a new discipline of economic sociology, which will generalize the economist's abstraction of exchange to the more universal notion of a "transaction," and will study economic organizations and their interaction in a less abstract way and with more variables than has been done in economics proper. The field of industrial relations pioneered this sort of thing. There are indications now of a genuine integration of economics and politics, in the study of the political aspects of decision-making processes in "economic" organizations such as firms, and in the study of rational decision-making in political organizations like governments. Much needs to be done to bring economics and anthropology together; this, however, is being forced on both by the development of the specialized study of economic development and cultural change. Even stranger rapprochements may be in the making. Economics has contacts with biology at many points. In theory, the biologist's view of the organism has many relevant similarities to the economist's view of a firm or a household, and the biologist's notion of an "eco-system" of interacting biological populations has much in common with the economist's idea of an economic system. Even in the realm of economic policy, however, the problem of conservation requires the concept of man as an agent in the biosphere, and it is wise for man not to forget his biological base.

Professor Pigou, the grand old man of British economics, is reported to have defended his existence as an economist by saying, "We do economics because it is fun." The remark may arouse derisive laughter from those whose memories are confined to a dreary textbook in Introductory Ec. Nevertheless, for those who have been in the game economics in the past twenty-five years has been fun, and more than fun. There has been a sense of intellectual excitement, of living through a "classic" period. There has also been a sense of urgency, a feeling that time was short, that great problems of vital importance for human welfare had to be solved and solved quickly. This sense of urgency is perhaps less today than it was in the grim days of the 1930's—the urgent problem now is not depression and economic collapse, but war and total collapse! The time may even come, as Keynes himself suggested, when the technical problems of economics will not be interesting because they will have been solved, and man can go on to the real business of life without all this fussing about the organization of scarce resources. That time, however, is not yet. Mammon is not yet tamed. Depressions may still break out; inflations may still plague us; progress may lag; injustice may wax; organizations may get out of hand; poverty lingers with us; fecundity and ferocity may still dash the cup of plenty from our lips; and we still have a long way to go before we establish securely in the organization of society that Hidden Hand which transmutes the dross of Self-Interest into the gold of General Welfare. But the taming is under way, and Mammon-taming is a fine career.

Economic Libertarianism*

I shall try to look at what I call the limits of libertarianism, particularly in regard to the role of exchange in the organization of society. I think freedom is a bit of a red herring here. The really crucial question is the role of exchange as an organizer. This is what the economic liberals, if we can call them that, care about. It is both the successes and the limits of this role of exchange which represent the real issue.

I recognize three major organizers in society. An organizer is something like a social gene. It is a relationship which organizes role structures in society and hence is capable of developing organization. I distinguish three of these organizers. I call them the threat system, the exchange system and the integrative system.

The Three Organizers of Society

The threat is an ancient organizer. This is the idea that you had better do something nice for me or I shall do something nasty to you. It frequently is effective. It can result in what I call the threat-submission system. This is found in the slave economy, for example. It is particularly powerful in the organization of civilization, which I regard as something resulting fundamentally from agriculture and exploitation. With agriculture, we get a food surplus from a food producer, and exploitation takes it away from him. Thus we get civilization, which I regard as a deplorable state of man, roughly from 3000 B.C. to 3000 A.D., which is now in the process of passing away. It is

* In: *Conference on Savings and Residential Financing, 1965 Proceedings* (Chicago: U.S. Savings and Loan League, 1965), pp. 30–42.

This paper was delivered as part of a dialogue between Professor Milton Friedman and myself at a conference organized by the U.S. Savings and Loan League in Chicago on May 6, 1965. Because it originated as a transcription I have taken the liberty of editing the published version rather more than some of the other papers, but it still retains the flavor of a verbal argument. Nevertheless, it represents several points of view which are not expressed in any other papers, and the oral style gives it a certain liveliness.

the condition where we have agriculture and a food surplus plus a coercive system which, through either the priest or the king, takes the food surplus away from the food producer. With this surplus we feed philosophers, armies, artisans and builders, and so make cities and civilizations.

Exchange is a much more powerful organizer with a much wider horizon. The threat system has a low horizon of development; it can produce classical civilization but it cannot do anything better. The exchange system is as old as the threat system. The first traders probably snuggled up to the temples, the forts and the castles. They have always been despised. As Milton Friedman has said, the traders have always had a bad press. But they have gradually developed an enormous world-wide system of exchange and specialization which, as Adam Smith pointed out, makes everybody better off because exchange, if it is really free exchange, does not happen unless both parties are better off. This does not mean, of course, that there is no conflict in exchange, but that is another question.

The integrative system is harder to define, but I think it is at least as important as the other two systems. It involves such things as status, identity, love, hate, benevolence, malevolence, legitimacy—the whole raft of social institutions which define roles in such a way that you do things because of what you are and because of what I am, that is, because of some kind of status or respect.

The important thing about the integrative system is that it is a necessary matrix of the other two. The threat system is fairly ineffective unless it can be put into an integrative matrix, that is, unless the threats can be legitimized. Naked threats are extraordinarily ineffective as a social organizer. You have to coat them with a kind of plastic coating or something of legitimacy before they can be very effective. Incidentally, this is why we are so ineffective in Viet Nam, where we have an enormous amount of threat with practically no legitimacy. Exchange can take place only if there is an atmosphere of trust, confidence, respect and, indeed, equality. Exchange is an extraordinarily equalitarian institution in the sense that in exchange the two parties look eye to eye. In contrast, the threat system tends to produce inequality of status, with one party dominant and the other submissive.

Economic libertarianism quite rightly emphasizes the benevolent and developmental qualities of exchange. As Friedman suggests, it is perhaps the subtle nature of this system which causes it to have a bad press and to be unappreciated. But I argue also that the political weakness of libertarianism as a doctrine arises partly because of the failure of the libertarian to recognize explicitly that exchange is only one of the organizers of social life and that, if it is to operate success-fully, it must operate in a setting in which both the threat system and the integrative system are realistically taken into account.

No Social System without All Three Organizers

No social system exists, I maintain, without all three organizers. Even if we take the most idealistic Utopian community, there is always an element of threat, for instance, of expulsion. Even in the family there is a certain element of threat. In any institution there are elements of exchange. There are always balance-of-payment problems. There is always a problem of terms of trade, of what you get for what you give. I argue also that in any social system there have to be some integrative elements or the system simply will not operate at all.

I suggest that the greatest threat to the exchange system is the claim that it can do everything. This leads to the equally absurd claim that it can do nothing. The real problem here is to appraise it in its setting and to get the right kind of setting for it.

I illustrate this with the problem of sexual relations. The market solution to this problem is prostitution. This usually is not regarded very favorably, even though it is an ancient industry and a very per-sistent one. But it is very difficult to build this into the integrative system, although there have been attempts to do so. For instance, in India there is (or was) temple prostitution, and in our society there is Hollywood. But there is always a little edge to this; we always feel that it is not quite respectable. And the reason is that the sexual rela-tionship is a subtle and a complex one which involves large integrative elements. It is not just like buying a shirt; you do not "simply" buy this sort of thing, because it is too complicated, even though there are elements of exchange in it.

In marriage, for instance, the element of exchange is very funda-mental; that is, if the balance of payments in a marriage gets out of whack, the marriage is in trouble. If one (or both) of the parties feels that he (or she) is giving everything and is getting nothing, a balance-of-payments problem exists. So there is a market element in a marriage, but it is wrapped up in an enormous integrative package of religion, ethics, love, security and all this great big ball of wax which I call the integrative system.

A slight element of prostitution carries over into many aspects of the exchange system. For instance, we do not really approve of mer-cenaries. We do not really approve of corruption, even though in political life in a highly politicized, centrally planned society the only thing that makes the thing work at all is corruption. If the threat system is overexpanded, the only way that the exchange system gets around it is by corruption. Even in this country I suspect that corruption has been an important, positive element in enabling people to do sensible things. If somebody sitting at a desk can prevent your doing something which is perfectly sensible to do and you consistently slip him something under the desk, this is the exchange system. Corruption is the market economy operating in political life. However, even though it is sensible, it has an element of prostitution about it. That is why we find it a little hard to approve.

Management of Threat System a Major World Problem

Perhaps one of the major problems that the world faces today is the management of the threat system, particularly in international relations. We are all aware that we are facing a major crisis in the international system. Traditional, unilateral national defense has really broken down as a system in the face of nuclear weapons. Nuclear weapons have done for national defense what gunpowder did for the baron. Europe is full of ruined castles. The reason they are ruined is gunpowder. You do not have to believe in the materialistic interpretation of history to believe that gunpowder made a great difference.

Certainly the weapons system has a profound impact on the social system. We cannot develop a new weapons system without changing radically the whole social system, and we have developed a weapons system that is so new and so radical that no social institution will remain unchanged as a result. I am quite sure that what may be called the classical institutions of national defense have broken down. We realize this only dimly. We realize this through the development of interest in arms control and disarmament agencies, but we have not had the kind of disaster that will really bring this home.

Unquestionably we are heading for such a disaster. The probability that a large proportion of the people and property of the United States will be destroyed in the next 25 years is quite high. We all know this. We do not want to recognize it, but this is the plain fact of the matter. We have not adjusted our image of the world to the realities of the weapons system. There are still people who think they can live in castles; there are still people who think we can have civil defense. The plain fact is that this is nonsense. We are in a totally different world from the one into which you and I were born.

My great complaint against the economic libertarians is that they offer no solution to this problem, whereas traditionally they should. On the whole, the economic liberals of the 19th century, like Cobden and Bright, were anti-imperialistic and antimilitaristic, although in the absence of any really good theory of threat system they did not get far with it. Great Britain, which is supposed to be the home of economic liberalism, actually was the most militaristic country in the 19th century, judged by the number of wars it was engaged in. Even in the 19th century, economic liberalism was accompanied by an extreme willingness to use the threat system on people outside. The liberal is a man who does not believe in coercion at home, but who does believe in it abroad. This inconsistency seems to be at the heart of libertarianism, even in this country. It is an inconsistency that brings libertarianism into disrepute.

If the liberals are hawks rather than doves, then they are trapped in their own system, because hawkism leads to socialism. The only place where creeping socialism has been significant in the United States is the Department of Defense. This department actually is the second largest centrally planned economy in terms of GNP. If we list centrally planned economies we have, in order of size, the Soviet Union, the U. S. Department of Defense and then the People's Republic of China. The Department of Defense is full of bright young people, and their knowledge is terribly frightening. I sometimes wonder what would happen if Mr. McNamara were the Pope. The attempt to introduce rationality into what is fundamentally a heroic and nonrational organization can easily be quite disastrous.

The bright young people in the Department of Defense recognize that, in a sense, the jig is up and that they are not going to defend anybody. We must move toward arms control and disarmament if we are going to live; and if we do this, what becomes of the Department of Defense? What the bright young people in the Defense Department want to do is to keep this the 10% socialist sector of the economy that it now is, and divert it into the civilian economy. The Department of Defense, they argue, is the only place where we do not have to worry about labor unions; hence it can go in for all sorts of technology and is not trapped by all the restrictions of the civilian economy.

Welfare State: Expansion of the Integrative System

The other weakness of economic libertarianism, I argue, is a failure to understand or to come to terms with the integrative system, especially as reflected in the welfare state. It seems to me there should be no hostility between the libertarians and the welfare state. They are strictly complementary goods, if they are properly understood. This is because the welfare state represents an expansion of the integrative system in the sense that it involves the responsibility of each for all. This is an element in human life and in human motivation that cannot be denied and cannot be neglected.

There are, of course, things that are very worrisome about it. I agree absolutely with Friedman that most government activity in this direction subsidizes the rich against the poor. Most of our redistribution goes the wrong way. I can give you a shocking example—public education. I am an employee of a socialized industry, a state university. I always tell my colleagues in the business school that they had better be careful what they say, for they are employees of a socialized industry, too! Actually, I'm quite in favor of state universities. I am in favor of a mixed system here. We would not have had the quantity, or perhaps even the quality, of education that we have had if it had not been for this mixed system combining public and private institutions.

However, the whole public education system is a device for subsidizing the rich. I became particularly aware of this last year in Japan when I had to pay for the education of my own five children. This took 25% of my income, and was really quite rough. Now I am home and I find my taxes incredibly low. I am really being subsidized to the extent of $2,000 to $3,000 a year by the system of public education. And who is subsidizing me? It is the little widows and the orphans and all the poor little people who own little houses and who run rooming houses. Even though I am not rich, I am not as poor as they are. I am being subsidized by people who are considerably poorer than I am. Every time we try to redistribute income by subsidizing prices, this is what we run into.

We have the same thing in agriculture. Our whole agricultural policy is a device for subsidizing the rich at the expense of the poor. The poverty in agriculture arises from having little or nothing to sell. If you have nothing to sell, it does not matter what price you do not sell it at. So, if we "do something for agriculture" by raising prices, the more a farmer has to sell, the more he is subsidized by raising prices. So it is the rich farmer who gets most of the subsidy, and the poor farmer gets practically none.

There are many other examples of subsidy of the wealthy. I am not quite sure about the income tax. Some studies of the rich at our Survey Research Center, not yet published, are extraordinarily interesting. They reveal that the rich in this country are (a) almost inconceivably stingy and (b) quite surprisingly stupid. The extent to which they actually pay avoidable taxes is quite surprising.

National State the Strongest Integrative System

The national state is by far the strongest integrative system in the world today. One of the aspects of the integrative system is what may be called the "grants" economy. There are two parts to our economy: the exchange economy, in which you get a *quid* for a *quo*; and the grants economy, in which all you get is *quid*—you do not pay any *quo*. The grants economy is between 5% and 15% of the total American economy. It is difficult to tell precisely, because of the fact that many things that look like grants in the short run actually turn out to be exchanges in the long run. Most social security, as Friedman suggests, is a compulsory exchange rather than a part of a grants economy.

Even so, the grants economy is important and it is growing. Included in this economy are such things as foundation grants, government grants, pensions, relief payments, aid to dependent children and so on. The grants economy is extremely important in the family. The family is a grants economy of considerable magnitude. You do not expect your children to support you in your old age anymore, that is, if you are wise. In the old days the family was a social security institution, but today it is not. You shovel money out to your children in great quantities, but you do not expect to get very much of it back. The family certainly is still far and away the most important element of the integrative system. After that is the national state.

Socialism is an incredibly weak integrative system, as the Chinese-Russian split indicates. The great "workers of the world" idea and the ideology about the common interests of the proletariat is just hogwash; there is nothing to it. The Russians have done practically nothing for the Chinese. They have lent them about one cent per Chinese per annum, and the Chinese have had to pay this back with interest at times when they were broke. No wonder the Chinese do not like the Russians! If I were a Chinese, I would not like the Russians either.

The socialist camp is a weaker integrative system than the French Union. The French shovel out 2% of their GNP to the old French colonies. Just look at a place like Cayenne. It lives almost wholly on French social security. That is its major industry. Its imports are about nine times its exports. The French are romantically generous; I cannot imagine why they do it. The British are almost as bad—or as good. And we do a fair amount of it ourselves—about ½ of 1% of GNP. But we do not shovel out nearly as much as the French; we are really very stingy.

The Christian church is an integrative system to some extent. And

Judaism is a great integrative system. I sometimes think the Jews are the only generous people in the world. They are the only people who really work at it. For example, look at the way they have supported Israel. It is one of the most extraordinary examples of the grants economy in the integrative system.

In general, humanity represents an extremely weak integrative system. Note the United Nations. The ordinary budget of the United Nations is about the same as that of the University of Michigan and only a quarter of that of the Department of Sanitation of the city of New York. In the exchange economy we get what we pay for, and we get the amout of world peace that we are willing to pay for. This is what we are prepared to pay for in the way of world integration, and this is why there is no real solution to any of our problems.

Exchange Economy Needs Integrative Matrix

I am suggesting that the exchange economy can operate successfully only if it is in a suitable integrative matrix. Schumpeter saw this very clearly. He argued that the reason capitalism will not survive is that nobody loves it. The institutions of the exchange economy do not produce in themselves the integrative system which will support it. The integrative system has to come out of religion, or nationalism, or education, or the family or something of that kind. Exchange in itself is such an abstract and stripped kind of relationship that it will not develop a very strong integrative system. Suppose you say, "Ask not what General Motors can do for you; ask what you can do for General Motors." This may be all right for General Motors, but it sounds a little silly. We do not expect exchange organizations to be very strongly integrative.

There is a bank in Michigan which had a motto, "The Bank That Puts People First." I have never believed this; if I believed it, I would take out my money and put it in another bank. I do not want a bank to put people first; I want it to put money first. I do not want a bank to be lovable; I want it to be efficient. I want it to be nice to me and not snarl at me; I do not mind bankers being polite, but I do not want them to slobber over me. There is a kind of abstract exchange relationship here which, within its limits, is entirely legitimate. The world of bankers will not produce the kind of institutions which can support them; you have to rely on the other institutions to provide this.

Adam Smith saw this. I am very fond of Adam Smith. But it is rather depressing to go back to him, because it makes you realize how little we have learned. It has been nearly 200 years since he wrote, yet on the subject of economic development we have said little that Adam

Smith did not say. He has a wonderful passage in which he denounces the division of labor. He has built up the advantages of the division of labor, exchange and how specialization produces wealth. Then he has second thoughts about it. Let me read this lovely passage:

"The man whose whole life is spent in performing a few simple operations, of which the effects too are, perhaps, always the same, or very nearly the same, has no occasion to exert his understanding, or to exercise his invention in finding out expedients for removing difficulties which never occur." [There is the learning process. This is why we have to be free to sin. I agree with that.] "He naturally loses, therefore, the habit of such exertion, and gradually becomes as stupid and ignorant as it is possible for a human creature to become. The torpor of his mind renders him, not only incapable of relishing or bearing a part in any rational conversation, but of conceiving any generous, noble or tender sentiment and consequently of forming any just judgment concerning many even of the ordinary duties of private life."

He goes on to say that a worker under these conditions is utterly incapable of being a citizen. Here is Adam Smith attacking the division of labor because it produces too much specialization. Actually, automation is going to get us out of this problem. It is the computers now that are torpid and stupid. A computer can be as stupid as it likes because we probably are not going to give it the vote for at least 50 years.

Then Adam Smith said: "No two characters seem more inconsistent than those of trader and sovereign." Here he is arguing for the idea that you cannot run a government as if it were a business; you have to keep business out of government. The people who make a Bible out of Adam Smith had better go back and read him again. They might find it disconcerting.

I agree with Friedman that the greatest enemies of the free market are businessmen and intellectuals. I hope that the cold war between them is reaching the stage of peaceful coexistence; I suppose this Conference is a sign of it. I hope even more that the cold war between business and government in this country will reach a stage of coexistence. A great problem of this country is that the business community is neurotic. It is neurotic because of the Great Depression. It had an enormously traumatic experience in the 1930s. As a result, the leaders of the business community today are depression-fixated in the same way that the leaders of government are Munich-fixated. These are our two greatest dangers today. Again, it is a matter of "learning things that ain't so." We do this all the time.

Two Concepts of Freedom

Let me just add a note on the question of freedom. This is a crucial and important question. I suggest that there are three concepts of freedom. One is the concept of power. This is defined as "what limits behavior." It is very close to the concept of wealth itself. The wealthy are free and the poor are not. The Indian peasant has no freedom at all; he is in an absolute box. The most important road to freedom is development; it is just plain getting rich. This is a most important concept of freedom.

On the other hand, this is not the only concept of freedom. There are other things which limit us. There are legal limitations, moral limitations and even psychological limitations that box us in.

There is another concept of freedom which is a matter of the legitimacy in our minds of the limitations that box us in. We are always going to have to operate within limitations; so long as there is scarcity, we cannot have absolute freedom. This is fundamental.

However, the question as to whether one accepts these limitations as legitimate is enormously important. For instance, I accept the limitation of the traffic light. We all stop for a red light. This is a limitation on our freedom, but we accept it because we recognize that it is a limitation which in effect produces more freedom. If we did not have any traffic lights we should probably be dead, and there is a nothing less free than being dead.

Let me give another example. I was in Japan and Korea last year, and I very much wanted to go to China. Because I am an American citizen, I cannot go to China. If I were a Canadian or an Australian or a Britisher or a Frenchman, I could go to China. But because I am an American citizen my freedom is seriously impaired, and I am hopping mad about it. I feel that it is outrageous that the State Department can prevent me from going to China or to Cuba just because of a little thing like a passport. Every time I look at my passport I chafe mentally. I deny the legitimacy of this limitation upon my freedom.

Legitimacy is a much more important concept than power. It is a more important system than the threat system. It is the dynamics of legitimacy that really determine the future of the world. In our social system we have to understand how things gain legitimacy and how they lose legitimacy. I am quite in sympathy with the question which Milton Friedman raises: How is it that exchange, the free market, which is a very successful institution, finds it so hard to develop, keep and retain legitimacy? I do not quite know.

The role of the market in finance and financial institutions is of particular interest. We have Yugoslav economists coming through Ann Arbor frequently. They all seem to say the same thing. They all say how wonderful Adam Smith is and they tell us that we do not appreciate the wonders of the free market and the price system. But if we ask them whether they are going to set up a stock exchange, they turn a bit shy. Nevertheless, in the socialist countries there is a very marked creeping capitalism developing because they are beginning to understand and appreciate the virtues and importance of the price system and of the market economy. But they are not showing any signs whatever of developing anything that looks even remotely like a free market in finance.

What we need is a cost-benefit analysis of the financial system. The financial system performs a real function which has to be performed in any society. If it is not done one way, it has to be done in another. But we do not really know the relative costs and benefits of alternative methods of performing this function. When such a study is made, I shall not be at all surprised if the answer comes out on our side of the fence. Until we know the answer to this question, we are in a weak position in arguing with the Yugoslavs. There is a certain amount of evidence, I think, that bankers are richer than they need to be. Possibly we could get this kind of service more cheaply. There may be obstacles to freedom of entry. This may result in this particular service being performed more expensively than it really needs to be. But it might still be cheaper in the long run than a centrally planned economy.

Social Security: Legitimatized Coercion

On the subject of social security, which I favor, I am prepared to quarrel with Friedman, who is a bit more radical than I am. He wants a negative income tax, or whatever he calls it. He wants to "shovel it out" regardless, and I am somewhat sympathetic to this. I wish somebody would try the pivoted income tax, one under which those above a certain income pay taxes and those below a certain income get subsidies. This would simplify the whole problem and we could get rid of all social security and all welfare payments and we would have an enormous amount of freedom. It would be fun to try such a system and see what would happen. It would satisfy the requirements of the integrative system that there are income limits below which people cannot be allowed to fall, and it would permit freedom which could be used wisely or unwisely.

The existing social security system is open to severe criticism on precisely the grounds that Friedman suggested; that it is, for instance, a bad bargain for the young. I am not altogether opposed, however, to the use of what might be called legitimized economic coercion. The tax system is a threat system. If there were no penalties for not paying taxes, and if we tried to run the government like the Red Feather, with voluntary contributions, it might involve difficulties. Even the United Fund has a bit of the threat system in it: You *want* to give to the United Fund, do you not, says the foreman. There is a bit of a tax element in it.

Friedman has neglected what might be called legitimatized coercion. We accept coercion because we are better off if everybody is coerced. Law is legitimatized coercion. There are certain aspects of life in which there are enormous advantages of monopoly. This may well be true in social insurance; if everybody is in it, it is much cheaper for everybody. Under such circumstances, where there are substantial economies of scale and substantial economies of monopoly, it may be perfectly rational to vote to be coerced.

But this is not inconsistent with the fundamental principles of economic liberalism, if economic liberalism involves a sensible appraisal of the value of exchange as a social organizer. If this is what being an economic liberal means, then I am an economic liberal. After all, my middle name is Ewart. I was born in Liverpool on the same street as William Ewart Gladstone. If that does not make me a liberal, what does?

General Systems and Society

A Conceptual Framework for
Social Science[*]

The noble concept of the unification of science has always attracted
the imaginative thinker. It is a concept, however, which has proved
disappointing, and perhaps even positively dangerous in practice. It
has led either to grandiose overall systems like those of Bacon and
Comte, which remain empty because the bulging and slatternly
corpus of knowledge obstinately refuses to fit the neat corsets of the
system builders, or it has led to something much more dangerous—
pseudo-systems which have been satisfying to the mind without being
sufficiently true to reality. The Aristotelian system was one such. In
the social sciences there are the Marxian system and also that of
Veblen. Both these represent premature syntheses in social science—
integrations of bad economics, bad sociology and anthropology, bad
political science. Nevertheless, because they are syntheses they exert
remarkable power over the minds of men, to the ultimate detriment
of intellectual progress. They are comfortable mental inns on the long
dark road of knowledge; it is little wonder that men seek their warmth
and shelter, and that they settle down in them and refuse to continue
their journey.

For all its dangers, however, the impulse to integrate will not be
denied. It may well be that we move fastest along our narrow specialized trails. Still, the trails are converging. There are three signs of this
convergence. One is the development of hybrid specializations. In
the natural sciences, for instance, physical chemistry developed between physics and chemistry some three or four generations ago;
biochemistry, biophysics, astrophysics, and geophysics are latecomers.
In the social sciences the first hybrid to develop was social psychology
(political economy, alas, was stillborn), and there are signs that we

* *Papers of the Michigan Academy of Science, Arts and Letters* 37,
1951. Published 1952.
This paper was presented at the meetings of the Michigan Academy of
Science, Arts and Letters in April, 1951.

may be on the threshold of separate disciplines of economic sociology, economic psychology, and political psychology. The second sign of convergence is the development of applied fields which cut across the specialized disciplines. Labor relations, for instance, is a field which cuts across economics, sociology, social psychology, psychology, law, political science, and engineering. International relations is a field which cuts across economics, political science, social psychology, sociology, and law. In the process of contributing to an applied field the specialized disciplines can hardly avoid contributing to one another. Finally, even in pure theory there are signs of increasing dissatisfaction with the narrow models of the pure disciplines. Especially is this true in economics, where we are beginning to realize, for instance, that the firm is not merely an economic institution maximizing profit, but is a complex social organism with sociological, psychological, and political aspects which must be brought into view if an adequate theory is to be developed. All these signs suggest that the time may be approaching when, in spite of the dangers involved, a new attempt at synthesis needs to be made. It is not the purpose of this short paper to make such a synthesis! Nevertheless, some lines may be indicated along which a synthesis seems to be growing.

The theoretical structure of virtually every science consists of, first, a theory of some *individual*, which is the basic unit of study of the science, and, secondly, a theory of *interaction* among these individuals. The individual is the unit of behavior of the science, behavior being defined as the change in the individual in response to changes in its environment. Thus the physicist studies electrons; the chemist, atoms and molecules; the biologist, cells, organs, and organisms; the psychologist, organisms in terms of their behavior as aggregates; the sociologist, groups, families, and churches; the economist, firms and banks; the political scientist, towns, counties, and states. The study of the behavior of individuals in response to changes in their environment inevitably leads to the study of *interaction*, for the environment of any one individual consists of other individuals. Behavior, therefore, is always interaction; a change in one individual constitutes a change in the environment of others, which in turn constitutes a change in the environment of the first.

There is emerging from a great many different sciences something like a general theory of an individual, or of behavior on the one hand and a general theory of interaction on the other. By this I do not mean that we expect to find a *single* theory into which individuals as diverse as electrons, molecules, cells, rats, men, families, nations, philosophies, poems, and universes can all be put. Such a theory would either have to be so general as to be contentless or it would be a strait-jacket into which reality would have to be forced. What is emerging is not a single theory of immense generality, but, rather, a continuum or a spectrum of theoretical structures and concepts— not necessarily in one dimension—in which the theoretical structure of one science overlaps with those of related sciences, and all throw some sort of light on one another. In a similar way I believe a general structure of the theory of interaction is likewise beginning to emerge from a number of different sciences.

At the base of the theory of the individual is the concept of behavior itself, that is, of predictable change in response to a controlled environment. At the level of physics and chemistry even the definition and the taxonomy of the individual are determined not by direct observation but by a study of behavior; what is observed is usually an entirely different thing from the individuals (e.g. atoms, electrons, protons, and mesons) which are being studied. Nobody has ever observed an atom, much less one of the smaller particles; their existence is inferred from certain regular patterns of behavior, and their classification depends not on the direct observation of differences in appearance but on the observation of differences in behavior. This is true largely even at the level of cytology and bacteriology; the taxonomy of bacteria depends mainly on their reactions rather than on their appearance through a microscope. As we rise in the scale of complexity of the individual the taxonomic structure comes to rest more and more on direct observation, and less on reaction; nevertheless, there is a question here whether the significant taxonomies do not always rest on reaction classifications and whether the purely observational taxonomies in the biological and social sciences are not sometimes misleading.

Probably the next most general concept which is encountered in the theory of the individual is that of homeostasis, that is, the interpretation of behavior in terms of some equilibrium state which the individual "seeks" to maintain. The theory of valency in physical chemistry is an example of this principle at a very simple level, that is, an interpretation of the behavior of atoms or ions in terms of stable electron rings. At the level of the biological organism the concept is most illuminating. Even at the simplest levels of life the behavior of the organism in response to changes in its environment can be interpreted largely in terms of the attempt to restore an optimum condition in physical and chemical terms. As we rise in the scale of complexity the number of "homeostatic" mechanisms in the organism ever increases, until in the human body their number runs into dozens—or, if we count mental processes, perhaps into hundreds. Thus we have equilibrium values of such variables as body temperature, blood count, sugar concentration, water concentration, acidity, and calcium concentration; a disturbance from the equilibrium value due to a shift in the external environment sets off a chain of reactions which have the effect of insulating the body, and especially the most delicate structures, such as the brain, from these external changes. If we go into a cold room our teeth chatter, we stamp up and down

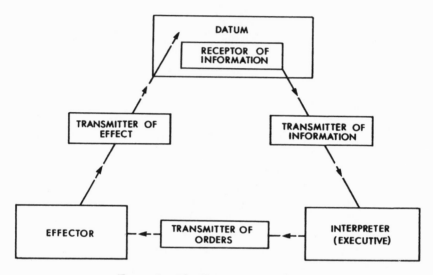

FIGURE 1.   The Homeostatic Mechanism

and so on—exercises some of which are involuntary, and some semivoluntary, but all of which are designed to release heat from the muscles. If we go into a hot room we become lassitudinous, the sweat glands open, respiration increases and so on—all these reactions being designed to cool us off.

Any homeostatic mechanism requires six parts, as shown in Figure One. There must first be the *datum*—the object of stabilization. Suppose we take as an example the homeostatic control of house temperature by a thermostat. The datum in this case is the temperature of the air around the thermostat. Secondly, there must be a *receptor* of information about the datum—the thermostat itself. There must be a *transmitter of information* from the receptor to an *interpreter* —in this case the wire connecting the thermostat to the furnace control. There must likewise be a transmitter from the interpreter of the information to an *effector* (the furnace) and a transmitter of the effect from the effector (the pipes and radiators) back to the datum. Then, if there is a divergence between the actual and the equilibrium value of the datum, this information is received and transmitted to the interpreter, which sets in motion the effector, which affects the datum in a direction calculated to diminish the divergence between the actual and the ideal value. Thus, if the house is cold (temperature below the set value), the thermostat registers this fact, transmits it to the furnace control, which sets the furnace in motion, which heats up the house; if the house is too hot, the thermostat registers this information, transmits it to the control, and shuts off the furnace. The mechanism may, of course, be much more complex than this, even in such a simple thing as a furnace control, but the system described is the basic element in all such arrangements, and anything which can be described as an organism, whether biological or social, will have arrangements of this kind.

I shall give two examples from the social sciences—the firm and the state. The firm is an organism consisting of an interpreter (the executive), who receives information through the accounting system, the budget system, the market-research system, Kiplinger letters, gossip on the golf course, and so on. As a result of his interpretation of this information certain decisions are made which are transmitted to the production and sales organizations and result in certain actions. These actions produce effects on the datum (sales, prices, and profits), which in turn are picked up by the receptors and transmitted to the executive as information, which again produce decisions. The simplest possible theory of the firm is the theory of "homeostasis of the balance sheet," in which we suppose that there is some composition of the balance sheet which the firm wishes to maintain. Then changes in the data, occasioned, for instance, by sales of goods, are transmitted to the effector in the form of a message to *replace* (by production) the goods sold; this replacement restores both the goods and the money items in the balance sheet to their initial level.

At the political level we can suppose also that there is some "state" of an organism, such as a nation, at which discontent is a minimum. A divergence from this happy condition results in discontent, which is eventually transmitted through the political and constitutional machinery into a need for action on the part of government (the effector) —the action presumably being directed toward reducing the discontent and restoring the body politic to contentment.

It should be observed that every homeostatic mechanism involves cycles. The amplitude of the cycle depends mainly on the sensitivity of the mechanism. If the mechanism is highly insensitive, large cycles will be set up because of the lag between the receptor and the effector. If some elements of the system are too sensitive, there is also a possibility of large cycles; generally, however, most cycles are the result of inadequate sensitivity. Thus the many cycles which are observed in economic and social life may be regarded as the result of an inadequate homeostatic mechanism; the so-called business cycle is largely a result of inadequate homeostatic mechanism in the monetary and fiscal system; the "war cycle" is a result of the absence of homeostatic mechanisms in international relations; the cycle of liberal and conservative governments in a two-party system may also be regarded as a homeostatic cycle.

Homeostasis does not, of course, exhaust the theory of the individual; indeed, it represents only the very first approximation. We cannot be content with merely observing that some state is maintained; we must raise the question of *what* state is maintained. Answers to this question involve problems of growth and decay, of learning and accretion, of survival and evolutionary development. Such questions arise in connection with almost any organism, from the simplest biological organism to the most complex social organization. The social sciences have given far too little attention to them; especially is this true of economics, where the theory of the firm remains at a level of static equilibrium (maximization), is only just beginning to advance toward a theory of a homeostatic mechanism, and has scarcely begun to include theories of growth and decay, life cycles, and learning. It is hardly an exaggeration to say that in the world of the economists man never learns anything; he just knows it already. Thus there is practically no discussion in economic literature with which I am familiar of how business men become aware of the nature of the demand which faces them.

I now pass on to the second broad field of theory in which integration seems to be taking place; this is in the study of the interaction of individuals and populations of individuals. In the study of individual behavior we assume that the environment is given, independent of the individual himself, and that we can examine the response of the individual to changes in that environment without worrying about the effect of this response on the environment itself. Where the individual is small in relation to his environment, this aspect of behavior is usually sufficient. Where, however, we are considering a whole system, and especially when there are few individuals interacting, we must recognize that the environment of each individual consists of other individuals, and that each individual himself comprises part of the environment of others. Ecology is the general science which studies these interactions, that is, which studies whole systems of individuals. Its general principles apply not only to biological systems but also to social systems. Any system, in fact, which can be regarded as a system of interacting populations can be regarded as an ecosystem. The general theory of such systems is formally quite simple, though the topology of particular systems may present numerous difficulties. If there are n populations, $x_1, x_2 \ldots x_n$, interacting, we simply write the equilibrium magnitude of each population as a function of the size of all the others. This gives us immediately a set of n equations which can theoretically be solved for the n unknowns to give a general equilibrium value for each population. There may, of course, be various restrictions placed on the solution; we may not admit negative values, for instance, zero being the lower boundary of each variable, or there may be lower boundaries established by "niches" which shelter some populations from the rigors of interaction.

These complexities, however, are nothing compared with the complexities introduced when the interaction is not direct, in the sense that the responses are to changes in the present environment, but indirect in the sense that the responses are to uncertain expected future changes in the environment. This is a problem which rarely if ever arises in the biological sciences, since it is essentially a phenomenon of consciousness—even of a fairly advanced level of consciousness. In human interaction, however, the problem of uncertainty and anticipation must be faced; the environment to which an individual reacts is not merely an external but an internal, subjective environment. It is at this level that we run into the type of problem considered in the economic theory of oligopoly or, more generally, in the theory of games. It is clearly of enormous importance in political science and in the study of group interaction of any kind. Unfortunately, the difficulty of the subject is at least as great as its importance; still, it is a rapidly developing field and holds great promise for the future.

I am not proposing this twofold scheme of the theory of the individual on the one hand and of interaction on the other as a complete framework for all science, or even for all social science; there are many studies which do not easily fit into it, especially in psychology. I believe, however, that, like the framework provided by the periodic table in chemistry, it may serve to point up new directions of inquiry by providing a structure in which there are some obvious missing segments. I have found this to be true in my own field of economics. I would be surprised if it is not true of others.

Toward a General Theory of Growth[*]

I

The growth phenomenon is found in practically all the sciences and even in most of the arts, because almost all the objects of human study grow—crystals, molecules, cells, plants, animals, children, personalities, knowledge, ideas, cities, cultures, organizations, nations, wealth, and economic systems. It does not follow, of course, from the mere universality of the growth phenomenon that there must be a single unified theory of growth which will cover everything from the growth of a crystal to the growth of an empire. Growth itself is not a simple or a unified phenomenon, and we cannot expect all the many forms of growth to come under the umbrella of a single theory. Nevertheless all growth phenomena have something in common, and what is more important, the classifications of *forms* of growth and hence of theories of growth seem to cut across most of the conventional boundaries of the sciences. In addition there are a great many problems which are common to many apparently diverse growth phenomena.

It is convenient to start with a threefold classification of growth phenomena. We have first what might be called *simple* growth, that is, the growth or decline of a single variable or quantity by accretion or depletion. In all that follows it should be understood that growth may be negative as well as positive, decline being treated merely as negative growth. In the second place we have what might be called *populational* growth, in which the growing quantity is not regarded as a homogeneous aggregate, but is analysed into an age distribution. Growth is regarded as the excess of "births" (additions to the aggregate) over "deaths" (subtractions from the aggregate), and the analysis of the process is conducted in terms of functions which relate births and deaths to the age distribution. Finally we have what might be

[*] *Can. Jour. Econ. Pol. Sci.* 19, 3 (Aug. 1953): 326–40.
This paper was presented at the annual meeting of the Canadian Political Science Association in London, Ontario, June 3, 1953.

called *structural* growth, in which the aggregate which "grows" consists of a complex structure of interrelated parts and in which the growth process involves change in the relation of the parts. Thus in the growth of a living organism, or of an organization, as the "whole" grows, the form and the parts change: new organs develop, old organs decline, and there is frequently growth in complexity as well as in some over-all magnitudes. Problems of structural growth seem to merge almost imperceptibly into the problems of structural *change* or development, so that frequently "what grows" is not the over-all size of the structure but the complexity or systematic nature of its parts. Thus the "growth" of a butterfly out of the chrysalis involves an actual decline in over-all magnitudes such as weight or volume, but certainly seems to come under the general heading of phenomena of growth or development.

These three "forms" of growth constitute three different levels of abstraction rather than a classification of actual growth phenomena. Growth phenomena in the real world usually involve all three types. Thus a phenomenon of simple growth such as, for instance, the growth of a capital sum put out to interest, or the growth in the inventory or stocks of a single commodity are in fact part of, and ultimately dependent upon, much more complicated structural processes. Similarly, populational growth as in the case, say, of a human population, never takes place without changes in the organizational structure of the society, that is, in the kinds and the proportions of its "parts"—its organizations, jobs, roles, and so on. Thus all actual growth is structural growth; nevertheless, for some purposes of analysis the structural elements may be neglected and the growing aggregate can be treated as a pure population, and for other purposes even the populational aspects can be neglected and the growth can be treated as simple growth.

II

Turning first then to the analysis of simple growth, the main problem here is that of finding a "law" of growth which will serve to describe the growth curve, that is, which will express the size of the growing variable as a function of time. Perhaps the simplest case of simple growth is growth at a constant rate, for example, the growth of a capital sum at a constant rate of interest. In this case the growth function is the simple exponential $P_t = P_0 (1 + i)^t$, where P_0 is the original sum, P_t the amount into which it has grown in t years at a constant rate of growth i, growth being added at the end of every year. If growth is continuous the function becomes $P_t = P_0 e^{it}$.

Continuous growth at a constant rate, however, is rare in nature and even in society. Indeed it may be stated that within the realm of common human experience all growth must run into *eventually* declining rates of growth. As growth proceeds, the growing object must eventually run into conditions which are less and less favourable to growth. If this were not true there would eventually be only one object in the universe and at that point at least, unless the universe itself can grow indefinitely, its growth would have to come to an end. It is not surprising, therefore, that virtually all empirical growth curves exhibit the familiar "ogive" shape, the absolute growth being small at first, rising to a maximum, and then declining eventually to zero as the maximum value of the variable is reached. Many equations for such a curve have been suggested, though none seem to rest on any very secure theoretical foundation. The most familiar is perhaps that of Raymond Pearl, which graphically is a cumulative normal frequency curve. In any such equation the most important constants are (i) one which measures the total amount of growth, that is, the difference between the initial and the maximum value of the variable, and (ii) one which measures the time taken to grow from the initial position to a value reasonably close to the maximum. All that growth equations can do, however, is to describe growth; they are never capable of interpreting or understanding it.[1]

III

Turning now to the second level of growth analysis, that of population growth, we find that fairly detailed and complex analyses are possible. A population may be defined as "an aggregation of disparate items, or 'individuals,' each one of which conforms to a given definition, retains its identity with the passage of time, and exists only during a finite interval."[2] "Birth" occurs when an item begins to conform to the definition which encloses the aggregation, and "death" when the item ceases to conform to this definition. A definition may be thought of as a closed

---

[1] My recent acquaintance with the work of Dr. S. A. Courtis suggests that this judgment may be much too severe. An empirical "growth law" which fits many cases has at least the virtue that it calls attention to possible unknown sources of disturbance in cases where it does not fit—just as the law of gravity led to the discovery of the outer planets. Courtis's law ($y = ki^r$) may well be of use in this way. See S. A. Courtis, "What Is a Growth Cycle?" *Growth*, I, no. 3, May, 1937.

[2] K. E. Boulding, "The Application of the Pure Theory of Population Change to the Theory of Capital," *Quarterly Journal of Economics*, XLVIII, Aug., 1934, 650.

fence: everything inside the fence belongs to the defined population; birth consists in crossing the fence into the enclosure; death in crossing the fence out of the enclosure. The population concept as thus defined is a perfectly general one, and applies not only to human or animal populations, but to populations of automobiles, poems, stars, dollars, ideas, or anything that is capable of definition.

Population *analysis* is only useful in the case of aggregates where birth and death rates can be regarded as some function of the *age composition* of the population. The age composition can be expressed most simply as a series of age groups, $a_1, a_2, \ldots, a_n$, where a_1 is the number of individuals between the ages of 0 and 1 "year," a_r is the number between the ages of $r - 1$ and r "years" old. The "age" of any individual is of course the time which has elapsed since birth. The "year" can of course be made as small as we like: in the limit the age composition reduces to a continuous function. If then the number of births and the number of deaths *in each age group* can be expressed as functions of the age composition, $a_1, \ldots, a_n$, the whole course of the population can be traced as far as patience and arithmetic hold out— or the assumed functions do not change. The simplest "birth function" is $B = b_1 a_1 + b_2 a_2 + \ldots + b_n a_n$. This assumes that each age group makes a specific and constant proportional contribution to the total number of births where $(b_1, \ldots, b_n)$ are constants. Similarly the simplest "death function" is $D = d_1 a_1 + d_2 a_2 + \ldots + d_n a_n$, where the number of deaths in each age group is assumed to be a constant proportion of the numbers in the group. Given such a death function, a "survival function" for any given "cohort" of births can be derived, a "cohort" being all those individuals who have a common "year" of birth. Thus of a number of births B in year 0, Bd_0 will die and $Bs_1 = B(1 - d_0)$ will survive into year 1: of these $B(1 - d_0)d_1$ will die and $Bs_2 = B(1 - d_0)(1 - d_1)$ will survive into year 2; similarly $Bs_{r+1} = B(1 - d_0)(1 - d_1) \ldots (1 - d_r)$ will survive into year $r + 1$. If the population is finite (that is, composed of mortals), we must have $d_n = 1$: that is, none of the oldest age group survive into the next year.

Probably the best way to illustrate the process of population analysis is by an arithmetical example, as the algebraic treatment is both easy and clumsy. Suppose a population of three age groups, a birth function $B = 3a_2 + 8a_3$, and a survival function $s_1 = 1$, $s_2 = 0.8$, $s_3 = 0.4$, and suppose we start with a population of 100 in the first age group, 40 in the second, and 10 in the third. The course of the population will be as in Table I.

TABLE I

Year	Births	Age Group 0–1	1–2	2–3	Total
1	120 + 80 = 200	100	40	10	150
2	240 + 160 = 400	200	80	20	300
3	480 + 320 = 800	400	160	40	600
4	960 + 640 = 1600	800	320	80	1200

Thus in the first year the number of births is $40 \times 3 + 10 \times 8$, or 200; of this cohort of 200 births all 200 survive into year 2, and are then in the first age group: $160 = (200 \times 0.8)$ survive into year 3, and are then in the second age group, and $80 = (200 \times 0.4)$ survive into year 4 and are then in the third age group. Given the number of births and the age composition of year 1 we can get immediately the age composition of year 2; the 200 births of year 1 become the 200 0–1 year olds: the 100 0–1 year olds become the 80 1–2 year olds, and the 40 1–2 year olds become the 20 2–3 year olds. From this age composition we can then derive the birth cohort of year 2 $(80 \times 3 + 20 \times 8)$. Similarly from the birth cohort and the age composition of year 2 we derive the age composition of year 3, and from that the birth cohort of year 3. The process can clearly be repeated for an indefinite number of years.

Table I has been arranged so that the population grows exponentially, doubling every year. It will be observed that the birth cohort likewise doubles every year, as does the number in each age group. Such a population may be said to be in "equilibrium exponential growth." If the rate of growth is 1, of course, the population is stationary and exactly reproduces its composition every year. If the rate of growth is less than 1 the population is declining, but the same principles apply. Now, however, suppose that instead of starting with the age composition of Table I we started with a distorted composition, as in Table II.

It will be seen that although the underlying laws of development of the population are exactly the same as in Table I, the immediate course of the population is very different. Instead of growing steadily, the population grows in a series of leaps and checks; indeed, from the second to the third years it actually declines, in spite of the fact that the underlying dynamics of the population imply a doubling every year! It will be observed, however, that in the present case the irregularities of the growth rate diminish as time goes on, and the age

TABLE II

Year	Births (3a$_2$ + 8a$_3$ =Total)			Age Group 0–1	1–2	2–3	Total
1	30 +	800 =	830	10	10	100	120
2	24 +	40 =	64	830	8	5	843
3	1992 +	32 =	2024	64	664	4	732
4	153 +	2656 =	2809	2024	51	332	2407
5	4857 +	208 =	5065	2809	1619	26	4454
6	6741 +	6480 =	13221	5065	2247	810	8122
7				13221	4046	1120	18387

distribution becomes less distorted. This is because the birth function has coefficients for more than one age group, so that the contribution of the initial age composition gets "mixed" as time goes on. If the birth function only had coefficients for a single age group the "cycle" in the growth curve would perpetuate itself.

A simple algebraic expression of the above principles follows. Let the age composition in year t be $a_1, a_2, \ldots, a_n$, these being the numbers in the age groups $0–1, 1–2, \ldots, (n-1)–n$. Suppose a birth function

$$(1) \qquad B_t = b_1 a_1 + b_2 a_2 + \ldots + b_n a_n.$$

Suppose also a series of survival coefficients, $s_1, s_2, \ldots, s_n$, where s_n is the proportion of the births of any year t that survive into the year $t + n$. Then for the year t we have

$$(2) \qquad a_1 = s_1 B_{1t-1}, \, a_2 = s_2 B_{t-2}, \, \ldots, \, a_n = s_n B_{t-n}.$$

Combining (1) and (2) we have

$$(3) \qquad B_t = b_1 s_1 B_{t-1} + b_2 s_2 B_{t-2} + \ldots + b_n s_n B_{t-n}.$$

Suppose now that we have a population in equilibrium exponential growth (or decline) at a rate g. Then we must have:

$$(4) \qquad B_{t+1} = g B_t, \text{ whence } B_{t+r} = g^r B_t.$$

Inserting the appropriate values from (3) and cancelling B_t we have:

$$(5) \qquad \frac{b_1 s_1}{g} + \frac{b_2 s_2}{g^2} + \ldots + \frac{b_n s_n}{g^n} = 1.$$

This equation can be solved for g to give the equilibrium rate of growth corresponding to any set of birth and survival coefficients. For a population in stationary equilibrium $g = 1$, and we have

(6)
$$R = \sum_{1}^{n} b_r s_r = 1.$$

R may be called the "growth potential" of the population; the population must eventually grow, be stationary, or decline according as R is greater than, equal to, or less than 1. If sex ratios are neglected R is the same as the net reproduction ratio of a human or animal population, that is, it is the average number of births which eventually come from a unit of any given cohort of births in a population in equilibrium exponential growth.

Suppose now that the birth function contains only a single coefficient, b_r. If the initial age composition of the population is $a_1, a_2, \ldots, a_n$, births in year t_0 are $b_r a_r$. In year t_r then the rth age group will have $b_r a_r s_r$ individuals in it, and the number of births will be $b_r^2 a_r s_r$. In the year t_{2r} the rth age group will be $b_r^2 a_r s_r^2$, and the number of births $b_r^3 a_r s_r^2$. In the year t_{kr} the number of births will be $b_r a_r (b_r s_r)^k$. Similarly in the year t_1 the rth age group will be

$$b_r \, a_{r-1} \frac{s_r}{s_{r-1}},$$

and the number of births will be

$$b_r^2 a_{\,r-1} \frac{s_r}{s_{r-1}}.$$

In the year t_{kr+1} the number of births will be

$$b_r \, a_{r-1} \frac{s_r}{s_{r-1}} (b_r \, s_r)^k.$$

It is clear that the birth cohorts and also the total population will repeat the pattern set up by the first r years, multiplied by the growth factor in all succeeding periods of r years. If however there is more than one birth function coefficient, the effect will be "damped."

The assumption of constant birth and survival coefficients gives us at least a first approximation to the dynamics of human or animal populations. The fact, however, that such an assumption results in exponential growth (or decline) means that it cannot be more than a first approximation for, as we have seen, exponential growth cannot go on forever. In order to achieve growth patterns of an ogive or logistic form it is necessary to assume that the birth or survival coefficients are themselves functions of the total population or of time, one or both eventually decreasing with increase of population, or lapse of time. A period of growth can then be attributed to a rise of

$$R = \sum_{1}^{n} b_r s_r$$

above 1; the ultimate cessation of growth comes about because the growth of the population itself carries R down to 1 again. This is illustrated in Figure One. We postulate an R-curve rr relating R to the

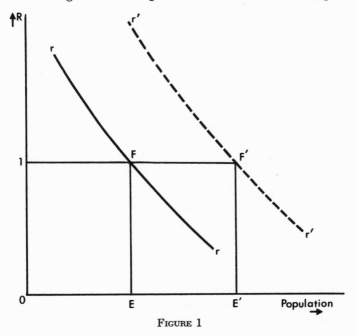

FIGURE 1

total population. The equilibrium population is OE where $EF = 1$. Suppose now that conditions change—life, say, becomes easier. The R-curve moves to the right to a new position $r'r'$. The equilibrium population is now OE', where again $E'F' = 1$. The exact dynamics of the shift from E to E' of course depend on the nature of the birth and survival functions.

Birth and survival functions need not, of course, be confined to age compositions. In many populations other variables are significant. For instance, for populations of capital goods (e.g., automobiles) we may assume as a first approximation that the object of "births" (production) is to hold the total population either constant, or increasing at a constant rate. In that case the number of births in any year will be equal to the number of deaths, plus the number necessary to maintain the desired increase in the total population. On such an assumption within any given pattern of growth of the total population, considerable fluctuations are possible in birth cohorts, if there are distortions in the age distribution. Thus consider the following population table:

TABLE III

		Age Composition			
Year	*Births*	0–1	1–2	2–3	*Total*
0	100	100	100	100	300
1	100	100	100	100	300
2	200	100	100	100	300
3	100	200	100	100	400
4	100	100	200	100	400
5	200	100	100	200	400
6	100	200	100	100	400

Here we suppose a population of "one-hoss shays," with three age groups, and survival coefficients of 1, 1, 1, 0: all deaths occur at the end of the third year. We suppose an initial population of 100 in each age group, 300 in all. This is maintained by 100 births every year, as we see going year 0 to year 1. Now in year 2 it is decided to increase the population to 400, and in order to do this 200 births are "made." In year 3 we then have an age composition of 200, 100, 100. However, only the 100 in the third age group "die," so that only 100 need to be born in year 4. In year 5, however, the 200 that were born in year 2 die, and have to be replaced by another 200. It is clear that a perpetual cycle is now set up, with 200 births every three years and 100 in the intervening years. This cycle could only be avoided by raising the total population by equal amounts each year for a three-year period. If the survival distribution is more normal, however, so that some of the survival coefficients are less than 1, the effect will again be damped and the intensity of the cycle will diminish.

Very interesting and important problems arise (which are too complex to be examined in detail here) when the growth functions of one population depend upon the size of other populations. This, of course, is the theory of ecological interaction. At the level of comparative statics, that is, the comparison of two positions of equilibrium, the theory is not too difficult, but the dynamics of such systems easily become very complex. Figure Two, however, illustrates the principle on which such systems operate.

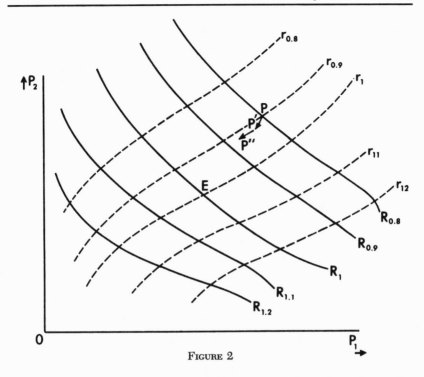

FIGURE 2

We suppose two different populations, P_1 and P_2. Size of population P_1 is measured along the horizontal axis, P_2 on the vertical axis. The solid line R_1 then shows all those combinations of P_1 and P_2 at which the R (growth potential) of population 1 is unity. Similarly the line $R_{1.1}$ shows those combinations for which $R = 1.1$ for population 1, and similarly for the other solid lines. The dotted lines similarly represent those combinations of P_1 and P_2 for which the growth potential of population 2 is 1, 1.1, etc. In the figure as drawn P_2 inhibits the growth of P_1, that is, the larger the population of P_2 the less will be the growth potential of P_1 for each level of P_1 as shown by the family of solid lines. P_2 is a predator or parasite on P_1. Cases in which both populations are mutually competitive, or in which both are mutually cooperative, can be analysed by the same technique. The point E where the R_1 and r_1 curves intersect is the point of general stationary equilibrium, that is, the point at which the populations in equilibrium will coexist without growth or decline of either. Consider, however, the combination of populations represented by the point P. At this point $R = 0.8$, $r = 0.9$. Both populations will therefore decline, unless their age structures are very distorted. P_1 will decline more than P_2, and the two populations will move following the vector PP'. From P'

another movement will take place to, say, P'', and so on until the equilibrium is reached. Lines of movement of the populations such as $PP'P''$ may be called "vector lines," and the family of such lines is a good rough description of the dynamics of the system. Examples will be found in my *Reconstruction of Economics*, chapter I.

I V

The analysis of structural growth is much more complicated than the analysis of populational growth, and is much more difficult to reduce to a neat set of propositions. Structural growth includes such complex phenomena as the growth of crystal structures, the growth, division, and differentiation of cells, the growth of organisms, of organizations, of language and other mental structures, of buildings, and of societies. We would hardly expect such diverse phenomena to reduce themselves to a uniform simple scheme. Nevertheless it is striking how many of the problems which rise to special prominence in one field of study also carry over into others, and it is not impossible to formulate some principles of great generality.

The first of these we may call the principle of nucleation, following a term which comes originally from physics. Any structure has a minimum size, which is its "nucleus." Once a nucleus has been formed, it is not too difficult to understand how additions to the structure are made. The formation of the nucleus itself, however, presents many problems which are quite different from those involved in the growth of an already established structure. Thus there is a minimum size of crystal, depending on its complexity: in smaller aggregations of atoms than this minimum there are not enough components to make up the minimum structure. In the case of the cell the problem of nucleation is almost completely unsolved: as far as we now know, all living matter grows from living matter. We know something about how the complex societies of subordinate structures which comprise the living nuclei can grow, divide, and differentiate as "going concerns." We know practically nothing about how such an immensely complex organization ever came to be established in the first place, and up to the present we have not been able to reproduce that mysterious initial act of nucleation. In the social sciences the nucleation problem also exists; here it manifests itself as the problem of innovation, in the Schumpeterian sense. Once a form of organization is established, whether a type of production or a kind of enterprise, a cult, a school, a party, or any distinct type of institution, it is not too difficult to imitate. The initial innovation, however, is something of a mystery, which does not fall easily within the smooth rubrics of historical necessity. We do not understand very well what it is that makes the genuine innovators—those mysterious individuals who establish religions, cultures, nations, techniques, and ideas. In society as in physics, however, we find that very small amounts of "impurities" (say one Edison per hundred million) produce effects fantastically disproportionate to their quantity, because of the nucleation principle. It is also not perhaps too farfetched to speak of "super-cooled societies," where the external conditions call for change to a new state of society, but where the rate of nucleation is so small that the change does not take place.

Another principle which emerges from the study of nucleation is that the nucleus does not have to be homogeneous with the structure that grows around it; thus the speck of dust at the heart of the raindrop! Consequently *impurity* in a universe is a very important factor in explaining change. Examples of this principle are numerous in society. Colleges nucleate around sects, farm organizations around county agents, trade unions around socially minded priests. One cannot be a student of society for long without observing what I have sometimes called the "Pinocchio principle." Some agent or organization sets up a "puppet" in the form of some other kind of organization. Before long however the "puppet" begins to take on a life of its own, and frequently walks right away from its maker. Here we see the principle of "heterogeneous nucleation" actively at work in society. The principle of nucleation applies even to the learning process, which can be thought of as the growth of a "mental structure." Thus in learning a language it is necessary for the language to "nucleate" in the mind of the learner before it can become anything more to him than an unusable bunch of unrelated words. Even in learning economics the student frequently finds that for the first few months the subject makes practically no sense to him, and then quite suddenly he experiences a "conversion"; what had previously been disconnected parts somehow fall into place in his mind, and for the first time he "sees" the subject as an organic whole. The application of this idea to the phenomenon of religious or political conversion would make a most interesting study.

The second general principle of structural development might be called the principle of non-proportional change. As any structure grows, the proportions of its parts and of its significant variables *cannot* remain constant. It is impossible that is to say, to reproduce *all* the characteristics of a structure in a scale model of different size. This is because a uniform increase in the linear dimensions of a structure will increase all its areas as the square, and its volume as the cube, of the increase in the linear dimension. Thus a twofold increase in all the lengths of a structure increases its areas by four times and its volumes by eight times. As some of the essential functions and variables of structure depend on its linear dimensions, some on its areal dimensions, and some on its volumetric dimensions, it is impossible to keep the same proportions between all the significant variables and functions as the structure grows.

This principle has two important corollaries. The first is that growth of a structure always involves a *compensatory* change in the relative sizes of its various parts to compensate for the fact that those functions and properties which depend on volume tend increasingly to dominate those dependent on area, and those dependent on area tend increasingly to dominate those depending on length. Large structures therefore tend to be "long" and more convoluted than small structures, in the attempt to increase the proportion of linear and areal dimensions to volumes. It follows therefore that as a structure grows it will also tend to become longer and more convoluted. Architecture and biology—two sciences which are much more closely related than might appear at first sight—provide admirable examples. A one-room schoolhouse, like the bacterium, can afford to be roughly globular and can still maintain effective contact with its environment—getting enough light and nutrition (children) into its interior through its walls. Larger schools, like worms, become long in relation to their volume in order to give every room at least one outside wall. Still larger schools develop wings and courtyards, following the general principle that a structure cannot be more than two rooms thick if it is to have adequate breathing facilities. This is the insect level of architecture (skin-breathing). The invention of artificial ventilation (lungs) and illumination (optic nerves) makes theoretically possible at any rate much larger structures of a "globular" or cubic type, with inside rooms artificially ventilated and lit, just as the development of lungs, bowels, nerves, and brains (all involving extensive convolution to get more area per unit of volume) enabled living matter to transcend the approximately three-inch limit set by the insect (skin-breathing) pattern. In the absence of such devices further growth of the structure involves splitting up into separate buildings (the campus) of which the biological analogy is the termite or bee colony.

The second corollary follows immediately from the first: if the process of compensation for structural disproportion has limits, as in fact seems to be the case, the size of the structure itself is limited by its ultimate inability to compensate for the non-proportional changes. This is the basic principle which underlies the "law of eventually diminishing returns to scale" familiar to economists. Thus as institutions grow they have to maintain larger and larger specialized administrative structures in order to overcome the increasing difficulties of communication between the "edges" or outside surfaces of the organization (the classroom, the parish, the retail outlet) and the central executive. Eventually the cost of these administrative structures begins to outweigh any of the other possible benefits of large scale, such as increasing specialization of the more directly productive parts of the organization, and these structural limitations bring the growth of the organization to an end. One can visualize, for instance, a university of a hundred thousand students in which the entire organization is made up of administrators, leaving no room at all for faculty.

It is interesting to note that the principle of compensation may operate in two very distinct ways—in the direction of attempt to *solve* the problems posed by large scale or in the direction of an attempt to *avoid* these problems. Thus the critical problem of large-scale organization is that of the communications system (nerves and blood!). This being a "linear" function tends to become inadequate relative to the "surface" functions of interaction and production as the organization grows. One method of compensation is to increase the proportion of the organization which is devoted to the communications system as the organization grows larger (the modern army, David Reisman has remarked, marches not on its stomach but on the punched card). Another method however is to diminish the *need* for communication by developing autonomy of the parts or rigid and ritualistic patterns of behaviour. Thus a very large church organization, such as the Roman Catholic Church, not only has to permit a good deal of autonomy to its various parts (in this case, national churches), but can only maintain its structure at the cost of extreme rigidity in its basic operations. The Pope doesn't have to communicate with the priest in the wilds of Bolivia because the mass is removed from the agenda of discussion! In this connection it might be noted also that great size in itself leads to relative invulnerability, and hence very large organizations do not face the same problems of uncertainty and adjustment which face smaller organizations or organisms. The whales and elephants of the universe can afford to have fairly placid dispositions and insensitive exteriors.

A third principle of structural growth follows somewhat from the second, but is sufficiently distinct to warrant a separate status. This might be called the D'Arcy Thompson principle, after its most famous exponent.[3] It is the principle that at any moment the *form* of any object, organism, or organization is a result of its laws of growth up

---

[3] D'Arcy W. Thompson, *On Growth and Form* (2nd ed., Cambridge, 1952).

to that moment. Something which grows uniformly in all directions will be a sphere. Something which grows faster in one direction than in others will be "long." Something which grows faster on one side than on the other will twist into some sort of spiral. The shape of an egg is related to its flow down the oviduct. Examples can be multiplied almost indefinitely, and the contemplation of these beautiful and subtle relationships is perhaps one of the most refined delights of the human mind. It is clear that the principle applies in general not only to organisms, but to organizations, though its applications here are more complex and perhaps less secure. An aggressive chairman or department head will cause his department to grow relative to the total structure. Scientific inquiries follow growth patterns which are laid down by previous studies and by the interests of scientists. Economic and technological development follows patterns which in turn determine the structure of an economy. Law grows like a great coral reef on the skeletons of dead cases.

Growth creates form, but form limits growth. This mutuality of relationship between growth and form is perhaps the most essential key to the understanding of structural growth. We have seen how growth compels adjustments to changes in relative proportions. It is also true that occasionally growth stops because of "closure"—because the growth itself seals off all the growing edges. We see this frequently in the world of ideas where self-contained ideologies (such as Marxism) exhibit closure in the sense that any development outside the narrow circle of the self-contained system is inhibited. It is often the "loose ends" of systems that are their effective growing points—too tight or too tidy an organization may make for stability, but it does not make for growth. This is perhaps one of the most cogent arguments for toleration in the political sphere; the morbid passion for tidiness is one of the greatest enemies of human development.

There is, I believe, a fourth principle of structural growth, detailed evidence for which it is difficult to find in the biological sciences, but which is clearly apparent in the growth of man-made structures, especially, oddly enough, in building. It may perhaps be called the "carpenter principle." In building any large structure out of small parts one of two things must be true if the structure is not to be hopelessly misshapen. Either the dimensions of the parts must be extremely accurate, or there must be something like a carpenter or a bricklayer following a "blueprint" who can adjust the dimensions of the structure as it goes along. If, for instance, we are building a structure out of a thousand identical parts, the tolerable variability of each part would have to be about one thousandth of the tolerable variability of the whole structure, if we were simply adding part to part without making any adjustments on the way. It is only possible, however, to build a brick wall or a wooden house, with bricks and with boards that are in themselves highly variable, if there is exercised during the process of growth a "skill" of adjustment, that is, of adjusting the structure as it grows in conformity with some plan or requirement. It may perhaps be hazarded that the genes perform some such function in the growth of living organisms, though what is the machinery by which these little carpenters of the body operate is still unknown. In social and intellectual structures, however, the principle is of great importance, for the whole development of these structures may be affected profoundly by the existence of a "plan" and of an apparatus by which the growing structure is constantly conformed to the plan. The construction of a building, a machine, or a bridge is an obvious example. The process of academic learning is another example. In the learning of a language, for instance, the existence of a grammar exercises a profound effect on the capacity of the student to develop originality. In any subject, the presence of a textbook exercises somewhat the same influence as a grammar on the process of learning, and the instructor is the intellectual carpenter, trimming the student's mind off at frequent intervals by means of quizzes and examinations. What we have here is essentially a homœostatic process, the divergence which excites action being the divergence at any time between the actual condition of the structure and the "planned" condition.

Even where a detailed "plan" of development is not available the existence of some kind of ideal structure with which present reality may be compared exercises a profound influence on growth, especially in the sciences. One need only cite, for instance, the influence exerted on the progress of chemistry by the existence of the periodic table of elements, an ideal structure which in the beginning had many "holes" (undiscovered elements), but which was gradually filled up as the process of chemical research was directed into filling the obvious gaps in the structure. It may, indeed, be regarded as one of the prime functions of "theory" in any field to set up these ideal structures which are in fact incomplete. In this connection it may be observed that one of the principal advantages which may be derived from interdisciplinary research is the development of a "general theory" which will fulfil this function of the "ideal structure" for knowledge as a whole.

A fifth principle of structural growth emerges fairly clearly from economics, though here also its application to the biological or physical sciences is quite unproved. This may be called the "principle of equal advantage." It governs the distribution of the "substance" of a structure among the various parts of the structure. We assume first that the "atoms" of a structure can be ordered according to a parameter which we label, for want of a better term "advantage," this being defined operationally as a "potential" such that units will tend to flow towards locations of higher, and away from locations of lower, advantage. We then postulate that the advantage of a unit in any location is an inverse function of the relative quantity of units in that location —that is, the fewer the merrier! This implies a concept something like the "demand" for any given location—demand in this case fulfils something of the function of the "plan" under the fourth proposition. We then postulate a principle that "demand" tends to be satisfied, that is, if there are differences in advantage to units ("industries") in different locations, units will tend to move from the low-advantage locations where there are "too many" to the high-advantage locations where there are "too few."

In economic systems the principle of equal advantage, and the fact that the "advantage" parameter can be approximately related to monetary reward, enables us to give reasonably satisfactory explanations of two phenomena which are common in biology, but very little understood. These are the phenomena known as functional substitution and regeneration. If one organ of a living organization is removed, there is an observable tendency for other organs to take over the function of the missing organ. At lower levels of life, also, the organism seems to have a remarkable capacity for the regeneration of lost parts; tadpoles can grow new tails and starfish new limbs. The healing of wounds and of broken bones is an example of the same phenomenon at a somewhat less spectacular level. In the economic system it is possible to observe fairly closely what happens when an "organ" (industry) is cut off, say, by prohibition. In the first place if regeneration of the severed industry is prevented by the cauterizing action of law, other "industries" will begin to take over the functions of the destroyed industry (speakeasies, bathtub gin, etc.). If now the prohibition is removed, the old industry rapidly grows back again into the body economic, under the stimulus of profit (advantage). One may again hazard a guess that biologists will have to look for a variable akin to profit at the level of the cell if they are fully to understand the phenomenon of functional substitution and regeneration.

It is interesting to observe that the "carpenter principle" and the "advantage principle" are to some extent alternative ways of effecting the organization of a society, the first, of course, corresponding to the communist planned economy and the second to the capitalist market economy. In the planned economy, growth is organized by the principle of conformity to the plan: industries which are lagging behind the plan get extra attention to make them catch up, much as a child is taught in an authoritarian educational system. In the market economy, growth is organized by the principle of advantage: it takes place in the directions that "pay off" to the individuals who initiate it or are able to take advantage of its initiation, the "pay off" being derived from "profit," that is, an excess of value of product over cost. There is a certain analogy here perhaps with "progressive" education.

We have not, of course, exhausted a subject so ramified and so universal as growth in five summary propositions, though it may be hoped that there is here presented some indication that general theories of growth are possible. It remains in the compass of a short paper to indicate some of the loose—and therefore growing!—ends of the subject. We have not, for instance, considered the problem of the possibility of equilibrium *rates* of growth in an organism or system such that higher (or lower) growth rates may seriously disturb the functioning of the system even to the point of its collapse and "death." There is evidence in the plant world that too rapid a rate of growth kills the organism; indeed, some very effective weed killers have been developed on this principle, using growth hormones. The growth theories of Harrod and Domar suggest that in the economic system there are "appropriate" rates of growth of a system as a whole which will yield continuous full employment. These theories also suggest, however, that there is nothing inherent in the nature of an unstabilized market economy which will guarantee these appropriate rates of growth. There is a suggestion, indeed, that under some circumstances a continuous equilibrium rate of growth may be impossible, because certain elements, consumption, for example, do not keep pace with the rise in capacity and so force *accelerated* growth on other elements, such as investment, if the system is to maintain full employment. These problems may all turn out to be problems in compensation for structural changes through increasing size, such as we have noted earlier, but particularly where equilibrium seems to require acceleration in certain growth rates some quite peculiar problems may be involved.

The problems of the transition from rapidly growing systems to more or less stationary ones are also very general, and need careful study at many levels. The character of a system frequently has to change not merely because it gets big, but because it stops growing. Thus when a religious movement passes from its initial phase of rapid expansion into the phase of slow or even negative growth it has to make profound adaptations: what is appropriate organization in a "movement" is not necessarily appropriate in a "sect." Any system which passes from a rapidly growing phase to a more stationary one, whether it is a religion, a labour organization, a business firm, a nation, an economic system, or a civilization comes face to face with somewhat the same kind of adjustment. David Reisman makes the growth phase of a culture the principal determinant even of the typical character of its individuals, attributing "tradition-directed" behaviour to low-level, slowly growing, or stationary populations with high growth potential, "inner-directed" behaviour to rapidly growing populations, and "other-directed" behaviour to high-level, slow-growing, or stationary populations. These connections may seem a little far-fetched, but there can be no doubt that the type of growth which any system exhibits will affect most if not all of its major characteristics.

In conclusion one may hazard a guess as to the growth patterns of the sciences. The remarkable universality of the principles enunciated here in regard to a general theory of growth indicates that perhaps there is emerging from the welter of the sciences something like a "general theory," something which is a little less general and has a little more empirical content than mathematics but which is more general and therefore, of course, has less content than the content of specific sciences. Mathematics is itself, of course, a "general theory" in that it applies wherever quantitative concepts and relationships are encountered. The sort of general theory which I have in mind, however, is a generalization from aspects of experience which include more than mere abstract quantity and which are common to many or even to all of the "universes of discourse" which constitute the various sciences. Growth is one such aspect: organization is another; interaction is another. When, and if, such a general theory comes to be written it will be surprising if the general theory of growth does not constitute an important chapter.

General Systems Theory—
The Skeleton of Science*

General Systems Theory[1] is a name which has come into use to describe a level of theoretical model-building which lies somewhere
between the highly generalized constructions of pure mathematics and
the specific theories of the specialized disciplines. Mathematics attempts to organize highly general relationships into a coherent system,
a system however which does not have any necessary connections with
the "real" world around us. It studies all thinkable relationships abstracted from any concrete situation or body of empirical knowledge.
It is not even confined to "quantitative" relationships narrowly defined
—indeed, the developments of a mathematics of quality and structure
is already on the way, even though it is not as far advanced as the
"classical" mathematics of quantity and number. Nevertheless because
in a sense mathematics contains all theories it contains none; it is the
language of theory, but it does not give us the content. At the other
extreme we have the separate disciplines and sciences, with their
separate bodies of theory. Each discipline corresponds to a certain
segment of the empirical world, and each develops theories which
have particular applicability to its own empirical segment. Physics,
chemistry, biology, psychology, sociology, economics and so on all
carve out for themselves certain elements of the experience of man
and develop theories and patterns of activity (research) which yield

* Management Science 2, 3 (Apr. 1956): 197–208.
    This paper was written especially for Management Science and was
reprinted in General Systems, Yearbook of the Society for General Systems
Research, vol. 1, 1956. It has been reprinted in a number of collections
since then.
    [1] The name and many of the ideas are to be credited to L. von
Bertalanffy, who is not, however, to be held accountable for the ideas of
the present author! For a general discussion of Bertalanffy's ideas see
General System Theory: A New Approach to Unity of Science, Human
Biology, Dec., 1951, Vol. 23, p. 303–361.

satisfaction in understanding, and which are appropriate to their special segments.

In recent years increasing need has been felt for a body of systematic theoretical constructs which will discuss the general relationships of the empirical world. This is the quest of General Systems Theory. It does not seek, of course, to establish a single, self-contained "general theory of practically everything" which will replace all the special theories of particular disciplines. Such a theory would be almost without content, for we always pay for generality by sacrificing content, and all we can say about practically everything is almost nothing. Somewhere however between the specific that has no meaning and the general that has no content there must be, for each purpose and at each level of abstraction, an optimum degree of generality. It is the contention of the General Systems Theorists that this optimum degree of generality in theory is not always reached by the particular sciences. The objectives of General Systems Theory then can be set out with varying degrees of ambition and confidence. At a low level of ambition but with a high degree of confidence it aims to point out similarities in the theoretical constructions of different disciplines, where these exist, and to develop theoretical models having applicability to at least two different fields of study. At a higher level of ambition, but with perhaps a lower degree of confidence it hopes to develop something like a "spectrum" of theories—a system of systems which may perform the function of a "gestalt" in theoretical construction. Such "gestalts" in special fields have been of great value in directing research towards the gaps which they reveal. Thus the periodic table of elements in chemistry directed research for many decades towards the discovery of unknown elements to fill gaps in the table until the table was completely filled. Similarly a "system of systems" might be of value in directing the attention of theorists toward gaps in theoretical models, and might even be of value in pointing towards methods of filling them.

The need for general systems theory is accentuated by the present sociological situation in science. Knowledge is not something which exists and grows in the abstract. It is a function of human organisms and of social organization. Knowledge, that is to say, is always what somebody knows: the most perfect transcript of knowledge in writing is not knowledge if nobody knows it. Knowledge however grows by the receipt of meaningful information—that is, by the intake of messages by a knower which are capable of reorganizing his knowledge. We will quietly duck the question as to what reorganizations constitute "growth" of knowledge by defining "semantic growth" of knowledge as those reorganizations which can profitably be talked about, in writing or speech, by the Right People. Science, that is to say, is what can be talked about profitably by scientists in their role as scientists. The crisis of science today arises because of the increasing difficulty of such profitable talk among scientists as a whole. Specialization has outrun Trade, communication between the disciples becomes increasingly difficult, and the Republic of Learning is breaking up into isolated subcultures with only tenuous lines of communication between them—a situation which threatens intellectual civil war. The reason for this breakup in the body of knowledge is that in the course of specialization the receptors of information themselves become specialized. Hence physicists only talk to physicists, economists to economists—worse still, nuclear physicists only talk to nuclear physicists and econometricians to econometricians. One wonders sometimes if science will not grind to a stop in an assemblage of walled-in hermits, each mumbling to himself words in a private language that only he can understand. In these days the arts may have beaten the sciences to this desert of mutual unintelligibility, but that may be merely because the swift intuitions of art reach the future faster than the plodding leg work of the scientist. The more science breaks into subgroups, and the less communication is possible among the disciplines, however, the greater chance there is that the total growth of knowledge is being slowed down by the loss of relevant communications. The spread of specialized deafness means that someone who ought to know something that someone else knows isn't able to find it out for lack of generalized ears.

It is one of the main objectives of General Systems Theory to develop these generalized ears, and by developing a framework of general theory to enable one specialist to catch relevant communications from others. Thus the economist who realizes the strong formal similarity between utility theory in economics and field theory in physics[2] is probably in a better position to learn from the physicists than one who does not. Similarly a specialist who works with the growth concept—whether the crystallographer, the virologist, the cytologist, the physiologist, the psychologist, the sociologist or the economist—will be more sensitive to the contributions of other fields if he is aware of the many similarities of the growth process in widely different empirical fields.

[2] See A. G. Pikler, Utility Theories in Field Physics and Mathematical Economics, *British Journal for the Philosophy of Science*, 1955, Vol. 5, pp. 47 and 303.

There is not much doubt about the demand for general systems theory under one brand name or another. It is a little more embarrassing to inquire into the supply. Does any of it exist, and if so where? What is the chance of getting more of it, and if so, how? The situation might be described as promising and in ferment, though it is not wholly clear what is being promised or brewed. Something which might be called an "interdisciplinary movement" has been abroad for some time. The first signs of this are usually the development of hybrid disciplines. Thus physical chemistry emerged in the third quarter of the nineteenth century, social psychology in the second quarter of the twentieth. In the physical and biological sciences the list of hybrid disciplines is now quite long—biophysics, biochemistry, astrophysics are all well established. In the social sciences social anthropology is fairly well established, economic psychology and economic sociology are just beginning. There are signs, even, that Political Economy, which died in infancy some hundred years ago, may have a re-birth.

In recent years there has been an additional development of great interest in the form of "multisexual" interdisciplines. The hybrid disciplines, as their hyphenated names indicate, come from two respectable and honest academic parents. The newer interdisciplines have a much more varied and occasionally even obscure ancestry, and result from the reorganization of material from many different fields of study. Cybernetics, for instance, comes out of electrical engineering, neurophysiology, physics, biology, with even a dash of economics. Information theory, which originated in communications engineering, has important applications in many fields stretching from biology to the social sciences. Organization theory comes out of economics, sociology, engineering, physiology, and Management Science itself is an equally multidisciplinary product.

On the more empirical and practical side the interdisciplinary movement is reflected in the development of interdepartmental institutes of many kinds. Some of these find their basis of unity in the empirical field which they study, such as institutes of industrial relations, of public administration, of international affairs, and so on. Others are organized around the application of a common methodology to many different fields and problems, such as the Survey Research Center and the Group Dynamics Center at the University of Michigan. Even more important than these visible developments, perhaps, though harder to perceive and identify, is a growing dissatisfaction in many departments, especially at the level of graduate study, with the existing traditional theoretical backgrounds for the empirical studies which form the major part of the output of Ph.D. theses. To take but a single example from the field with which I am most familiar. It is traditional for studies of labor relations, money and banking, and foreign investment to come out of departments of economics. Many of the needed theoretical models and frameworks in these fields, however, do not come out of "economic theory" as this is usually taught, but from sociology, social psychology, and cultural anthropology. Students in the department of economics however rarely get a chance to become acquainted with these theoretical models, which may be relevant to their studies, and they become impatient with economic theory, much of which may not be relevant.

It is clear that there is a good deal of interdisciplinary excitement abroad. If this excitement is to be productive, however, it must operate within a certain framework of coherence. It is all too easy for the interdisciplinary to degenerate into the undisciplined. If the interdisciplinary movement, therefore, is not to lose that sense of form and structure which is the "discipline" involved in the various separate disciplines, it should develop a structure of its own. This I conceive to be the great task of general systems theory. For the rest of this paper, therefore, I propose to look at some possible ways in which general systems theory might be structured.

Two possible approaches to the organization of general systems theory suggest themselves, which are to be thought of as complementary rather than competitive, or at least as two roads each of which is worth exploring. The first approach is to look over the empirical universe and to pick out certain general *phenomena* which are found in many different disciplines, and to seek to build up general theoretical models relevant to these phenomena. The second approach is to arrange the empirical fields in a hierarchy of complexity of organization of their basic "individual" or unit of behavior, and to try to develop a level of abstraction appropriate to each.

Some examples of the first approach will serve to clarify it, without pretending to be exhaustive. In almost all disciplines, for instance, we find examples of populations—aggregates of individuals conforming to a common definition, to which individuals are added (born) and subtracted (die) and in which the age of the individual is a relevant and identifiable variable. These populations exhibit dynamic movements of their own, which can frequently be described by fairly simple systems of difference equations. The populations of different species also exhibit dynamic interactions among themselves, as in the theory of Volterra. Models of population change and interaction cut across a great many different fields—ecological systems in biology, capital theory in economics which deals with populations of "goods," social ecology, and even certain problems of statistical mechanics. In all these fields population change, both in absolute numbers and in structure, can be discussed in terms of birth and survival functions relating numbers of births and of deaths in specific age groups to various aspects of the system. In all these fields the interaction of population can be discussed in terms of competitive, complementary, or parasitic relationships among populations of different species, whether the species consist of animals, commodities, social classes or molecules.

Another phenomenon of almost universal significance for all disciplines is that of the interaction of an "individual" of some kind with its environment. Every discipline studies some kind of "individual"—electron, atom, molecule, crystal, virus, cell, plant, animal, man, family, tribe, state, church, firm, corporation, university, and so on. Each of these individuals exhibits "behavior," action, or change, and this behavior is considered to be related in some way to the environment of the individual—that is, with other individuals with which it comes into contact or into some relationship. Each individual is thought of as consisting of a structure or complex of individuals of the order immediately below it—atoms are an arrangement of protons and electrons, molecules of atoms, cells of molecules, plants, animals and men of cells, social organizations of men. The "behavior" of each individual is "explained" by the structure and arrangement of the lower individuals of which it is composed, or by certain principles of equilibrium or homeostasis according to which certain "states" of the individual are "preferred." Behavior is described in terms of the restoration of these preferred states when they are disturbed by changes in the environment.

Another phenomenon of universal significance is growth. Growth theory is in a sense a subdivision of the theory of individual "behavior," growth being one important aspect of behavior. Nevertheless there are important differences between equilibrium theory and growth theory, which perhaps warrant giving growth theory a special category. There is hardly a science in which the growth phenomenon does not have some importance, and though there is a great difference in complexity between the growth of crystals, embryos, and societies, many of the principles and concepts which are important at the lower levels are also illuminating at higher levels. Some growth phenomena can be dealt with in terms of relatively simple population models, the solution of which yields growth curves of single variables. At the more complex levels structural problems become dominant and the complex interrelationships between growth and form are the focus of interest. All growth phenomena are sufficiently alike however to suggest that a general theory of growth is by no means an impossibility.[3]

Another aspect of the theory of the individual and also of interrelationships among individuals which might be singled out for special treatment is the theory of information and communication. The information concept as developed by Shannon has had interesting applications outside its original field of electrical engineering. It is not adequate, of course, to deal with problems involving the semantic level of communication. At the biological level however the information concept may serve to develop general notions of structuredness and abstract measures of organization which give us, as it were, a third basic dimension beyond mass and energy. Communication and information processes are found in a wide variety of empirical situations, and are unquestionably essential in the development of organization, both in the biological and the social world.

These various approaches to general systems through various aspects of the empirical world may lead ultimately to something like a general field theory of the dynamics of action and interaction. This, however, is a long way ahead.

A second possible approach to general systems theory is through the arrangement of theoretical systems and constructs in a hierarchy of complexity, roughly corresponding to the complexity of the "individuals" of the various empirical fields. This approach is more systematic than the first, leading towards a "system of systems." It may not replace the first entirely, however, as there may always be important theoretical concepts and constructs lying outside the systematic framework. I suggest below a possible arrangement of "levels" of theoretical discourse.

(i) The first level is that of the static structure. It might be called the level of *frameworks*. This is the geography and anatomy of the universe—the patterns of electrons around a nucleus, the pattern of atoms in a molecular formula, the arrangement of atoms in a crystal, the anatomy of the gene, the cell, the plant, the animal, the mapping of the earth, the solar system, the astronomical universe. The accurate description of these frameworks is the beginning of organized theoretical knowledge in almost any field, for without accuracy in this description of static relationships no accurate functional or dynamic theory is possible. Thus the Copernican revolution was really the dis-

---

[3] See "Toward a General Theory of Growth," pp. 64–82.

covery of a new static framework for the solar system which permitted a simpler description of its dynamics.

(ii) The next level of systematic analysis is that of the simple dynamic system with predetermined, necessary motions. This might be called the level of *clockworks*. The solar system itself is of course the great clock of the universe from man's point of view, and the deliciously exact predictions of the astronomers are a testimony to the excellence of the clock which they study. Simple machines such as the lever and the pulley, even quite complicated machines like steam engines and dynamos fall mostly under this category. The greater part of the theoretical structure of physics, chemistry, and even of economics falls into this category. Two special cases might be noted. Simple equilibrium systems really fall into the dynamic category, as every equilibrium system must be considered as a limiting case of a dynamic system, and its stability cannot be determined except from the properties of its parent dynamic system. Stochastic dynamic systems leading to equilibria, for all their complexity, also fall into this group of systems; such is the modern view of the atom and even of the molecule, each position or part of the system being given with a certain degree of probability, the whole nevertheless exhibiting a determinate structure. Two types of analytical method are important here, which we may call, with the usage of the economists, comparative statics and true dynamics. In comparative statics we compare two equilibrium positions of the system under different values for the basic parameters. These equilibrium positions are usually expressed as the solution of a set of simultaneous equations. The method of comparative statics is to compare the solutions when the parameters of the equations are changed. Most simple mechanical problems are solved in this way. In true dynamics on the other hand we exhibit the system as a set of difference or differential equations, which are then solved in the form of an explicit function of each variable with time. Such a system may reach a position of stationary equilibrium, or it may not—there are plenty of examples of explosive dynamic systems, a very simple one being the growth of a sum at compound interest! Most physical and chemical reactions and most social systems do in fact exhibit a tendency to equilibrium—otherwise the world would have exploded or imploded long ago.

(iii) The next level is that of the control mechanism or cybernetic system, which might be nicknamed the level of the *thermostat*. This differs from the simple stable equilibrium system mainly in the fact that the transmission and interpretation of information is an essential part of the system. As a result of this the equilibrium position is not merely determined by the equations of the system, but the system will move to the maintenance of any *given* equilibrium, within limits. Thus the thermostat will maintain *any* temperature at which it can be set; the equilibrium temperature of the system is not determined solely by its equations. The trick here of course is that the essential variable of the dynamic system is the *difference* between an "observed" or "recorded" value of the maintained variable and its "ideal" value. If this difference is not zero the system moves so as to diminish it; thus the furnace sends up heat when the temperature as recorded is "too cold" and is turned off when the recorded temperature is "too hot." The homeostasis model, which is of such importance in physiology, is an example of a cybernetic mechanism, and such mechanisms exist through the whole empirical world of the biologist and the social scientist.

(iv) The fourth level is that of the "open system," or self-maintaining structure. This is the level at which life begins to differentiate itself from not-life: it might be called the level of the *cell*. Something like an open system exists, of course, even in physico-chemical equilibrium systems; atomic structures maintain themselves in the midst of a throughput of electrons, molecular structures maintain themselves in the midst of a throughput of atoms. Flames and rivers likewise are essentially open systems of a very simple kind. As we pass up the scale of complexity of organization towards living systems, however, the property of self-maintenance of structure in the midst of a throughput of material becomes of dominant importance. An atom or a molecule can presumably exist without throughput: the existence of even the simplest living organism is inconceivable without ingestion, excretion and metabolic exchange. Closely connected with the property of self-maintenance is the property of self-reproduction. It may be, indeed, that self-reproduction is a more primitive or "lower level" system than the open system, and that the gene and the virus, for instance, may be able to reproduce themselves without being open systems. It is not perhaps an important question at what point in the scale of increasing complexity "life" begins. What is clear, however, is that by the time we have got to systems which both reproduce themselves and maintain themselves in the midst of a throughput of material and energy, we have something to which it would be hard to deny the title of "life."

(v) The fifth level might be called the genetic-societal level; it is typified by the *plant*, and it dominates the empirical world of the botanist. The outstanding characteristics of these systems are first, a division of labor among cells to form a cell-society with differentiated and mutually dependent parts (roots, leaves, seeds, etc.), and second, a sharp differentiation between the genotype and the phenotype, associated with the phenomenon of equifinal or "blueprinted" growth. At this level there are no highly specialized sense organs and information receptors are diffuse and incapable of much throughput of information —it is doubtful whether a tree can distinguish much more than light from dark, long days from short days, cold from hot.

(vi) As we move upward from the plant world towards the animal kingdom we gradually pass over into a new level, the "animal" level, characterized by increased mobility, teleological behavior, and self-awareness. Here we have the development of specialized information-receptors (eyes, ears, etc.) leading to an enormous increase in the intake of information; we have also a great development of nervous systems, leading ultimately to the brain, as an organizer of the information intake into a knowledge structure or "image." Increasingly as we ascend the scale of animal life, behavior is response not to a specific stimulus but to an "image" or knowledge structure or view of the environment as a whole. This image is of course determined ultimately by information received into the organism; the relation between the receipt of information and the building up of an image however is exceedingly complex. It is not a simple piling up or accumulation of information received, although this frequently happens, but a structuring of information into something essentially different from the information itself. After the image structure is well established most information received produces very little change in the image—it goes through the loose structure, as it were, without hitting it, much as a sub-atomic particle might go through an atom without hitting anything. Sometimes however the information is "captured" by the image and added to it, and sometimes the information hits some kind of a "nucleus" of the image and a reorganization takes place, with far reaching and radical changes in behavior in apparent response to what seems like a very small stimulus. The difficulties in the prediction of the behavior of these systems arises largely because of this intervention of the image between the stimulus and the response.

(vii) The next level is the "human" level, that is of the individual human being considered as a system. In addition to all, or nearly all, of the characteristics of animal systems man possesses self consciousness, which is something different from mere awareness. His image, besides being much more complex than that even of the higher animals, has a self-reflexive quality—he not only knows, but knows that he knows. This property is probably bound up with the phenomenon of language and symbolism. It is the capacity for speech—the ability to produce, absorb, and interpret *symbols*, as opposed to mere signs like the warning cry of an animal—which most clearly marks man off from his humbler brethren. Man is distinguished from the animals also by a much more elaborate image of time and relationship; man is probably the only organization that knows that it dies, that contemplates in its behavior a whole life span, and more than a life span. Man exists not only in time and space but in history, and his behavior is profoundly affected by his view of the time process in which he stands.

(viii) Because of the vital importance for the individual man of symbolic images and behavior based on them it is not easy to separate clearly the level of the individual human organism from the next level, that of social organizations. In spite of the occasional stories of feral children raised by animals, man isolated from his fellows is practically unknown. So essential is the symbolic image in human behavior that one suspects that a truly isolated man would not be "human" in the usually accepted sense, though he would be potentially human. Nevertheless it is convenient for some purposes to distinguish the individual human as a system from the social systems which surround him, and in this sense social organizations may be said to constitute another level of organization. The unit of such systems is not perhaps the person—the individual human as such—but the "role"—that part of the person which is concerned with the organization or situation in question, and it is tempting to define social organizations, or almost any social system, as a set of roles tied together with channels of communication. The interrelations of the role and the person however can never be completely neglected—a square person in a round role may become a little rounder, but he also makes the role squarer, and the perception of a role is affected by the personalities of those who have occupied it in the past. At this level we must concern ourselves with the content and meaning of messages, the nature and dimensions of value systems, the transcription of images into a historical record, the subtle symbolizations of art, music, and poetry, and the complex gamut of human emotion. The empirical universe here is human life and society in all its complexity and richness.

(ix) To complete the structure of systems we should add a final turret for transcendental systems, even if we may be accused at this point of having built Babel to the clouds. There are however the ultimates and absolutes and the inescapable unknowables, and they also exhibit systematic structure and relationship. It will be a sad day for man when nobody is allowed to ask questions that do not have any answers.

One advantage of exhibiting a hierarchy of systems in this way is that it gives us some idea of the present gaps in both theoretical and empirical knowledge. Adequate theoretical models extend up to about the fourth level, and not much beyond. Empirical knowledge is deficient at practically all levels. Thus at the level of the static structure, fairly adequate descriptive models are available for geography, chemistry, geology, anatomy, and descriptive social science. Even at this simplest level, however, the problem of the adequate description of complex structures is still far from solved. The theory of indexing and cataloguing, for instance, is only in its infancy. Librarians are fairly good at cataloguing books, chemists have begun to catalogue structural formulae, and anthropologists have begun to catalogue culture trails. The cataloguing of events, ideas, theories, statistics, and empirical data has hardly begun. The very multiplication of records however as time goes on will force us into much more adequate cataloguing and reference systems than we now have. This is perhaps the major unsolved theoretical problem at the level of the static structure. In the empirical field there are still great areas where static structures are very imperfectly known, although knowledge is advancing rapidly, thanks to new probing devices such as the electron microscope. The anatomy of that part of the empirical world which lies between the large molecule and the cell however, is still obscure at many points. It is precisely this area however—which includes, for instance, the gene and the virus—that holds the secret of life, and until its anatomy is made clear the nature of the functional systems which are involved will inevitably be obscure.

The level of the "clockwork" is the level of "classical" natural science, especially physics and astronomy, and is probably the most completely developed level in the present state of knowledge, especially if we extend the concept to include the field theory and stochastic models of modern physics. Even here however there are important gaps, especially at the higher empirical levels. There is much yet to be known about the sheer mechanics of cells and nervous systems, of brains and of societies.

Beyond the second level adequate theoretical models get scarcer. The last few years have seen great developments at the third and fourth levels. The theory of control mechanisms ("thermostats") has established itself as the new discipline of cybernetics, and the theory of self-maintaining systems or "open systems" likewise has made rapid strides. We could hardly maintain, however, that much more than a beginning has been made in these fields. We know very little about the cybernetics of genes and genetic systems, for instance, and still less about the control mechanisms involved in the mental and social world. Similarly the processes of self-maintenance remain essentially mysterious at many points, and although the theoretical possibility of constructing a self-maintaining machine which would be a true open system has been suggested, we seem to be a long way from the actual construction of such a mechanical similitude of life.

Beyond the fourth level it may be doubted whether we have as yet even the rudiments of theoretical systems. The intricate machinery of growth by which the genetic complex organizes the matter around it is almost a complete mystery. Up to now, whatever the future may hold, only God can make a tree. In the face of living systems we are almost helpless; we can occasionally cooperate with systems which we do not understand: we cannot even begin to reproduce them. The ambiguous status of medicine, hovering as it does uneasily between magic and science, is a testimony to the state of systematic knowledge in this area. As we move up the scale the absence of the appropriate theoretical systems becomes ever more noticeable. We can hardly conceive ourselves constructing a system which would be in any recognizable sense "aware," much less self conscious. Nevertheless as we move towards the human and societal level a curious thing happens: the fact that we have, as it were, an inside track, and that we ourselves *are* the systems which we are studying, enables us to utilize systems which we do not really understand. It is almost inconceivable that we should make a machine that would make a poem: nevertheless, poems *are* made by fools like us by processes which are largely hidden from us. The kind of knowledge and skill that we have at the symbolic level is very different from that which we have at lower levels—it is like, shall we say, the "knowhow" of the gene as compared with the knowhow of the biologist. Nevertheless it is a real kind of knowledge and it is the source of the creative achievements of man as artist, writer, architect, and composer.

Perhaps one of the most valuable uses of the above scheme is to prevent us from accepting as final a level of theoretical analysis which is below the level of the empirical world which we are investigating. Because, in a sense, each level incorporates all those below it, much valuable information and insights can be obtained by applying low-level systems to high-level subject matter. Thus most of the theoretical schemes of the social sciences are still at level (ii), just rising now to (iii), although the subject matter clearly involves level (viii).

Economics, for instance, is still largely a "mechanics of utility and self interest," in Jevons' masterly phrase. Its theoretical and mathematical base is drawn largely from the level of simple equilibrium theory and dynamic mechanisms. It has hardly begun to use concepts such as information which are appropriate at level (iii), and makes no use of higher level systems. Furthermore, with this crude apparatus it has achieved a modicum of success, in the sense that anybody trying to manipulate an economic system is almost certain to be better off if he knows some economics than if he doesn't. Nevertheless at some point progress in economics is going to depend on its ability to break out of these low-level systems, useful as they are as first approximations, and utilize systems which are more directly appropriate to its universe—when, of course, these systems are discovered. Many other examples could be given—the wholly inappropriate use in psychoanalytic theory, for instance, of the concept of energy, and the long inability of psychology to break loose from a sterile stimulus-response model.

Finally, the above scheme might serve as a mild word of warning even to Management Science. This new discipline represents an important breakaway from overly simple mechanical models in the theory of organization and control. Its emphasis on communication systems and organizational structure, on principles of homeostasis and growth, on decision processes under uncertainty, is carrying us far beyond the simple models of maximizing behavior of even ten years ago. This advance in the level of theoretical analysis is bound to lead to more powerful and fruitful systems. Nevertheless we must never quite forget that even these advances do not carry us much beyond the third and fourth levels, and that in dealing with human personalities and organizations we are dealing with systems in the empirical world far beyond our ability to formulate. We should not be wholly surprised, therefore, if our simpler systems, for all their importance and validity, occasionally let us down.

I chose the subtitle of my paper with some eye to its possible overtones of meaning. General Systems Theory is the skeleton of science in the sense that it aims to provide a framework or structure of systems on which to hang the flesh and blood of particular disciplines and particular subject matters in an orderly and coherent corpus of knowledge. It is also, however, something of a skeleton in a cupboard—the cupboard in this case being the unwillingness of science to admit the very low level of its successes in systematization, and its tendency to shut the door on problems and subject matters which do not fit easily into simple mechanical schemes. Science, for all its successes, still has a very long way to go. General Systems Theory may at times be an embarrassment in pointing out how very far we still have to go, and in deflating excessive philosophical claims for overly simple systems. It also may be helpful however in pointing out to some extent *where* we have to go. The skeleton must come out of the cupboard before its dry bones can live.

The Relations of Economic, Political, and Social Systems*

The raw material of social systems is the history of mankind. The record of history, however, is no more than raw material. In order to have knowledge of social systems we must abstract out of the almost infinite complexity of this record those elements which exhibit enough regularity to be subject to analysis. Social systems, that is, are essentially abstractions from reality; without these abstractions, however, we cannot hope to understand reality. A system is anything that is not chaos, and even though history seems highly chaotic at times, we have an intuitive feeling that it is not pure chaos. If it is not chaos, there is system in it, and if there is system in it, there is some hope that the system may be perceived and understood.

All systems potentially consist of three elements which might be labelled necessity, chance, and freedom. In the case of systems which have worked themselves through time into a virtual equilibrium, the elements of chance and freedom are practically non-existent and the element of necessity is all that remains. The solar system is a good case in point. In the formation of this system there may well have been important elements of chance which determined how many planets there should be, how large they should be, and in what orbits they should lie. In so far as the system was created it will have elements of freedom in it also, but this we must leave to the theologians. At present, however, the elements of chance and freedom have almost been eliminated, with the notable exception now of political astronomy. It is necessity that rules the stars or, at least, the planets. Their orbits can be described by difference or differential equations of only the second order. Given the position of the solar system yesterday and

* *Social and Economic Studies* (Jamaica) 11, 4 (Dec. 1962): 351–62.

This paper was presented at a conference on Political Sociology in the British Caribbean, held at the University of the West Indies, Jamaica, December, 1961.

today, we can theoretically find an equation which will predict exactly its position tomorrow; given today and tomorrow, we can then predict the next day, and so on indefinitely into the future. It is this stability in the relationship between the positions of the system in successive time periods which constitutes *necessity* in mechanical systems and which gives us, therefore, the power of prediction. We can predict eclipses because they belong to a system in which the elements of chance and freedom are almost wholly eliminated.

As we move from the physical into the biological systems, the element of chance becomes more important in the dynamic process. We cannot predict the life history of an infant of any kind in the way that we can predict the movement of the planets. We can predict a limited range of life histories but we cannot tell in advance out of this limited range which one will be realized. We know that a kitten will not grow up into a dog, but his life history as a cat has many possible variations, none of which can be predicted in advance. It may be a hungry alley cat or a sleek house cat; it may be ferocious or gentle, depending on its experiences. In a living organism we may, perhaps, regard its genetic constitution as embodying the element of necessity in its development, for its genetic constitution is something which it cannot change. Its development depends also, however, on environmental factors, some of which may be subject to necessity but many of which can only be attributed to chance. Systems of this kind are called "stochastic" systems and they are by no means absent even in physics. As we move from the physical through the biological into the social sciences, however, the stochastic element becomes more and more important. Such systems may be expressed by stochastic equations in which there is some random component; money invested at a constant rate of interest in a safe bank grows, according to a simple law of necessity, at a constant rate of growth. Money invested in speculative enterprises grows according to a stochastic system. There may be a constant growth component in it, but from day to day or from year to year a number is picked, as it were, out of a hat and added or subtracted. The actual day-to-day course of the system, therefore, is fundamentally unpredictable, even though the general tenor of its way may be predicted.

The third component of general systems, freedom, is virtually unknown at the physical level except in mixed socio-physical systems. It begins to become important as we reach the higher organisms in biology and it becomes of great importance in social systems. By freedom I mean that element which is introduced into the system by the existence of knowledge structures, or images, and especially by the existence of an image of the future. Freedom is the process by which an image of the future is consciously realized. If I am in Jamaica in December, 1961, it is not because of any mechanical necessity, such as that which moves the planets, for my movements are too complex to be described by differential equations except, perhaps, of an infinite degree. Nor is it satisfactory to explain my appearance in Jamaica on the grounds that my movements constitute a random walk. I may flatter myself, but I am pretty sure that my movements around the face of the earth do not have the mathematical characteristics of a purely random path, that is, a path in which the direction, extent, and changes of movement are determined by the throw of the dice. The mere fact that I return home again occasionally is sufficient to destroy the random walk explanation, simply because a random walker returns home much less often than I do. There must, therefore, be some other explanation of my movements, and this can only be found in the fact that I have an image of the future at any moment of time and that I tend to act in such a way as to make the future conform to my image. If my image of the future involves going to Jamaica in December, 1961, sometime before this date I will make preparations; I will buy a plane ticket; at the right time I will go to the airport, get on the plane, and eventually arrive in Jamaica. There are, of course, stochastic elements in this process which may interrupt it; I may have a heart attack, the plane may crash, or the world may come to an end; these stochastic elements, however, lurk in every system, but it is one of the great objects of knowledge to lessen their incidence and to lower their probability.

We must recognize, therefore, that in any system which has an important element of freedom in it, knowledge about the system always changes it. We run into this even in the physical sciences in the famous Heisenberg principle, according to which the attempt to inform ourselves about the position or velocity of an electron changes its position or velocity. As we move towards the social sciences, knowledge about the system and information collected from the system becomes a more and more important part of the system itself. This does not mean, however, that knowledge is impossible or that the systems are uncontrollable. Indeed, the possibility of control of social systems arises only as knowledge about them increases. I am by no means a Marxist and, indeed, I regard Marxism as a very dangerous simplification of social dynamics, but I have a lot of sympathy with what Engels called the "leap from necessity into freedom." We begin to make this leap when our knowledge of social systems rises to the point at which some sort of control becomes possible so that the future is no longer solely in the hands of necessity and chance. We can then form images of the future of society as well as of our own personal lives which have some chance of coming about, a chance which is great enough to make it worthwhile pursuing conscious efforts towards the future that we have in mind. The more inaccurate our knowledge of the social system, of course, the less the element of freedom in it; we may think that we are directing our actions towards a certain future when, in fact, our actions have the effect of taking us away from this future rather than towards it. Nevertheless, the idea that we can plan for a future of society as well as in our own personal lives is, perhaps, one of the most important ideas of the nineteenth century, and it is an idea that we owe in no small measure to Marx himself.

If we are going to reduce the almost inconceivable complexity of human history to manageable, systematic form, we must break up the social system, at least conceptually, into sub-systems, recognizing, of course, but at the same time keeping in the back of our minds, the fact that these sub-systems are not independent and that they constantly interact with each other. A large number of these sub-systems may be identified, but I propose to discuss only four of them which I regard of primary importance. These four I shall label population systems, exchange systems, threat systems, and learning systems. In all of these we can trace the same three general elements of necessity, chance, and freedom.

In population systems we consider, first of all, the total stock of all those objects or items which are significant from the point of view of social systems. We may consider also the composition of the stock, that is, its division into various significant categories. Then we consider the dynamics of the stock, that is, its change through time, as this is determined by additions to and subtractions from the stock. The fundamental law of necessity in such a system is that the increase in any stock over a period of time must be equal to the additions to the stock less the subtractions from it, or "births" into it minus "deaths" out of it. This identity is a mechanical necessity which can be avoided neither by chance nor by freedom.

The most significant population system is, of course, the population of human beings themselves. It is possible to make projections of human population and its distribution by area, race, sex, or any other composition by assuming fairly simple relationships between births, deaths, immigration, emigration, and so on into the various groups. These projections represent the element of necessity in population systems; they all take the form of saying that, if certain parameters of the system remain the same, then its course will be as projected. These projections, however, are not predictions, because of the chance elements in the system. The parameters themselves, such as the age-specific birth and death rates, are always subject to unpredictable change, and those who believed that the population projections were, in fact, predictions have been grievously disappointed by the experience of the last twenty-five years. Nevertheless, the projections are important, for they give us the range of possible futures and they enable us to make propositions of the form, "If there is no change in these parameters, then the future will be like this." We can say, for instance, to use a very crude example, that if the population of Jamaica continues to increase at its present rate, it will double, roughly, every forty years. Population systems also enable us to make projections about the distribution and composition of populations. Cohort analysis enables us to predict, within reasonable margins of error, what the age composition of the population is likely to be in the future. In the United States, for instance, the fact that there were so many more babies born in the forties than there were in the thirties has now created a crisis in the educational system because of the distortion in the age distribution of the population. This is a crisis which was both predictable and predicted. On the other hand, it is extremely dangerous to assume that birth and death rates will continue at present rates or will follow any prescribed course into the future. The failure of the population predictions of the forties were based largely on this mistake.

It is not only to human populations, however, that population analysis applies. It can be applied to anything which has a stock and which has additions to or subtractions from that stock. It can be applied, therefore, to the whole world of capital goods and of commodities; it can be applied even to such things as ideas and images. The famous proposition that capital can only increase if production exceeds consumption is identical in form with the basic identity of all population analysis. A good deal of the theory of economic development rests on this identity. The rate of capital accumulation can be increased only by increasing production or by diminishing consumption. Frequently, the latter is the only alternative open. So we run into the iron law of development; that development implies parsimony, whether involuntary or imposed.

It is clear that population systems broadly interpreted cover a large part of the field of social dynamics; nevertheless, they do not cover it all. As we move from demography into economics, for instance, we find that the concept of exchange becomes more and more important. Exchange systems may, perhaps, be regarded as a sub-division of population systems as they essentially involve the redistribution of existing stocks of things among people. Exchange systems, however, have peculiarities of their own which perhaps justify their classification as a special sub-system. Exchange is a basic form of human interaction; it is basic, not only to economic life, but also to all social relationships, such as marriage, friendship, and all kinds of collective action. We think of it fundamentally as an exchange of "goods" and its basic proposition is, "I will do something good for you if you will do something good for me." It is a positive-sum game in which all parties can be better off, but it is also a curious mixture of cooperative and competitive elements. It is cooperative in so far as there is gain to both parties; it is competitive in so far as the distribution of this gain depends on the terms of trade, that is, on the ratio of exchange, and any movement in the ratio of exchange makes one party relatively better off and one party relatively worse off than they were before.

Exchange systems can become seriously disturbed by changes in the medium of exchange. Inflation or deflation in the monetary system, for instance, disturbs the whole system of exchange because of the fact that many exchange relationships involve a time interval between one transaction and its reciprocal transactions. Exchange, of course, always consists of two transfers or transactions, but these do not have to occur at the same time. In a debt relationship, for instance, or in the implicit exchange among the generations in which the middle aged support the young in expectation that they themselves will be supported when they are old, and support the old in repayment of the support that they received when they were young, there is a substantial time interval between one transfer and the transfer which completes the exchange. If, in the interval, there is a general social change, for instance, in the price level, the whole system of transfers over time is disturbed. Inflation discriminates against the creditors, deflation against the debtors, and economic development can easily discriminate against the generation that initiates it. Marriage and friendship both may be wrecked by disappointment in deferred exchange, though in this case, the commodity may simply be affection or approval. Political parties and political structures, likewise, are involved in this time exchange; a political party makes promises and, if these are not fulfilled, the voters may take their revenge at the next election. The whole dynamics of society and the dynamics of population systems themselves are profoundly affected by the operations of the exchange system. Thus, the great depression in the United States, which resulted fundamentally from a breakdown in the exchange system, had profound effects on the birth rate, on future populations, and on the accumulation of capital.

Exchange systems, again, have certain elements of necessity in them. The relative price structure, for instance, is not arbitrary and cannot be changed at will without severe repercussions on the society. The closer we get to perfect competition, the greater the element of necessity in the system and the more all-pervasive and compelling is the "law of supply and demand." We cannot force the price structure away from some equilibrium position without producing serious consequences in the way of shortages and surpluses of commodities. As we move towards monopoly, and especially towards oligopoly or bilateral-monopoly, however, the element of chance in the system becomes more important. Where we have bargaining, there will be a range of prices at which a bargain may be struck, but there is no way of predicting in advance where within this range the bargain will actually be found. Under these circumstances there is a genuinely stochastic element in the dynamics of a price system which cannot be neglected. There are also, however, elements of freedom in it. The equilibrium price structure is not an absolute necessity; it can be changed under appropriate governmental action and pressure. It can be distorted by price control and by taxation. Within limits, the consequences of these distortions can be predicted, and the control of the price system may well be an instrument by which we move towards some image of the future. We may wish, for instance, to make vice expensive and virtue cheap, and we may be able to do this both through the tax system and through direct prohibitions or encouragements. We may look into the future and decide that some commodity, for instance, water, which is plentiful now, is going to be scarce in the future. We may wish, therefore, to distort the present price system in order to anticipate the future scarcity. The present price system, for instance, affects the course of future technology; if we make something expensive it is likely to be economized. This is one argument, for instance, for distorting the price system in favor of higher money wages. Then a "disequilibrium" system would create dynamic change. Even though high wages create unemployment, it may be better to have unemployment than low wages because, if labor is scarce, it will be economized and it is the economizing of labor which constitutes the essence of economic development. These elements of freedom in the price system are not well understood or worked out, but they undoubtedly exist, and the more explicit we can be about them the better our policy is likely to be. The argument that the price system must lie wholly in the realm of necessity is not, I think, acceptable to modern ears.

We have still by no means encompassed all the relationships of society and here, again, even though what I have called "threat systems" may be viewed as a special case of exchange systems, they nevertheless present so many peculiarities that they deserve to be singled out for special treatment. An exchange system is based on a transfer of goods, a threat system on the transfer of "bads." An exchange system, as we have seen, is based on the proposition "If you do something good for me, I will do something good for you." A threat system is based on the proposition, "If you do not do something good for me I will do something bad to you." Threat systems are the basis of politics as exchange systems are the basis of economics. Political power fundamentally is based on threats. Actual political life, however, is made up of a curious mixture of exchange systems and threat systems. In part, and perhaps in the largest part, government is always by consent, that is, by exchange. We give up some of our personal sovereignty to the state, as we give up some of our personal income in taxation because we feel that the state does something for us in exchange. It gives us protection, identification, an enlarged personality, and other benefits and, in so far as it does this, the system may quite properly be regarded as a system of exchange. This, however, is not the whole story. Man early discovered that threats were a powerful method of social organization. We can, indeed, conceive of classical civilization as essentially a threat system based on the fact that, with the invention of agriculture, the food producer produced more than he could eat himself or rather, than he needed to eat himself, and that with the food surplus the ruler was able to feed an army or a coercive organization which would then compel the food producer to give up the food that would feed the agent that coerced him. As long as this is unchallenged, this is a very stable social system. As the civilizations of the Mayans and of Mohenjodaro testify, the threat, of course, need not always be a physical one. It can also be spiritual. Many of the early civilizations seem to have been based on spiritual threats, that is, on the capacity of a priesthood to threaten people with spiritual damnation, if the did not turn over their food surpluses to the social organization.

Slavery in the early colonial system was a good example of the threat system in an almost pure form. With the surplus which the slave produced over his subsistence, the master could employ a coercive power with which he could threaten the slave's life. As long as the

slave preferred slavery to death, and as long as the master was able
and willing to use the means of coercion at his disposal, the system
continued. The demise of the system occurred, not so much because
of any internal instability, but because of the fact that both its moral
and its economic base were eroded by the development of more profitable systems of social organization, namely, a system of exchange. An
exchange system is fundamentally more productive than a threat system simply because the exchange of goods encourages the production
of goods, whereas the threat of ill discourages the production of goods.
While a one-sided threat system is internally stable, threat systems in
themselves develop instability because of the fact that they become,
not one-sided but bi-lateral. The proposition, "If you do not do good
to me, I will do bad to you," becomes "If you do bad to me I will do
bad to you." It is hard to keep a monopolistic threat system intact, and,
against one threat system, another threat system tends to be aroused.
Threat systems, therefore, constantly decline into war systems or deterrence systems which seem to have an inherent instability in them. This
is the main reason for the rise and fall of civilizations, and the long
cycles which have characterized human development for the last five
thousand years. We are now at the extreme end of this period in which
the threat system has become so universal that it threatens to destroy
us all.

Any account of social dynamics would be incomplete if it did not
include learning systems. Learning, of course, is involved in all the
other systems but here, again, it has peculiarities of its own which
make it desirable to single it out. A learning system may be defined
broadly as a social process by which the image of the world possessed
by the individuals of the society comes to change. At each moment
each individual has an image of the world which includes an image
of space, of time, of the past and the future, of his role in society, of
things that are expected of him, the things he expects of others, his
obligations and his rights, and so on. This image largely determines
his behavior. If people find themselves in situations where their
behavior does not reinforce their image, then either their image must
change or they will find themselves in a new situation. If a man thinks
he is Napoleon and acts as if he were Napoleon, when in fact he is not,
he will soon find himself segregated in a mental hospital in which his
role is acceptable. We might add that if he thinks he is Napoleon when
he is Napoleon he finds himself at Saint Helena. Society moves and
changes by an enormous interaction of images, behaviors, disappointments, role fulfilments or unfulfilments, and the constant interaction of
images on society and society on the images.

The most significant thing that has happened, perhaps in the whole history of mankind, is the formalization and systemization of the learning process itself in what we know as science. This has resulted in an enormous acceleration of change in the image. In folk culture the image is very resistant to change. If messages are received which are inconsistent with the image, they are generally rejected. Because of this stability in the image, a primitive society in which the processes of learning are not specialized, provided that it is left to itself, is likely to be very stable and will reproduce itself generation after generation. The specialization of the learning process has introduced an enormous dynamic into human society in the last four hundred years and has now placed us in a pace of social change so rapid that now we go through in a single year a change in the basic parameters of the social system at least equivalent to what took a hundred years in the age of classical civilization.

This specialization of the learning system offers both great hope and great danger to mankind. It offers hope because it is only out of this specialization that we can hope to understand the nature of social systems and, hence, move from the realm of necessity into the realm of freedom. It is only by the specialized activities of the knowledge seekers, especially in the social sciences, that we can hope to understand the social system sufficiently well to be able to control it and to be able to move into a positive image of the future through our own volition and policy. Otherwise, we are merely slaves of necessity or victims of chance. On the other hand, the very specialization of the learning process and the rapidity of change make it all the more difficult to understand and especially to get widespread understanding of the nature of the change itself. Let us imagine what the world would be like if the parameters of the physical systems in which we operate changed as rapidly and as unpredictably as the parameters of the social systems. Suppose, for instance, that on Monday the gravitational constant was low, whereas on Tuesday it was high; we would literally never know how to get out of bed. On Monday we fly through the window and Tuesday we would crack our head on the floor. To live at all in a world like this we would have to have an elaborate system of scientific information; we would have to have a gravimeter by the bedside to tell us before we even got up whether to make a desperate leap or a gentle movement.

This, however, is precisely the fix we are in in social systems. Their significant parameters such as, for instance, the price level, the productivity of labor, the range of the deadly missile, or the proportion of communications received outside the family, change constantly and often with great rapidity. Under these circumstances, it is extremely difficult to know how to operate and it is not surprising that we make serious mistakes. Under these circumstances too, however, it is all the more important to devise accurate and unbiased methods of sifting information and of condensing information into forms which are readily appreciated. We desperately need a social systems equivalent of the gravimeter by the bedside. In economics we have this to some extent in the form of national income statistics. It was still possible in the United States in 1931 to argue about whether there was a depression or not. Today, we cannot have a turndown for two or three months without this fact coming to the attention of all the significant decision-makers in this society. In international systems we have not yet reached this position; we have, in fact, a system of information which is almost designed to be corrupted. Both diplomats and intelligence agencies produce an extremely biased picture of the truth, by nature of the social system which they themselves inhabit, and until we can get more accurate and more "scientific" information in international systems the chance of handling them well is very slim.

In religious systems, in family life, and in the broader learning process by which the images, skills, and ideas of society move from one year to the next our information processes are not organized at all. Because of this, public expenditures, especially in the field of health, education, and welfare, are usually made very inefficiently. In the United States, at any rate, we seem to have a very fundamental principle, that while we are willing to spend a lot of money to see that public funds are spent honestly, we will not spend a dollar to see that they are spent wisely. Until this situation is rectified, one must remain highly sceptical about the advantages of any substantial expansion in the public sector, even in the most developed economies of the capitalist world. As a corollary one might say that there is no socialist country in which an expansion of the private market sector would not result in a marked increase in economic efficiency, even thought this might not result in the desired rate of social change.

I should perhaps, add a fifth system to the four I have already outlined, though I am hesitant to do this because we understand so little about it. The four systems outlined above, however, do not encompass an important social phenomenon which could variously be described as social integration, affection, altruism, or even by the simple word "love." Love systems are those in which the individual comes to identify his own desires with those of another. These are important in the explanation of the institution of the family, of the church, and of nationalism, of the phenomena of philanthropy and self-sacrifice, and of all those areas of life where we do not merely exchange or threaten but in which we *identify*. A sense of identification, of course, participates in both exchange and threat systems; the love of country, like the love of a spouse, has elements of exchange in it or perhaps even of threat. These elements do not encompass the whole picture, however, and I suspect that we have to include an autonomous element of integration if we are to obtain a full description of social systems.

The complaint may be made with some justice that I have not dealt adequately with the title of the paper, in that my classification and hierarchy of systems does not correspond closely to the division between the economic, the political, and the social. My only defence to this charge is that I believe that the distinctions I have made are more elemental and important than the usual distinctions on which the customary division of the social sciences are based. It is true, of course, that economic systems concentrate around the phenomenon of exchange, and, if we like, we can identify exchange systems with economics. Economic systems cannot wholly be understood, however, apart from the economic operations of the government, especially through the systems of unilateral transfers in taxes and subsidies. In order to understand this element in the economic system we have to invoke either threat systems or love systems. The budgets of states are arrived at by an extremely complex process of exchange, threat, and philanthrophy; the same is true, as a matter of fact, for the budget of individuals.

Similarly, even though we may wish to make a certain identification of political science with threat systems, these also do not quite encompass its traditional field. Government is by consent as well as by threat; in order to explain government by consent we have to introduce either exchange systems or love systems. We consent also because we identify our own interest with those of the coercer. Even in international relations where we might suppose that threat systems reign supreme we find that there are examples of the systems of stable peace, for instance between the United States and Canada, in which the threat system has been so completely overlaid by other relationships that it has ceased to be important or, at least, visible.

Social systems are less clearly demarcated traditionally from political or economic systems. This has always caused difficulties, for the sociologist has never quite decided whether he is studying everything about the social system or whether he has a demarcated field within it. Sociologists like George Homans attempt to make exchange the basis of all social relationship. I suspect this is quite inadequate and that even in the most elementary forms of social interaction, threat systems and love systems are important and that all these, of course, exist in the setting of population systems and learning systems. It would certainly be tidy if the sociologist could be designated to study love systems as the core of his discipline, that is, the systems by which integration takes place. To put the matter in another way, the principle subject of sociology would then be alienation which is, of course, the opposite of integration. This division of labor is probably too tidy and most sociologists would object to it. However, it does seem to me that the problem of how, in the course of social interaction, we learn or fail to learn to identify with other people and with other organizations is peculiar to the "sociological" part of social systems.

As for the interaction among these various systems, it would take, of course, a large volume even to summarize them. I will take but a single example from the problem of economic development. Economic development as a process can be described fairly accurately by means of population systems. Its principal measure is the increase in *per capita* income which is, of course, the birth rate of commodities per person or the amount of commodities to which the average individual gives birth in the course of a year's activity. There is a somewhat mechanical economic theory of economic development which is essentially an application of population analysis, arising out of the assumption that income is a function of total capital and that the increase in capital is a function of the differences in income and consumption. This mechanical theory, however, is descriptive rather than predictive. In order to give it flesh and blood we must have some notion about the role of the exchange system, especially as reflected in the price structure, in this process. We must know also something about the role of threat systems, that is, the possibility of the use of the coercive power. On the whole, it may be said that the capitalist development rests on exchange systems and socialist development on the threat systems, but this, as usual, is too simple a point of view and many modifications would have to be made. It can be said also, I suspect, that a prerequisite of economic development is a certain minimum of social integration. Economic development always involves costs to certain parts of the population. It is a painful process which may involve a gross injustice to a whole generation who sacrifice for growth in order that the next generation or so may enjoy the benefits. Such a system is impossible unless there is a strong sense of social identification. In traditional capitalism the sense of identification is supposed to be found through the family. The present generation is expected to be parsimonious because the parents identify with the children or even the great-grandchildren who will enjoy the fruits of the parsimony. The family, that is, is a love system extending through time. Socialist development attempts to expand this sense of identification to the whole society, at least as embodied in the élite party. There is a thin dividing line, however, between love systems and threat systems and there is a constant tendency for one to pass into the other. Thus, capitalist development has seldom proceeded very far without the exercise of police power, and socialist development seems to be even more dependent on coercion, as the record of Stalin shows. It is in the study of the subtle interweaving of these various systems of society, therefore, that the best hope of understanding of social systems and, therefore, ultimately, their control lies.

A Pure Theory of Death: Dilemmas of Defense Policy in a World of Conditional Viability*

Death as a System Boundary

Death is a subject which is more often associated with the macabre half-light of Gothic fancy than with the sunshine of reason, science, and general systems research. It is, however, a phenomenon which is common to many systems and there is no reason why it cannot be examined in the light of systems dynamics. It may be defined as a system-break or a point of no return in the dynamic course of a system. It is a semi-permeable boundary around a system which has the property that it can be crossed from the inside to the outside but cannot be crossed from the outside to the inside. When the dynamic course of a system carries it beyond this boundary, therefore, it can never return. The system is excluded forever from the old paths.

Death may be followed by transfiguration or it may not. A system that crosses a death boundary may reform itself within another boundary. Sometimes, however, a system passes the irreversible boundary into sheer disintegration and nothingness. This raises, of course, the ancient conundrum about when is a system not a system, when does a set of variables in the course of their dynamic development stop being System A and start being System B. I doubt very much if any answer can be given to this question in logic; it can only be given in experience and in utility. We divide the great system of

* In: *Behavioral Science and Civil Defense*, Office of Behavioral Science, National Academy of Sciences (Washington, D.C.: National Academy of Sciences, 1962), pp. 53–69. National Research Council Publication 997.

This paper was presented at a conference in Washington, D.C. April 1961 organized by the Disaster Research Group of the National Academy of Sciences, National Research Council on Behavioral Science and Civil Defense.

the universe into sub-systems such as people, animals, plants, things, and organizations—largely for our own convenience and because it pays us to do so. I shall argue that there is nothing wrong with this although it may seem untidy to the pure logician; there is nothing wrong, that is to say, with the payoffs of arbitrary classification, provided they do not turn out to be a cheat and disappointment. I will take, therefore, a fairly naive view of the universe as consisting of a large number of reasonably identifiable sub-systems, the boundaries of which I shall derive from experience rather than from logic.

The poetic images of death give us an important clue to its ubiquity as a systems phenomenon. A pitcher goes to the well once too often and is shattered; Humpty-Dumpty falls from his wall; and all the king's horses and men cannot put him together again. A clock stops; a flame is blown out; all these events are simple models of death at low systems levels. A static pattern like a china vase exists through time until some point where too great a strain is put upon it and it disintegrates never to be reassembled. A simple cyclical-mechanical system like a clock endlessly repeating a pre-ordained cycle may stop because one small link in the causative chain is broken, and to start it again requires the incursion of a much more complex system in the shape of the watchmaker. All clocks left to themselves eventually stop. This is a consequence of the great and universal law of increasing entropy. If they are to be restarted, entropy must be diminished from outside. The flame is a still closer analogue of life. It is one of the simplest of the open systems; it is a system, that is, with a role structure. At each point in the flame, there is a chemical state which can well be described as a role. The molecular occupants of this role are continually passing on to the state immediately above and are continually renewed from the state immediately below. An open system is a system in which a given structure is maintained in the midst of some kind of a throughput of role occupants. When the flame is out, the role-structure disappears. The candle and the oxygen may still be there, but the temperature is not high enough to maintain the role-structure of the flame. There is a physical boundary here within which the flame can exist and outside of which it cannot exist. The candle may be burnt out; that is, the food supply which provides the molecular occupants for the first roles in the system may disappear. The waste products may accumulate to the point where the last molecular occupants of the last role cannot leave it, and this stops the flow of material through the system. The surrounding temperature may be reduced to the point where the chemical reactions which sustain the system can no longer be carried on. This is what happens when we blow out the flame. In any case, once a flame is blown out, it cannot reestablish itself. The system has passed a one-way boundary through which it can never return under its own dynamic. If the system is to be reestablished, it must be through the act of some outside system. Usually energy must be supplied to the system, although in some cases the reestablishment of a system may involve the withdrawal of energy. In all cases entropy must be withdrawn from it, and organization supplied.

Life as a Homeostatic System

The taxonomic boundary that separates non-living from living systems is perhaps hard to draw, as a fine line. We do not have to cross very far over it, however, before we are aware that we are in a new country and in a new type of system. It is the peculiar characteristic of life, as Schroedinger has said, that it feeds on entropy. The flame cannot defend itself against the wind. If it dies, it can only be reestablished from outside.

A living system, by contrast, is capable of at least minimum defense against its environment. It exhibits, that is to say, the phenomenon of homeostasis. Homeostasis is something a little different from mechanical equilibrium (of which it is the Greek translation). In a homeostatic system, information begins to play an essential role. Because of this, homeostatic systems are self-sustaining in a way that mechanical systems cannot be. If a clock runs down, it has to receive energy from outside; if it breaks, it has to receive organization from outside, that is, negative entropy. A living system is not passive in regard to its environment; it goes out and seeks sources of energy, and because it has information as an essential element it can create organization within itself. When a candle is burned out, the flame simply comes to an end: it does not wander around the room looking for a new candle. When even the simplest living thing is hungry, it seeks food. It does not simply maintain itself passively as an open system. When its open system is threatened, either by the absence of inputs or the inability to get rid of outputs, it indulges in at least scanning or seeking behavior in the endeavor to find a new environment in which it can survive.

Four Degrees of Homeostasis

We may distinguish perhaps four kinds of homeostasis. We have first, the homeostasis of a state, cybernetics. This is a type of system, of course, which extends below the threshold of life and there are many examples of non-living cybernetic or control systems of which the thermostat is the most often cited. Even non-living cybernetic systems, it should be observed, involve information as an essential variable. They must have the following components:

(1) An ideal state of the system (the temperature at which the thermostat is set); (2) a receptor, that is, an apparatus for perceiving the actual state of the system and recording the divergence between the actual and the ideal states (the thermometer); (3) a communication system which can communicate the information acquired by the receptor (2), and (4) an executive or decision-maker who can interpret this information and transform it into instructoin to (5) an effector (the furnace) which can effect the environment. All living organisms and all social organizations exhibit a great variety of these cybernetic or state-maintaining systems, and a great deal of behavior, although by no means all of it, can be explained by cybernetic models.

The second aspect of homeostasis is role-maintenance, that is, the maintenance of an occupant in each role of the system. The simplest level of an open system is one in which we have a structure of roles, holes, or slots in each of which is some kind of occupant, and which are connected by lines of transportation along which occupants can move. In a simple, one-way open system, each role is connected by a line of transportation to some role below and to some role above. As the current occupant of the role passes to the role above, a new occupant must be received from the role below. In the flame, the gases pass from one chemical zone to the one immediately above it and each zone receives the appropriate molecules from the one below and passes them on to the one above. In the river, another interesting example of a non-living open system, each segment of the river receives water, gravel, sand, vegetation and fish from a segment immediately above, and passes similar items on to the segment immediately below. In a university, sophomores become juniors and are continually recreated by freshmen. In any self-maintaining organization, a job which has become vacant either because of death, removal, or promotion of its occupant has to be filled either from another position in the organization or from the outside. At the simple biological level, as we have seen, such phenomena as hunger and thirst, and from the point of view of the species, sex, can be regarded as role-maintaining activity. In an industrial organization, the personnel office is the role-maintaining organization at lower levels; at the higher levels of the organization, the peer group tends to be the role-maintaining apparatus. The self-perpetuating board of trustees is, of course, the ideal type of the role-maintaining peer group.

A third and still higher organizational level of homeostasis might be described as "maintenance-maintenance." This is the apparatus for maintaining the role-maintenance apparatus itself. Thus, at the biological level, food-growing can be thought of as maintenance-maintenance, whereas mere food-seeking is role-maintenance. The food-grower sees to it that there is a supply of food for the food-seeker to find. Food-growing clearly represents a higher level of organization than mere food-seeking, and it is no accident that food-growing, that is, agriculture, signalized the passage from pre-civilized societies to civilization. The movement from civilization to post-civilization through which we are now passing reflects perhaps a fourth degree of homeostasis, in which, for instance, scientific research enables us to grow more food more easily and so support a still higher level of organization. Scientific research then is seen as the maintenance or even the improvement of the maintenance-maintaining activity.

Organizations as Defense against Death

It is not unreasonable to think of these increasing degrees of organization and homeostasis as successive levels of depth in defense against death. The flame has no defense against death. If its environment changes to the point where is goes out, it simply goes out. A simple cybernetic system has some defense against changes in the environment. When the weather gets cold, the furnace works harder, and the temperature of the house is maintained. Cybernetic systems, that is, build little islands of stability in a changing world. Even at this level, we can perhaps distinguish between two systems of defense which might be labeled "flight" and "fight." In flight, a worsening of the immediate environment which is perceived as dangerous is followed by a removal of the system to a new environment. If the system has receptors which inform it as to whether the environment is getting worse or getting better, and if there is a continuous field of more or less favorable environments, this procedure can be quite successful. The snake, who is too hot in the sun, for instance, will crawl into the shade. In cold weather he retreats into the warmer ground. By contrast, the so-called warm-blooded animals maintain an internal environment which is in a degree independent of the external environment. When the external environment worsens, they do not necessarily flee (although in practice fight and flight responses are frequently combined), but they put more energy into the system in order to maintain a favorable internal environment even when the external environment is unfavorable. When we get cold, we burn more fuel, we insulate ourselves, our teeth chatter, we become more active, and so on. When we become hot, we perspire, we relax, we seek the shade, and so on. Similarly, the firm which finds itself in an increasingly unfavorable market environment—which finds, for instance, its inventory of product accumulating or finds that it cannot sell its output except at a loss—will develop new forms of activity. It may cut back its output; it may go in for price-cutting; it may go in for a sales campaign; it may even merge with another firm. All these are possible defenses against its death, that is, the dissolution of the organization.

The Theory of Conflict and Viability

Up to this point, we have assumed that the state of the organization is simply part of a generalized state of nature, and that the defenses against death are defenses against the "worsening" of an abstract external environment. We must now move one step towards reality and suppose that the environment includes other organizations or organisms. The system then becomes much more complex, since we now have a system of interaction among organisms. The defenses against death then involve not merely defenses against a worsening external environment, but defenses against other organisms. We now move into the theory of conflict, in which death may be the result of a loss of a conflict or of the dominance of one party over another. This is the system, of course, which is of peculiar interest from the point of view of national viability or national defense. It is derived largely from the economic theory of duopoly or oligopoly.

I have developed it in some detail in my book entitled ·*Conflict and Defense*[1] and I shall only summarize it here. The essential concept is an undefined variable which I call simply "strength." The only significance of this concept for the pure theory is that it serves to define the dominance relationship. One of the systems is said to be dominant in any part of the field in which its strength is greater at that point than the other party. To fix our ideas and to bring us closer to the problems of the day, let us suppose that the systems are two nations and that they exist in a geographical field. For purposes of simplicity, let us suppose this is a straight line. The two nations are located at A and B in Figure 1. For each nation, we postulate a strength function over the field, represented by FHG for A and LKM for B. As we have drawn these functions in the figure, we have supposed that the maximum strength for each nation is at its home base.

---

[1] K. E. Boulding, *Conflict and Defense* (New York: Harper and Row, 1962).

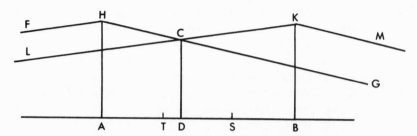

FIGURE 1. Areas of Dominance and the Boundary of
Equal Strength: Unconditional Viability

This is a reasonable but not a necessary assumption—that the strength of each nation is the greatest at its home base but declines as it goes away from home in any direction. The point of intersection of the two strength functions at C, is the boundary of equal strength D. Anywhere to the left of D, A is dominant, anywhere to the right, B is dominant. The situation of Figure 1 is what I would describe as mutual unconditional viability. Each party is dominant in its own territory and neither can destroy the other.

Consider, however, the situation of Figure 2. Here nation A is dominant over B at all points in the field including B's home base. Assuming that dominance implies the ability to destroy, then I would

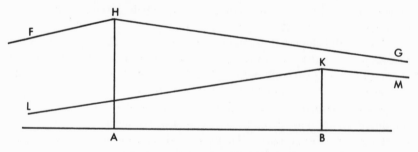

FIGURE 2. Conditional Viability

say that in this case, B was only conditionally viable. The condition here is that A is unwilling to use his power to destroy. Here we may distinguish two further sub-cases. If A has the power to destroy B, but it is not to A's interest to do so, we may call this secure conditional viability. If A has the power to destroy B and it would be in its interest to do so, but for some reason or other, either through ignorance or sheer lack of imagination, it refrains from doing so, this might be described as insecure conditional viability.

Consider now the extraordinary case of Figure 3, in which the strength of each country increases as it goes away from home. Here B is clearly dominant over A to the left of D whereas A is dominant

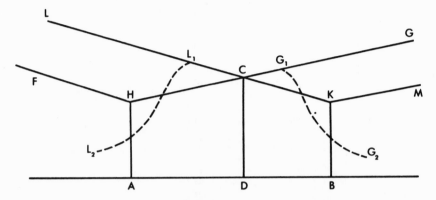

FIGURE 3. Mutual Conditional Viability

over B to the right of D. That is to say, each country can dominate the other one at the other's home base. This is what I would call mutual conditional viability, for each country can destroy the other. This is the sort of situation that we are moving to very rapidly on a world scale, if indeed we have not already arrived there.

In the case of military defense a further complicating factor arises. War may be defined as men throwing things at each other with malicious intent. In this kind of system, the range of the deadly missile is a variable of great importance. Thus, to return to Figure 1, if the range of the deadly missile is equal to AT or BS, the countries would still be unconditionally viable because each can dominate an area beyond its home base equal to the range of the deadly missile. If, however, we suppose the range of the deadly missile increasing, shall we say to AS (= BT), the situation reverses itself. Under these circumstances, neither country can dominate an area beyond its home base equal to the range of the deadly missile and neither of them, assuming that the missiles exist, is any longer unconditionally viable. If, under these circumstances, both had the deadly missiles, we have a situation which is known as deterrence, which is also roughly where we are today.

If the strength functions are linear, they can be described by two very important parameters. One is the home strength, AH or BK, that is, the strength at the home base. The other is the loss of strength gradient, that is, the slopes of the lines HF, HG, LK, and KM. With this simplification, we can now relate the viability conditions to the home strengths of the two nations concerned. Thus, in Figure 4, we measure the home strength of A along OA and of B along OB. Refer-

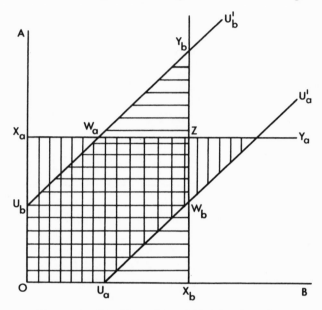

FIGURE 4. The Unconditional Viability Boundaries

ring now to Figure 5, we see that if A's strength function HG passes through K, B is only just unconditionally viable. This condition

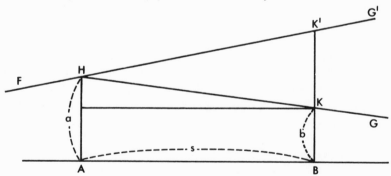

FIGURE 5. Situation on B's Unconditional Viability Boundary

is expressed by the equation $a - b = cs$, where a and b are the respective home strengths, s is the difference between the nations (equal to AB) and c is the loss of strength gradient or the slope of the line

HK. In Figure 4, this is the equation of the line U_b U^1_b. This is an unconditional viability boundary for B. At any combination of home strengths above and to the left of this 45° line, B is no longer unconditionally viable because A can dominate him at its home base. That is, we have a condition like Figure 5. Similarly the line U_a U^1_a is the unconditional viability boundary for A corresponding to the equation $b - a = cs$. This would be the situation in Figure 5, where BK^1 was the home strength of B and AH the home strength of A.

In Figure 4, let us further suppose that there is some level of home strength of A, OX_a and B, OX_b which these countries cannot exceed. This represents the economical, political, or psychological limit of their strength capability. We then have two further boundaries, X_a Y_a and X_b Y_b. The horizontally shaded area $OU_bY_bX_b$ is that part of the field within which B is unconditionally viable with respect to A. This area is shaded horizontally to show that B can move unilaterally in this direction, but not vertically. Similarly, the vertically shaded area $OX_aY_aU_a$ is A's area of unconditional viability. We have now divided the field into four regions. We have an area of mutual unconditional viability which is the cross-hatched area $OU_bW_aZW_bU_a$. We have two triangles, $U_aW_bX_b$ and W_aY_bZ in which B is unconditionally viable but A is not. There are two similar triangles vertically shaded in which A is unconditionally viable and B is not. Then there is the unshaded area of the field in which neither country is unconditionally viable, and we have mutual conditional viability.

Remembering now that $OU_b = OU_a = cs$ in Figure 4, we can see immediately the effect either of a decline in the loss of power gradient c or diminution of the distance between countries s or, more exactly, a diminution of what might be called the effective distance, which is the distance between them minus twice the range of the deadly missile, or the distance TS in Figure 1. Any of these things moves the lines $U_bU^1_b$ and $U_aU^1_a$ closer together in Figure 4, diminishing the cross-hatched area or the area of mutual unconditional viability. By the time either c or s reaches zero, the area of unconditional viability has been eliminated. This, again, I would argue, is close to the condition that we face today.[2] It is easy to develop variations on Figure 4 with different assumptions about the viability boundaries. The maximum home strength of each country, for instance,

---

[2] If r is the range of the deadly missile, the unconditional viability boundaries are $a - b = cs - 2cr$, and $b - a = cs - 2cr$. An increase in the range of the deadly missile therefore diminishes OU_b or OU_a in Figure 4 by twice the increase in range.

may be a function of the home strength of the other, in which case the lines $X_aX^1_a$, etc. may bend toward or away from one of the other axes. None of these various cases, however, destroys the fundamental conclusion regarding the systems-effect of a decline in the loss of strength gradient or an increase in the range of the deadly missile.

Viability in the Interpretation of History

These models may seem abstract, but they imply a whole interpretation of history, and, in particular, they imply a conclusion about the nature of the present crisis which is both startling and is certainly not generally accepted. The interpretation of history is that with each diminution in the loss of strength gradient as a result of improvements in methods of transport and as a result of a continual increase in the range of the deadly missile, the size of the unconditionally viable unit has been continually shrinking. We have now got to the point where the range of the deadly missile is close to 12,500 miles. This is the end of a long historical process. Unconditional viability has now disappeared from the earth. If we think of unconditional viability as the essence of what might be called the classical system of national defense, we can put the matter even more strongly by saying that the system of national defense has now come to an end. It has been succeeded by a quite different system which is the system of deterrence. This is, unfortunately, a system which is only metastable. It is stable for small disturbances, but not for large, like Humpty-Dumpty on the Wall. Unfortunately, also, there is no guarantee that disturbances will not be large enough to upset Humpty-Dumpty and then all the king's horses and men will never put him together again.

I think it can be demonstrated historically that where unconditional viability has disappeared in any human or organizational relationship, the system of deterrence which has succeeded it has turned out to be so disagreeable and unstable that the system has always either fallen back into defense, that is, into unconditional viability, because of some regression in technology, or else it has gone forward into a system that might be called community. This has been true, for instance, in the field of personal combat. We have achieved personal disarmament not by any agreement—the American constitution, indeed, explicitly guarantees the individual the right to bear arms —but by a disarmament race, initiated unilaterally by individuals because of the sheer personal danger of living under a system of deterrence. Unconditional personal viability disappeared with the crossbow and was completely finished off by the revolver. If anybody seriously wants to kill me, there is practically no way in which I can stop him. There is, perhaps, a certain second-strike capability in the hands of the law, but certainly not in my hands, as I know of no way of killing a man after I am dead. But even the operation of the law is highly uncertain, and it is doubtful whether it acts as much of a deterrent. It certainly does not succeed in preventing homicide, although it does perhaps succeed in limiting it. We have now arrived at the same condition of conditional viability in regard to the relation of nations to which we have long been accustomed in the relation of persons. Unconditional viability has disappeared, and with it the whole classical concept of national defense. Unless we can go forward into world community, we are almost bound to slip back. The only way to go back to national defense, however, is through a widespread technological collapse as a result perhaps of a nuclear war.

Adaptive Systems Survive Periods of Transition

The moral of all this rather abstract argument is that we live in a time of history of quite unprecedented system-change. The only period in history which remotely approaches what we are now going through is the transition from pre-civilization to civilization which began about 3000 B.C. In periods of very rapid change, it is the adaptive systems that survive rather than the simple equilibrium systems. The difference between these is illustrated in Figure 6. Here we suppose that each

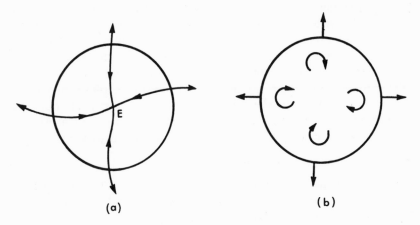

(a)   (b)

FIGURE 6. Adaptive Systems

point in the plane of the paper represents a different state of some system or organization. In each case, the heavy circular line represents the "death boundary." Within it, all the points represent the states in which the system is viable. Outside it, the system is not viable and will disintegrate or be transformed. The lines with arrows represent the possible dynamic paths of the system. In Figure 6(a), which is an equilibrium system, all the dynamic paths lead to an equilibrium system at E, within the death boundary. As long as E is within the death boundary, that is, in the viable area, the organism will survive indefinitely. If, however, the death boundary shifts so that E is no longer within the viable area, the organism has no defenses against this shift and will not survive.

In Figure 6(b), we see by contrast an adaptive system. Here, as the dynamic course of the system turns it toward the death boundary, this fact is "perceived" and forces are brought into play to turn the system away from it. There may or may not be a single position of equilibrium within the death boundary. This does not matter, however, as the system is defended against passing the death boundary by its adaptive nature. If there is a shift in the position of the death boundary, the system perceives this and adapts accordingly. A good example of an adaptive system would be a man in a car driving towards a railway crossing with a red light flashing. His behavior and the resulting motion of the vehicle is a function of the distance between the vehicle itself and the perceived death boundary. An equilibrium system by contrast would be a vehicle proceeding at a constant rate of speed no matter whether the danger signals were flashing or not. Clearly, the more rapid the rate of system change, the more important it is for a system to be adaptive to survive. In the relatively stable world and in a relatively stable environment, equilibrium systems may have high survival value. They may indeed be better adapted to a particular stable environment than an adaptive system would be, for we almost always have to pay a certain price, in complexity if nothing else, for adaptivity. In the rapidly changing environment, however, equilibrium systems are continually finding themselves outside the viability zone and they have no recourse against this disaster.

The Crisis of National Defense

With these considerations in mind, let us take a look at the present crisis of the system of national defense. I have argued that we are here facing a true system-breakdown in national defense, in that no nation is now unconditionally viable, and national defense implies a world system in which unconditional viability is possible. There are several possible adaptations to this situation. We may attempt to restore unconditional viability and the system of national defense. Two approaches are generally suggested to this problem. One is arms control, world organization, and the elimination of war as a social system. The other is the development of defensive weapons or other defensive apparatus to reduce the strength of the potential enemy in the neighborhood of the home base of the defender. Let us suppose that in Figure 3, by defensive measures, we could lower the strength-line KL to KL_1L_2 and the line HG to HG_1G_2. Unconditional viability has now been restored, for each party is stronger than the other at home, provided that the defensive measures are not so expensive as to destroy the internal viability of the nations concerned. This, in essence, is the theoretical base of those who would argue that we should go underground in the face of a nuclear weapon. The feasibility of this proposal is partly technical, partly psychological and ethical. I am no expert in the technical feasibility of these proposals. I am, however, highly skeptical about them, even if they are technically feasible, for the price of defense under these circumstances seems to be absurdly high. Furthermore, if there are any lessons from history, it is that defensiveness of this kind is always obtained at an extremely high cost, especially in mobility and other forms of adaptiveness. Neither the turtle nor the knight in armor ever got very far, and though the tank had a brief success, its day seems to be over. The truth seems to be that the concentration of effort on defensiveness in this sense, that is, on city walls, Maginot lines, armor plate and civil defense, either is inimical to survival or, if it succeeds, succeeds only at a fantastically high cost in terms of the nature of the organism which is defended. If the continuance of the system of the sovereign national states implies that we shall all live on algae in caverns, then I say, "To hell with it." There must be better solutions to the problem than this.

The anti-missile missile represents a variant of the above case. This might be called the defensive-aggressive weapon, or the interceptor which is designed to destroy the enemy's deadly missile before it reaches its target. Here again, I cannot judge the present technical feasibility of such systems. I may be permitted, however, to express extreme skepticism about them. There is a profound tendency for defensive measures to become obsolete, and for offensive weapons to outrun them. The deadliness of the nuclear weapon is so great that I shall be extremely surprised if any defense for it is ever found. Just as firearms destroyed armor, and the revolver led to personal disarmament, now I suspect the nuclear weapon will likewise lead to the destruction of national sovereignty and to world disarmament. The final answer to those who advocate the practicability of nuclear war seems to me to lie in the purpose of such a war, which is to restore the system which produced it! If the price of national sovereignty is a nuclear war every generation or so, again I say, "to hell with it," for the loyalties on which national sovereignty depends will not stand up under these circumstances. The best form of loyalty to a hopelessly insolvent organization is to bankrupt it as soon as possible so that it may be reorganized into a viable form.

The Necessity for Adaptive Conflict Control

The world system in which we now live has a positive probability of nuclear disaster built into it, and though we do not know how great this probability is, it is certainly of an order of magnitude to be seriously disturbing, even if it is only one per cent per annum. Under these circumstances, it is desperately necessary to develop adaptive systems, especially adaptive social systems, which can diminish and rapidly eliminate the probability of this disaster. The attempts to build equilibrium systems of defense on stable deterrence seem to me to be doomed to failure. The world changes too rapidly and, as we have seen, it is the adaptive system, not the equilibrium system, that will survive under these circumstances. The adaptive system which is required here is a world system of conflict control. By this I mean social institutions which will be able to detect the dynamics of conflict situations and will be able to throw in counterweights, or countervailing forces, which will prevent these systems from reaching the crisis point of system-breakdown into overt violence involving the use of national armed forces. Such institutions already exist on the national level. In the less-developed countries this may take the form of conflict-suppression rather than control, which is dangerous in the long run. In the developed countries we have an extremely elaborate set of social institutions—the law, the courts, the regulative agencies, collective bargaining, arbitration, and so on—all of which are designed to divert conflicts into peaceful channels and to diminish the reactivity of conflict processes. At the world level, we have the beginnings of such institutions but they are not yet adequate, and we do not even have the information institutions which will warn us when we are approaching a system boundary. We desperately need something which will be the equivalent of national-income statistics in the field of international tensions. As it is now, we often do not know what is happening until it is too late. We should ask ourselves, for instance, by what world institutions could we have dealt with Hitler, and this, incidentally, is a most unusual and unlikely case which may not occur again for a thousand years. We must then seek to build these institutions and put our major efforts in this direction.

The Armed Forces as Destroyers of Defense

There are, of course, even more urgent tasks than the development of the long-run institutions of conflict control. My personal view is that the armed forces of the world have become a social system almost completely divorced from the states which they ostensibly defend and which pay for them. They have become a highly reactive dynamic and isolated social system and it is, paradoxically, the armed forces themselves that have destroyed the system of national defense which they are supposed to embody. Under these circumstances it is an urgent task to build organizational ligaments between the armed forces of the world. I have argued elsewhere that, just as we resolved the religious question by the ingenious device of separating the church from the state, to the great mutual benefit of both parties, so we must solve the question of war by the separation of the armed forces from the state. In this case, however, the armed forces will wither away unless they can find other functions, for an armed force is one organization which has no justification apart from the existence of another organization of like kind. It is this which makes the interaction of the world armed forces a unique social system.

The bargaining problems involved in this movement are difficult, but they are not insoluble; this, however, would have to be the subject of another paper. In the meantime, we must exploit and strengthen all the tacit agreements which we have. Bargaining is not necessarily a matter of explicit agreement. Most of the important bargains of social life are never made explicit, and many of them are even unconscious. The tacit "agreement" that we have with the Russians to do nothing really serious about civil defense, for instance, is an extremely important element of the stability of the present situation, as Schelling (1960) and others have observed.[3] If either side breaks this, the results might be disastrous for all. Tacit agreements, however, are somewhat insecure, and there is much to be said for trying to reinforce them

---

[3] The incredibly dangerous situation which resulted from Kennedy's civil defense program of late 1961, the quiet sabotage of this program by the good sense of the American public, and the inability of Leon Gouré to persuade us that mysterious doors in Moscow subways constitute a civil defense program appropriate to the nuclear age are all tributes to the stability of this "agreement," even though it may rest on little more than mutual inertia.

with explicit agreements, as long as the attempt to write explicit agreements does not destroy the tacit.

The Price System as an Adaptive Mechanism

In the present state of the world, one must look not only toward the postponement—one hopes the indefinite postponement—of disaster; one must also look beyond disaster. We should certainly give thought to the nature of the adaptiveness of the social and economic system to recovery from a nuclear disaster. We may face a certain dilemma in that activity which is directed towards more rapid recovery from a disaster may make that disaster itself more probable, just as insurance probably increases the number of fires. For the most part, however, I am optimistic enough to think that some measures which would make for recovery from disaster would also postpone it, or at least would not make it more probable.

The major victim of a nuclear disaster is likely to be large-scale organization of all kinds, private or public, as the central offices and records of large-scale organizations are almost all concentrated in large cities. Some relatively simple measures, however, in the way of the establishment of a monetary system, of some form of quick allocation of the equity in the remaining property among survivors, and of a minimum of law and order, would be sufficient to set in motion a rapid process of recovery. The system of private enterprise is peculiarly well adapted to such a situation. Even Communist Russia, for instance, had to adopt the New Economic Policy which involved a partial restoration of private enterprise in the 1920's after an extensive economic collapse.

The extraordinary recovery of West Germany from the holocaust of the second World War is a good example of the adaptability of systems of this kind, and their remarkable powers of recuperation. Such a system, of course, requires a certain minimum of government. It requires a reasonably stable monetary unit, and it requires reasonable security of property. Once these are assured, however, the price-profit system has extraordinary powers of regeneration and recuperation. Even though a nuclear war, for instance, would see the United States with an extreme maldistribution of resources, with far too much in agriculture and not enough in manufacturing, provided that the holocaust led to a considerable collapse of restrictive and regulative government institutions, recovery should be swift. If a price system can be established, agricultural prices and incomes would fall very low and there would be a very rapid migration out of agriculture into construction and industry. Very large payoffs would appear at the places in the society where they were needed, and resources would move accordingly. Recovery might even be assisted by the destruction of much of the apparatus of the Federal Government, or at least of its past laws, which on the whole would prevent adjustment and strangle developments under these circumstances.

Learning to Live with Conditional Viability

Even though I have a good deal of confidence in the adaptiveness of the social and economic system, I have very little confidence in the adaptive nature of the national state, and it is this institution which I think is really threatened by the existing technology. No national state, not even the United States or the Soviet Union, can guarantee to its citizens that minimum area of peace and security which alone can justify its sovereign existence. The political organization of the world is bankrupt. It is as obsolete as the sword. Unfortunately, we have no social institutions for bankrupting it decently and quietly, and for reorganizing it in a more stable and more satisfactory form. The present system is, I think, almost certain to end in catastrophe. The question remains, then, do we change the system before catastrophe or after it? If we prepare to change it before, we may be successful, in which case the catastrophe will be avoided. But even if the catastrophe is not avoided, preparation to change the system will bear fruit after the catastrophe, if this is not wholly fatal to mankind. It is the great genius of man that he is able to anticipate catastrophe in his imagination. He develops early-warning systems that warn him when he is approaching the cliffs. It is hoped that we can still do this in the crisis which now confronts us.

The problem is essentially one of learning under conditions of very rapid system-change. There is no doubt that this learning is going on. The Khrushchev doctrine of peaceful coexistence, incompletely thought out as it is, represents a very fundamental learning process within Marxism. Our own ideology is not so explicit, but still one can detect in our actions a certain learning process. The crucial question is, "Will it be rapid enough?" At the present time, the mass of the American people, and to a large extent what might be called the "establishment," still have an image of the world which is fundamentally obsolete. It is an image of the world in which national defense and unconditional viability still exist as they did for the United States before 1949. Among the more sophisticated, the realization is spreading that we have suffered a system-change, and that we must adapt our behavior accordingly. In particular, we must learn to live with conditional viability if we expect to survive as a society. This means a national posture very different from what we have been accustomed to in the past. It is a posture, however, which is not wholly alien to what is best in our tradition. It may be that in this day the ability to survive and to avoid the impending death of our society may depend upon our ability to learn certain skills which have long been preached but very little practiced—the skill, for instance, of loving our enemies, of saving our life through being willing to lose it, and of being meek, adaptable, and teachable. These, I think it can be shown, are the skills that lead to survival in an age of conditional viability. They are skills that we have not taken seriously. We have regarded them as platitudes and preachments. In the past, on the whole, we have relied on unconditional viability and national defense, and we have gotten away with it. Now, I suspect, we can get away with it no longer. We must unlearn the lessons of experience; the payoff function has changed and we had better find this out before it is too late.

My final plea, therefore, is that we correct a massive misallocation of our intellectual resources. We put most of our resources into the study of physical and biological systems, but very little of the study into social systems. It is here, however, that the problems lie. We have now got to the point, I believe, where major efforts in this direction would not only have a very high rate of return in terms of sheer dollars and cents, but might make the difference between life and death for our system. We can no longer rely on the machinery of state-maintenance, role-maintenance, or even maintenance-maintenance to defend us against death. We must go to the fourth level, the level of the metatask. We have spent too much time and energy in trying to find the best way of doing things that should not be done at all. We must now put a major effort in finding those things which should be done and which must be done if we are to survive.

Some Questions on the Measurement and Evaluation of Organization*

The concept of organization is perhaps the most central, and also the most puzzling notion in the scientific view of the universe. The great quest of the scientist is for *ordered structure* in space and time, whether this is in the nucleus, the atom, the molecule, the virus, the gene, the organ, the animal, the human person, or the social organization. An ordered structure capable of behavior and perhaps capable of growth is however precisely what we mean by an organization. All these ordered structures are essentially role structures—open systems with a throughput of components consisting of lower level organizations, in which however the components are forced by the related roles around them to play a certain role in the organizational structure. Thus individual electrons come and go in an atom, but once one is captured it must behave in a certain way until it is lost. Similarly atoms come and go in a molecule, but the molecule remains, molecules come and go in a cell, but the cell remains, cells come and go in a body, but the body remains; persons come and go in an organization, but the organization remains. What "remains" in the midst of all this flux of components is the "role," the "place," and the relations of roles one to another. A role is a hole, an organization is a related and orderly set of holes, and one sometimes catches a fleeting and slightly nightmarish vision of the scientific universe as a set of holes bounded and defined by other holes! The significance of almost anything, like that of a word, is derived largely from its context; everything, however, is the context for other things; context creates itself, *ad infinitum.*

* In: *Ethics and Bigness: Scientific, Academic, Religious, Political, and Military,* Harlan Cleveland and Harold D. Lasswell, eds., (New York: Harper and Bros., 1962), pp. 385–95. Copyright © 1962 by the Conference on Science, Philosophy and Religion in Their Relation to the Democratic Way of Life, Inc.

This paper was written for the Sixteenth Conference on Science, Philosophy and Religion in their Relation to the Democratic Way of Life and was discussed at a session of this conference on August 29, 1960 in New York City.

In the processes of the universe we seem to see two apparently opposite, though not essentially contradictory processes at work. One is the constant increase in entropy, that is in "chaos" or "disorder" as work is done and processes are carried out, according to the Second Law of Thermodynamics. Everything that happens destroys potential, and so makes "happening," which is made possible by potential differences of some kind, less possible. According to this image of the universe all processes in time lead eventually to a universe which is a kind of thin soup of undifferentiated matter and energy, all equally distributed, all at the same temperature, and in which nothing whatever can happen. This gloomy view of the ultimate future may be in process of modification by current controversies among the astronomers, but whatever the outcome of these, whether the Universe is a stationary state with continuous creation of hydrogen, as Hoyle supposes, or whether the more conventional views are correct, there is no doubt about the general validity of the increase of entropy with process.

We observe, however, another process at work in the universe which we call "evolution." This is a process by which the population of organizations comes to have more and more complex members in it. The elements evolve in the primordial explosion, at a certain point in time life appears, living forms grow in complexity and culminate in man; man himself forms social organizations which also evolve rapidly toward greater and greater complexity. Here is a process which seems to go in the opposite direction to that of "time's arrow" as measured by entropy. What is happening here is not that entropy is failing to increase, but that entropy itself is getting increasingly *segregated*. There are redistributions of entropy going on, leading to greater organization at some points no doubt at the expense of other points. "Life," as Schroedinger says, "feeds on entropy." In the course of the evolutionary process even though chaos continually increases and "unchaos" diminishes, out of these diminished reserves of order evolution builds increasingly complex castles. The universe on this view is like a rich man continually losing his capital, but in the process transforming his diminishing stock into ever more intricate and differentiated forms.

The first Question therefore which I want to raise is whether it would be possible to find a *measure* of the extent of evolution in the *distribution* of entropy. This would be in itself a measure of the degree of organization of the universe or of any part of it, though it would not in itself be an adequate description of organization. No single measure, of course, can describe a complex structure such as an organization. Nevertheless these "indices" which single out certain quantitative aspects are helpful in reducing the complexity of reality to a form which our inadequate minds can grasp. Thus a price index reduces a long list of prices to a single number, and expresses something "important" about the list. Similarly a measure of the degree or quantity of organization, if we had one, would be a useful way of symbolizing something essential and significant in these very complex structures.

It would provide, for instance, a rough measure of the rate of evolution. We have a certain intuitive sense that in the course of evolutionary change "something" is evolving; that there is, in other words, an evolutionary vector, and that it makes sense to say that evolution moves "faster" at some times than at others, or even that it occasionally reverses itself. From the hydrogen atom to the amoeba, and from the amoeba to man we seem to detect "progress," that is, increase in some quantity which measures progress. It may be that this "upwardness" is an anthropomorphic illusion, and that in some scale of values the retrogression from the ascetic simplicity of the hydrogen atom to the monstrous corruption of mankind may be deplored. It is not the value sign which matters here, however, but the vector, that is, the sense of both direction and magnitude. Few could deny that the process which leads from the hydrogen atom to the amoeba to man has both direction and magnitude, and that it would be very useful to have even a rough measure of the magnitude.

Several important problems might be closer to solution if we had a measure of evolutionary change. It is difficult, for instance, to test any theories of the machinery of evolutionary change, whether in biology or in the social sciences, without some measure of the extent of this change. Furthermore a simple measure of the quantity of organization would almost certainly force us to examine higher levels of organizational systems, simply because it would prove unsatisfactory in dealing with the complexities of the higher organizational forms. Consider, for instance, the view that the key to the understanding of the process of evolution is an analysis of the *teaching* process. Here is the one clearly observable process in the universe where the strict laws of conservation do not hold. Energy and matter can only be exchanged: knowledge can be *produced*. When a teacher teaches a class, if the hour has been successful, not only do the students know more as a result of the process, but the teacher frequently knows more, too! Teaching is in no sense an exchange, in which what the student gets the teacher loses. We can break down the teaching process perhaps into two others: the first might be called the *printing* process. It is the process by which a certain structure or organization is imposed on some carrier around it by simple transfer of pattern. The pattern of a page of type imprints itself on many pieces of paper in exactly the same shape. The gene evidently has this property of printing in three dimensions: its self-reproducing quality arises because it can attract to each atom of itself a like atom, which forms a mirror image of the structure, which then exercises the same power of imprinting itself and so reproduces exactly the original pattern of the gene. Similarly a teacher may simply "teach" verbatim something that he knows, like the multiplication table: this is "rote teaching," which results in rote learning.

There is also however a more fundamental process at work: I shall call it, for short, "inspiring." This is the process by which the teacher supports and cooperates with a process of internal growth in the mind of the student. This is also the process by which the gene organizes the growth of a phenotype or body quite unlike itself. It is the process also by which ideas and ideologies inspire the growth of cultures and societies. This is clearly a complex and puzzling process, which we understand very imperfectly at present. It has some similarities to the process by which a building is built to follow a blueprint— the blueprint, indeed, might be described as a special case of the "inspiring" process, for the building which it "inspires" is very different from the mere two-dimensional plan which maps it. The building of the body, however, or of a society, is inspired by more complex processes than that of the blueprint. The gene seems to be able to change its blueprint in the course of executing it, and society likewise does not develop toward a predetermined end, but according to certain broad principles of change and continuity in a process which is constantly liable to a shift in direction both from conscious images and from unconscious causes.

It is clear that in the "teaching" process we are dealing with something akin to the growth of organization. Knowledge, indeed, can be regarded as a form of organization. In its verbal expression it consists of a structure of related contexts, in each of which any "word" or symbol can play the appropriate role, provided that the code is understood. Thus "House," "Domus," "Maison," etc., are different words or symbols each of which however plays the same *role* in a language. One despairs, indeed, of ever getting any simple measure of the quantity of knowledge. Nevertheless a measure of the quantity of organization would be of some help here, and might be valuable in testing the "success" of a learning process.

These considerations may seem very abstract and remote from

the pressing problems of today. Nevertheless I hope to show that the questions I have raised lie at the heart of most of the major problems of our day. Consider, for instance, the problem of economic development. What we have here is a process of social evolution from an economy at a lower level of organization to one at a higher level. The difference between a rich and a poor society lies mainly in the level of organization which it has attained; rich societies are rich not usually because they are amply endowed with natural resources but because they have learned how to organize themselves into complex processes of production extended through time. Extreme poverty of resource base, of course, like that of the Bushmen or the Eskimos, may condemn any society which lives on it to a low level of organization and a low standard of living. Once these extremes are excluded, however, the level of organization of a society is overwhelmingly a function of its degree of organization. Iceland, which is a fairly well organized society, makes a moderately good living in a most unprepossessing natural environment; there are countries by contrast with fair climates and rich soil "where every prospect pleases" but man ekes out a miserable existence in dire poverty.

In the case of economic development we actually possess a rough measure of the degree of attainment of a society and of its rate of progress in the per capita real income. At first sight this seems to be wholly unrelated to the "distribution of entropy" measure which I suggested as a possible index of degree of organization. The relation is a subtle one, but I believe it exists. Consumption is clearly a process which increases entropy: we eat more highly ordered substances than we excrete, automobiles are more highly ordered than scrap iron, clothing is more highly ordered than rags or dust, and so on. Consumption means therefore reducing order to disorder: it is a typically "entropic" process. By contrast production is "anti-entropic." It takes soil and air and water and makes wheat and bread; it takes ore and rock and makes steel and machines; it takes fiber and makes cloth, or cloth and makes clothes. In each case the act of production is that of imposing a greater degree of order in one place, at the cost, however, of greater disorder elsewhere (mine tailings, waste materials, etc.). Production therefore is typical of the evolutionary process in that it segregates entropy and builds up highly ordered, low entropy "products" (commodities) at the cost, no doubt, of producing high entropy "wastes" elsewhere.

Per capita real income is a measure of the rate of production, in some index of units of commodities per unit of time. It is clearly therefore related to the rate at which entropy is being segregated in economic processes. We may ask, however, what about consumption? If all production is consumed, does not the entropy-increasing character of consumption just offset the entropy-decreasing character of production so that there is no net segregation of entropy or increase in organization? This raises the question whether increase in organization does not come from *accumulation*, that is, from the excess of production over consumption, rather than from production or consumption itself? On this view the rate of progress of a society would be measured by its rate of accumulation rather than by its real income: two societies might have the same real income, but if one consumed less and accumulated more than the other it would be advancing faster.

There is a good deal of truth in this view, especially if we take a broad enough concept of accumulation. There is some confusion of thought here even among economists because of a failure to distinguish between income in the sense of production or consumption, that is, additions to or subtractions from the capital stock, and income in the sense of "use" or enjoyment *of* a capital stock. Thus my enjoyment or use of furniture, houses, clothing, etc. is almost independent of their consumption—that is, the rate at which they wear out. I have argued in an earlier paper[1] that it is this enjoyment or use of a capital stock which is the true measure of human wellbeing, not the rate at which this stock is consumed or produced. Nevertheless there is likely to be a fairly monotonic relation between use or enjoyment, the total stock which is used or enjoyed, and the rate at which this stock is consumed or produced, especially under fairly constant techniques. We must bear in mind here that the capital stock consists not only of physical objects like furniture, but also of the furniture of our minds and the states of our bodies. Thus the acquisition of memories, the learning of information or skills, and the inculcation of pleasant states of mind is as much capital formation as the building of a dam. When we go to a movie we build a state of mind called "just having been to a movie." This state depreciates or is consumed just as a chair or a breakfast depreciates, and needs to be restored at suitable intervals.

I do not propose to resolve the question here whether economic organization or welfare can be discussed equally well in its "stock" aspect as capital or in its "flow" aspect as income. I am prepared to argue that both these aspects may be of importance, and that neither

---

[1] "Income or Welfare," *Review of Economic Studies*, Vol. 17, 1949–1950, p. 77.

can quite be reduced to the other. This dilemma also faces us, we may note, in general evolutionary theory. Is it the "stock" of organisms or species which is significant in measuring the rate of evolution, or is it some rate of "throughput" or metabolism which is most significant? We should not be much interested in a "stock" of things, however complex, which never "did" anything—that is, which had no throughput—evolution is more than the elaboration of skeletal forms. On the other hand *mere* busyness, mere throughput, mere metabolism is not the sole object of interest either; evolution is not merely the development of vast outputs of slop and enormous appetites and excretions. It is this curious combination of the development of intricate structures which do things that are significant to them, or to something, which constitutes the peculiar charm of evolution, and I am not prepared to argue at this point whether this apparent two-dimensionality can be reduced to one dimension or not.

The transformation of a society from a lower level to a higher level of organization is not a process of simple homogeneous growth (indeed, the fashionable term "economic growth" may be quite a misnomer) but is an evolutionary, developmental, and almost embryological process not unlike that of the development of a chicken within (and out of) the egg. The "egg" is the relatively undifferentiated, unorganized subsistence economy of small farmers and craftsmen, without large organizations, without much in the way of complex equipment or formal education. The "chicken" is the developed society, with large and complex organizations, complex accumulations of capital in the form of material, skill and educated and informed intelligence, and an extensive division of labor and differentiation of function. As the chicken grows, it gradually absorbs the "yolk"; subsistence farmers and unskilled laborers get jobs in larger organizations, they get education and skill and they end up as highly differentiated members of complex organizations. One of the problems which a developing society faces which is not usually faced by an embryo is that the "yolk" may revolt and refuse to be absorbed in the chicken: it may even carry the revolt to the point where the chicken is killed and the developmental process stops. Because of this possible resistance the developmental process in society requires a certain identification of the "yolk" with the whole developing society: the undeveloped people must either enjoy vicariously the pleasures of the developing middle class which they themselves are not enjoying, or they must identify themselves with the *hope* that they or their descendants will enjoy the fruits of progress, or they must be coerced into cooperation by the superior power and will of the developing part of society in control of the means of coercion. The first is the British pattern, the second the American, and the third (one fears) the Chinese.

The problem of the measure of the level of organization is quite crucial in the argument of the "cold war" between Communism and capitalist democracy. The Communists claim, in effect, that their system is at a higher level of social evolution, and a higher level of organization, than capitalism, and that it must therefore ultimately triumph, as all higher levels of organization have supposedly triumphed in the evolutionary process. We must beware, incidentally, of a tautology here: if we *define* "higher" by "survival," then of course the higher organism always survives! The "survival of the fittest" slogan is quite empty if fitness is defined as fitness to survive. This underlines the necessity of an independent measure of organization or "fitness" so that the proposition that the fit survive may be *testable* in experience. The Communist claim to be a higher level of organization rests mainly on the assumption that hierarchy is the only organizing instrument. The Communist society is a "one-firm state"—that is, a society organized hierarchically into a single economic organization. It is simply General Motors (or perhaps more realistically, the Pentagon, which is in terms of national income the world's third largest Communist society) expanded to include the whole economy, with the possible exception of a few Nepmen and some surreptitious private trade. A capitalist society by contrast is "ecological" where the Communist society is "organic." A Communist society is a true Leviathan, a vast social whale; a capitalist society is more like a pond with a great multitude of interacting organisms bound together in a system of mutual exchange, or markets.

The biological parallel gives us a certain reason for not accepting the Communist claim without very careful scrutiny. The key to the problem here is what the economist calls "diminishing returns to scale." In society, as in biology, it by no means always follows that "the bigger the better." Beyond a certain point in the development of a particular type of organism a further increase in size leads to a decline in efficiency, a decline therefore in the "Quantity of organization," and a lessened chance, we presume, of survival. Where this point comes at which diminishing returns to scale set in depends on the *type* of organization. Chemical elements seem to show diminishing returns in terms of stability as the atomic number increases, and beyond Bismuth (atomic number eighty-three) no stable (nonradioactive) forms are known. Inorganic molecules form larger structures than the elements, but these rarely exhibit molecular weights above 100. Organic molecules with carbon chains go much farther; cells are much larger organizations again, but again have a limit—no one-celled animal reaches more than microscopic dimensions. Differentiation of cells permits the growth of larger organisms: plants get to be quite large, though not very complex: insects achieve great complexity, but cannot break through the size barrier of about three inches in length, and their optimum size seems to be between the ant and the bee. The endoskeleton and the convolution of the lung, the bowels, and the brain permitted the construction of still larger complex forms in the vertebrates, culminating in the mammal, just as the steel frame (an endoskeleton) and air conditioning permits the development of larger buildings than solid walls (exoskeletons) and mere windows permit.

Now, however, the biological parallel, no doubt to our alarm, gives some possible comfort to the Communists. Admitting (which in general Communists do not) the existence of diminishing returns to scale beyond a certain point for *any one form* of organization, do we not see in the evolutionary process the constant transcending of an old size barrier by a new form of organization—the molecule transcending the element, the cell the molecule, the animal the cell, the vertebrate the invertebrate, the mammal the reptile? Can we not argue then that new and more perfect forms of social organization now have enabled us—or shortly will enable us—to transcend the old size barrier and establish, literally, a whale of a society in the Communist state? The question here is crucial to the world's future: it is however an empirical question which cannot be answered *a priori*, but only by studying the organizations themselves. Here again we see how useful would be an acceptable measure of the degree of organization against which we could test the hypothesis that diminishing returns to scale set in at a point far smaller than that of the whole society. It is on this hypothesis, if "returns" are interpreted broadly enough to include all things which are valued by men, not merely commodities, that a market (capitalist) society stands or falls by comparison with an organic (Communist) society.

Somewhere lurking in the wings of this whole argument is, of course, the whole problem of value. The bigger is not necessarily better, the more is not necessarily better, so what *is* better? This unfortunately is a question too important to be left to the philosophers, and too unanswerable to be left to anyone else. The value coordinate is clearly a scalar, like organization. We compare two constellations of perceived reality, and we say that one is "better" than the other, that is, is further "out" from some origin of goodness. In so far as we believe that the evolutionary process carries us not only to more organized systems but also to "better" systems we imply a generally monotonic relationship—which does not, of course, have to be linear—between degree of organization and "goodness." Such a relationship may of course be questioned—indeed even to state it so baldly looks like a reversion to the uncritical Spencerian optimism of the nineteenth century, and one can hardly question that for short, or even for fairly extended periods, evil may clothe itself in organization superior to good. Nevertheless it is surely an implication of the basic long-run optimism of most religious or even secular faiths that the course of evolution toward higher organization is also a movement towards the "good." If this seems homocentric it is at least not surprising in *homini*!

If large and complex constellations of organizations are to be reduced to a one-dimensional scalar of "goodness" we must have something like a "price system" of valuation coefficients by which the diverse and many dimensional elements of the constellation can be reduced to a single dimension of value. Thus suppose we ask whether a man who is loyal but stupid is "better" or "worse" than a man who is unfaithful but intelligent. The answer we give will clearly depend on the *value weights* which we give to the various qualities. If we give loyalty a low value weight and intelligence a high one, we are likely to rate the intelligent man "better" than the stupid one even if he is unfaithful: if we give loyalty a high value weight by comparison with intelligence the reverse result may obtain. Many of the difficulties of ethical valuation arise because of the absence of a "salient" and clearly agreed upon system of value weights. In economic valuation of course —as in, for instance, the valuation of a heterogeneous constellation of assets in a balance sheet—we have the advantage of a system of value weights given us initially by the structure of relative prices, even though we may modify this considerably in the evaluation process. In ethical valuations we do not have the same advantage, and the difficulties of ethical agreement are a direct result of the absence of an agreed system of value weights.

I would not wish to imply that a measure of organization would automatically yield a system of ethical value weights which would enable us to do perfect "ethical accounting." Nevertheless, because I have some confidence in the generally monotonic character of the relationship between organization and "goodness"—that is, that both generally increase together—I would argue that the development of a workable measure of organization would at least be a first step toward the construction of an ethical calculus. The want of this measure however may impede progress toward the solution of many problems, not only in biology and in the social sciences, but also in ethics.

Knowledge as a Commodity[*]

The idea that knowledge is itself an object of knowledge and is therefore a subject matter of science is slowly attaining respectability. By and large, the classical sciences—whether physical or social—such as Newtonian physics, Daltonian chemistry, or Ricardian economics do not include knowledge as an object of study. They can get away with this because the objects of study are so large and gross relative to the act of investigation that it can be assumed without difficulty that the act of investigation itself makes no impact on the subject matter that is being investigated. In twentieth-century science, however, at almost all levels, the problem of knowledge as part of the subject matter has become acute. The shadow of a generalized Heisenberg principle, according to which any attempt to investigate a scientific subject matter profoundly alters the material which is being investigated, now broods over the whole realm of science. Pierre Teilhard de Chardin goes so far as to characterize the present age as that of the "nöosphere" in which the dynamics of the surface of planet Earth are determined very largely by the web of knowledge which envelops it. Since the advent of mankind, the nöosphere, which is distinct from the biosphere which it inhabits, has become an increasingly important part of the Earth system, and innumerable biological, physical, and evolutionary events have to be referred to it. Without the nöosphere, for instance, we could not explain atomic explosions on earth, or the displacements of matter which constitute architecture, or the present distribution of living species. It is absurd to suppose that we can think of nature as a system apart from knowledge, for it is knowledge that is increasingly determining the course of nature.

[*] In: *Series Studies in Social and Economic Sciences, Symposia Studies No. 11* (National Institute of Social and Behavioral Science, June 1962), pp. 1–6.

This paper was presented under the auspices of the National Institute of Social and Behavioral Science at the meeting of the American Association for the Advancement of Science in Denver, Colorado in December 1961, co-sponsored by the American Economic Association.

For all its importance in the world system, knowledge is difficult to define and even more difficult to measure. It clearly is related to information, which we now can measure; and an economist especially is tempted to regard knowledge as a kind of capital structure, corresponding to information as an income flow. Knowledge, that is to say, is some kind of improbable structure or stock made up essentially of patterns—that is, improbable arrangements; and the more improbable the arrangements, we might suppose, the more knowledge there is. Unfortunately, this view, while it undoubtedly contains elements of truth, is far too simple. Knowledge is not merely a pile of bits of information; and the "wit" which seems to be the appropriate term for a unit of knowledge, is far more complex than a mere capitalized "bit." The idea of knowledge as an improbable structure is still a good place to start. Knowledge, however, has a dimension which goes beyond that of mere information or improbability. This is a dimension of significance which is very hard to reduce to quantitative form. Two knowledge structures might be equally improbable but one might be much more significant than the other.

Significance, again, may be a many-dimensioned quantity. It is, however, clearly related to what might be called the teleological property of knowledge—that is, the ability of a knowledge system to realize an image of the future which exists in the present. This is the element which this writer has sometimes called the element of freedom in systems and it is, of course, peculiarly characteristic of social systems. Necessity governed the solar system, at least until the advent of political astronomy; chance governed the biological systems until the advent of man. But with the coming of man into the world, a new kind of system developed because of the appearance of knowledge on a scale and complexity far beyond what had been achieved previously. The movements of a man cannot be reduced to necessity. They cannot, for instance, be described by any system of differential equations. They cannot be accounted for by chance, for they do not have the characteristics of a random walk. They must be accounted for by the introduction of knowledge, that is, of images of the world in which the image of the world is related also to a value function or some principle of ordering. One exists and moves about because of freedom—that is, because of an image of the world and an image of a role structure which involves consistency with other people's role structures. In a system of this kind, it is evident that knowledge plays an absolutely vital role, and that the movements of the system cannot be explained without it.

An economist is one who knows economics, and economics is primarily the science of commodities. A commodity is something which is exchanged and, therefore, has a price. It is usually something which can be produced and consumed—that is, created and destroyed. At times, knowledge possesses all these properties, and hence it can claim to be a commodity. It is, however, a very peculiar commodity and has very peculiar relations to other commodities.

Its first peculiarity is that it does not obey the law of conservation. In simple exchange, the commodities themselves are conserved. Exchange, that is, represents a redistribution of exchangeables among owners; just as in chemical exchange there is no loss of atoms, only a rearrangement of the old atoms into different molecules. In the classroom, the situation is extraordinarily different. When a teacher teaches a class, at the end of the hour the pupils know more and the teacher usually knows more, too. In the simplest form of rote learning, this corresponds very closely to an important process of nature which might be called printing. This is the process by which a certain structure is able to impose itself on the matter around it, as the type reproduces its pattern on innumerable pages of print. The gene reproduces itself by a process that is very much like three-dimensional printing. Printing can be done orally, as when a speech is memorized by the listeners; it can be done visually, as when we read a printed page or a map. Oral printing has sharp limits imposed by the number of people who can hear a single human voice. Visual printing has no such limits, which is why the invention of movable type produced an enormous acceleration in the rate of structural and technical change.

The multidimensionality of the knowledge concept may confuse us here if we are not careful. By the increase in knowledge we may merely mean that more people know a certain thing. We may also mean, however, that one person knows something that nobody knew before. We should really have two different expressions for these two quite different phenomena. We might, perhaps, call the former the "growth" of knowledge, and the latter the "increase." These correspond roughly to the two activities of teaching and research. The distinction, however, is not an altogether clear one. Once we leave the simple patterns of rote learning, the process by which the knowledge of a single individual increases is not wholly different from that of research. Knowledge beyond that of rote learning always requires a degree of understanding. It cannot simply be transmitted by a printing process. It always involves a growth process in the mind of the learner. This growth process, however, does not seem essentially different from the process by which a researcher obtains new knowledge from nature rather than from men or from books.

This self-multiplicative property of knowledge, by which it seems to transgress the fundamental law of conservation, may be the basic explanation, not only of phenomenon like economic development, but even of the whole evolutionary process. One of the paradoxes of evolution is how, in a universe that according to the second law of thermodynamics is running down, parts of it seem to be running up. The two learning processes we have outlined, the imprinting of patterns and the growth of understanding, correspond roughly to the fundamental evolutionary processes of reproduction on the one hand and mutation and selection on the other. In social systems it is clear that social evolution depends both on man's capacity to transmit large quantities of knowledge to his fellows and also on his ability to learn from nature—that is, to develop images or knowledge structures which correspond to "reality" in the natural world. His understanding likewise increases his freedom, for the test of "truth" in the image of nature is the ability which that image gives to realize images of the future. An image of the future which cannot be realized is fantasy—like flying carpets which are guided by incantations. One may have an image of the future which involves flying and have reasonable expectations of realizing this image. The realization, however, comes about because of knowledge of aerodynamics, structural engineering, the chemistry of combustion, and all the innumerable pieces of knowledge which have to be fitted together to make a modern airplane.

It is reasonable to assume, therefore, that economic development is primarily a learning process and that the capital goods in which it is embodied are merely material structures which reflect the mental structures out of which they come—though we may postulate, indeed, that all production comes out of knowledge and that it is precisely the nonconserving property of knowledge which enables us to produce anything in the first place. In the last analysis, the reproduction both of wheat and of automobiles may belong to somewhat the same category of systems, though the gene structure of automobiles is contained in the minds of men or in the drafting-rooms and libraries of automobile companies, whereas the gene structure of wheat is contained in the seed itself.

If the transmission of knowledge is analogous to production, the loss of knowledge is likewise analogous to consumption. The greatest consumer of knowledge, of course, is death. A very large part of the process of education is, in fact, mere replacement of depreciation—the depreciation which death imposes on the knowledge structure of society. An increase in the expectation of life, and especially of vigorous adult life, diminishes the cost of replacement of the knowledge structure of society. A society in which the average age at death is thirty cannot have as complex and intricate a knowledge structure as a society in which the average age at death is seventy.

Alternatively, a society with a low average age at death must spend a much larger proportion of its resources in simply replacing the knowledge which is lost by death than the society in which the expectation of life is high. Thus, in the society in which the expectation of life is only thirty years, about half the population will be below the age of fifteen. In a society, in which the expectation of life is sixty years, only a quarter of the population is below the age of fifteen. The sheer extension of the expectation of life, therefore, liberates resources for education and for increasing the community's stock of knowledge. A traditional society is static largely because the effort which is required to transmit the culture takes almost all of the available energy of the society which can be released for this purpose. Most of the energy of the society goes into simply keeping it alive. The high proportion of children in the population not only makes it difficult to spare anything from sheer subsistence, but also makes it difficult to transmit the culture. It is only as resources become available over and above what might be called knowledge subsistence—that is, a minimum necessary to transmit an existing culture—that a culture is likely to change. Once the change is begun, however, it has to take place at an accelerating rate, for every increase in knowledge permits the release of resources to develop a further increase in knowledge. When the increase of knowledge becomes specialized, as it does in a scientific society, the acceleration is all the greater. Thus, the most crucial knowledge of all is that which leads to the release of resources for the pursuit of knowledge.

The peculiarities which characterize the production and consumption of knowledge naturally carry over into its exchange. In the case of ordinary commodities, exchange both arises out of and justifies specialization. Because we specialize, we must exchange the specialized products. Because there is an opportunity for the exchange of specialized products, it pay us to specialize. The division of labor, as Adam Smith so justly observed, depends on the extent of the market; but the extent of the market likewise depends on the division of labor. Knowledge is not exempt from these commodity-like characteristics. Nevertheless, it also has some peculiarities. We are all familiar with the phenomenon of specialization in knowledge, but we have long since passed the point where one head could hold all the knowledge which is available to mankind. There are innumerable specialized fields of knowledge, just as there are innumerable specialized occupations and producers of commodities. Specialization in knowledge, however, does not automatically result in exchange—that is, in the exchange of knowledge for knowledge. This is because there is nothing in the field of knowledge which corresponds to the institution of money. For the most part, there are not even shop windows. Each specialist hoards his knowledge like a hermit in a cave, and he who wants a specialized piece of knowledge may have to search before he finds it. We have the paradox here which is implicit in the very concept of knowledge, that we have to know what we want to know before we can start looking for it. There are the things that we ought to know, and which we do not know that we ought to know, that remain largely unknown and unsought for. Because of this, specialization in knowledge is much less effective in increasing the total wealth of knowledge than is specialization in the production of commodities.

This situation is both alleviated and aggravated by the existence of organized professional disciplines. When the possessors of a certain form of specialized knowledge become a self-conscious group, with a professional organization, professional journals, and organized departments in the universities, communication is unquestionably facilitated within the discipline. When there is conversation, an alert ear picks up the message that it needs; and one of the main functions of an organized profession is the organization of conversation among its members. The very organization of a discipline, however, often tends to cut its practitioners off from other disciplines. Consequently, when problems arise which require pieces of knowledge from many different disciplines, we are extremely ill-equipped to handle them. One solution to this problem has been the development of new disciplines between the cracks of the old—physiochemistry, bio-chemics, social psychology, political sociology, and so on—hybrid disciplines which have developed between the cracks of the older disciplines, and occasionally even threatened to engulf the disciplines between which they grew.

Up to now, however, these hybrid disciplines have developed only between adjacent disciplines. When problems arise which require the cooperation of distant disciplines, we are extremely ill-equipped to deal with them. Thus, many problems of the present day—for instance, disarmament and arms control—require the cooperation of disciplines which are remote in academic structure and educational experience. They require, for instance, the cooperation of physicists and sociologists who have to deal with what are essentially socio-physical systems —that is, social systems with important physical constants. There is no interdiscipline of social physics, so we have no professional apparatus to handle problems of this kind. As a result, we find ourselves cursed with physicists who become amateur sociologists, and who offer all sorts of practical advice about social systems without professionally understanding them in the least; and you may even find an occasional sociologist who poses as an amateur physicist!

The problem here is partly one of the organization of communication and partly that of the development of specialized intellectual middlemen. Middlemen, unfortunately, seldom receive the status or the credit which their function in society deserves, and this seems to be as true in the intellectual life as in any other. The middleman tends to be despised by the specialist as shallow, even when he is performing a vital intellectual function. Similarly, the librarian and the bibliographer, who likewise contribute to this exchange function in the world of the intellect, seldom receive the respect and attention which the occupation intrinsically deserves. A perverse process then sets in. Because the intellectual middleman is not highly regarded, the occupation does not attract the best minds; because it does not attract the best minds, it is still less highly regarded. A society would be well advised to organize these professions of intellectual exchange in such a way that they have high prestige and that some of the best intellectual resources of the society are attracted into them. Otherwise, specialized intellectual resources may largely go to waste. The body of knowledge, instead of becoming a great organization capable of serving the needs of the society, becomes a set of little pigeon-holes—a mere pile of intellectual accumulations instead of an organic and operating whole.

If the exchange of knowledge for knowledge presents peculiarities and difficulties, the exchange of knowledge for money—that is, really for other commodities—presents a similar picture. If the pursuit and transmission of knowledge is to be a specialized function in society, it must be paid for. That is, the pursuers and transmitters of knowledge must receive commodities which are the product of other men. This, however, looks like the exchange of something concrete for something abstract. The gains to society which come from the pursuit and transmission of knowledge are apt to be diffuse. They are not easily appropriable, and it is hard to tell who gains and who does not—or how much each person gains. The pursuit and transmission of knowledge, therefore, has almost always been regarded as a peculiarly fit subject for the activity of government or some other agency representing society as a whole—such as an established church. Education and research, that is to say, tend to fall under what might be called the grant system of the economy rather than the exchange system. It is true, of course, that there are educational and research institutions which operate under the exchange system. There are language schools, dancing schools, secretarial schools, training institutions of many kinds, which operate essentially in the market economy, and which derive the bulk of their income from the simple sale of their services to customers. The society is rarely satisfied, however, to leave the education and research functions wholly to the operations of the market. It supports public schools through grants from governmental authorities, and it regards education as an extraordinarily suitable subject for private charity—which might be thought of economically as private government, that is, the private part of a grant system.

Each of these methods of organizing education and research presents problems of its own. Adam Smith observed (*The Wealth of Nations*, Volume II, Everyman Edition, page 250), "Those parts of education, it is to be observed, for the teaching of which there are no public institutions, are generally the best taught. When a young man goes to a fencing or a dancing school, he does not indeed always learn to fence or to dance very well, but he seldom fails of learning to fence or to dance. In England, the public schools are much less corrupted than the universities." The great advantage of education which is provided for a market is that if it is not provided, it is not paid for; and there is, therefore, a strong incentive to provide it. The same may likewise be said of research. Where education and research, on the other hand, are provided for through the grant system, or where they are provided by endowed institutions where there is no public check upon the performance of the duties, there is a strong tendency for the recipients of these bounties to excuse themselves and each other from the more difficult tasks. This is not to say, of course, that the public institutions are entirely without checks which are analogous, in a sense, to the checks of the market. The Parent-Teachers Association may keep a vigilant eye on the schools, and the foundations and government authorities which provide the funds for research are supposed to take some sort of pride in their successful expenditure. There is something like a "grants market" in which the seekers for grants and the donors of grants compete among themselves, the seekers for the donors, and the donors for the seekers. Where there are a large number of granting institutions and a considerable number of seekers after grants, we may reasonably expect that a mechanism not unlike that of perfect competition will develop, which will be in itself a considerable protection against gross abuses.

Nevertheless, the organization both of learning and of research in this country do not give us cause for unqualified self-satisfaction.

Quite apart from the sputnik trauma, there is reason to suppose that neither education nor research is directed towards solving the major problems of our society. Our educational system, extensive as it is, is not producing the kind of citizen who can handle the enormously difficult problems of our day in a mature and knowledgeable manner. Our research effort suffers from a gross maldistribution of intellectual resources. The major problems of our society, whether these be flood control, agricultural surpluses, urban unemployment, depressed areas, or the threat of nuclear annihilation, essentially lie in the field of social systems, or at least of sociophysical systems—that is, social systems with important physical constants. Our main intellectual effort, however, goes into physical systems or into biological systems. We spend enormous amounts of money on the physical sciences, and on medical research. We allot pitifully small amounts to the study of the social systems in which our problems lie. By and large, we can argue that this is a result of the failure of the grant system.

One hardly expects fundamental research into social systems and the problems of society to be paid for out of the exchange system. The benefits are too diffuse and the exchange system only operates well in the field of knowledge when the knowledge that is purchased is clearly and obviously of peculiar benefit to the purchaser. In the case of the study of social systems, therefore, it is the grantors, both governmental and private, who have fallen down and who have failed to realize the nature of their responsibility. This is not to absolve altogether the potential grantees who by and large have failed to make their cases sufficiently urgent and who have not been insistent enough on the importance of their efforts. It can be argued also that the study of social systems is only just reaching to the point where large investment would pay off. In the early stages of almost any body of knowledge, investment must be fairly small because the body of knowledge itself must grow according to its own laws, and before it can expand rapidly it must consolidate itself.

It is clear that what is needed in this field is a two-way entrepreneurship in the grants market. We are assuming that the bulk of knowledge-increasing activity will be supported in the grants sector of the economy rather than in the exchange sector. The grant sector, however, suffers from very imperfect competition. The endowed agencies which are, as it were, the makers of grants to themselves, are not subject to the stimulus of outside forces in an adequate degree and so have a strong tendency toward eventual corruption, like eighteenth-century Oxford. The granting agencies, such as foundations and governments, because of the absence of any clearly recognized standards of success in this operation, tend to fall into habitual or fashionable patterns of behavior. In the course of the communications network that surrounds them, the grantors come to have certain images as to what kinds of grants are safe. Respectability, therefore, grows at the expense of imaginativeness. Policies are decided mainly on a negative basis, by ruling out all the things that the granting agency will not do, and, as a result, risk-taking declines. The same phenomenon, unfortunately, happens too easily on the side of the grantees. Because of the difficulty of finding support for risky enterprises in the world of the intellect, there is a certain tendency for the intellectual community, which should be at the frontiers of knowledge, to settle down comfortably somewhat behind the lines. We still have not succeeded in institutionalizing satisfactorily the entrepreneurial, risk-taking element in the field of the advancement of knowledge. Up to the present this has largely been taken care of by the wide distribution of granting power and the existence of a marginal fringe, among both the grantors and the grantees. The more the whole operation is institutionalized, however, the smaller this marginal fringe is likely to get, and the less chance there is, therefore, of the kind of risk-taking which is likely to lead to the major advances.

Knowledge about knowledge has a peculiar multiplier or leverage effect on the growth of knowledge itself. The more we know about learning and the transmission of knowledge, and the more we know about the processes by which knowledge advances at the frontiers, the more efficient will be the use of resources, both in education and in research. One would think it would hardly be possible to waste resources in the investigation of the knowledge process itself; yet this is an astonishingly neglected field. Here again, it may be that knowledge about knowledge has to proceed slowly at first, and in a somewhat casual and unorganized way. The time, however, will surely come—and it may be here now—when a well-organized and well-financed attempt to increase our knowledge about knowledge would have enormous payoffs, simply because it would improve the efficiency of the knowledge industry at all points. It may well be that we are now at the point where enough experience has been accumulated in work on the psychology of learning and creativity, on the sociology of the professions and of research and educational organizations, and on the economics of education and research, that a major interdisciplinary effort in the study of knowledge processes is in order.

The Misallocation of Intellectual Resources[*]

Economists have always been interested in the problem of allocation of resources. It is, indeed, a central problem of their science. In equilibrium price theory, for instance, an equilibrium set of prices of all commodities, on the one hand, and of outputs of all commodities on the other, results in an equilibrium set of returns to factors such that there is no incentive for factors or resources on balance to switch from one occupation or from the production of one commodity to another. If there were no obstacle to the movement of resources, the returns to their use would be equal in all uses. Where there are obstacles to movement, returns to factors in the equilibrium situation may be unequal, provided that the differences are not large enough to overcome the obstacles to movement.

The weakness of this elegant schema, particularly when it comes to examining economic development and the dynamic course of an economy through time, is that it takes no explicit account of the intellectual resource and the learning process. In the classical economics, the three factors of production are identified as labor, land, and capital; labor is little more than manpower, analogous to horsepower—indeed, Adam Smith at one point speaks in the same breath of the laboring poor and the laboring cattle. Capital is conceived as a stockpile of commodities, and investment is simply the addition to these stocks by the process of producing more than is consumed. Land is little more than simple area. Alfred Marshall tried, somewhat unsuccessfully, to add a fourth factor of production which he called organization, which looks a little more like an intellectual resource. In all this scheme, however, there is very little explicit recognition of the fact that economic development is essentially a learning process, and that the nature and allocation of the intellectual resource is the key to it.

[*] *Proceedings, Am. Phil. Soc.* 107, 2 (April 1963): 117–20.
This paper was read at the meeting of the American Philosophical Society in Philadelphia, Pennsylvania on November 8, 1962.

The above statements should be qualified by the observation that Adam Smith, with his usual insight but also with his usual lack of an explicit analytical framework, comes very close to expounding what might be called an epistemological theory of development in his account of the effects of the division of labor. In the very first chapter of *The Wealth of Nations* he says,

"This great increase of the quantity of work which, in consequence of the division of labour, the same number of people are capable of performing, is owing to three different circumstances; first, to the increase of dexterity in every particular workman; secondly, to the saving of the time which is commonly lost in passing from one species of work to another; and lastly, to the invention of a great number of machines which facilitate and abridge labour, and enable one man to do the work of many."[1]

Each of these "three different circumstances" represents a learning process and an allocation of an intellectual resource. The increase in dexterity is a learning process in the lower nervous system. The diminution in what Adam Smith in another place calls "sauntering" as we go from one occupation to another also reflects the fact that there has to be a brief period of relearning when we take up a new pursuit, even if it is one we have pursued in the past; and the invention of machines is, of course, the most important learning process of all, and the only one which seems to have an almost unlimited horizon. Later in the chapter Adam Smith observes that improvements in machinery may in part come from the workmen who operate them (the suggestion box!), but then he goes on,

"Many improvements have been made by the ingenuity of the makers of the machines, when to make them became the business of a peculiar trade; and some by that of those who are called philosophers or men of speculation, whose trade it is not to do anything, but to observe everything; and who, upon that account, are often capable of combining together the powers of the most distant and dissimilar objects."[2]

In his tribute to the philosophers Adam Smith foreshadows the increasing importance of research and development as a source of economic progress. These important hints which were dropped by Adam Smith, however, were not much taken up by subsequent econo-

---

[1] Adam Smith, *The Wealth of Nations*, 7, New York, Modern Library edition, 1937.
[2] *Ibid.*, 10.

mists, and it is only very recently that the problem of the intellectual resource as opposed, say, to the mere accumulation of capital has risen to prominence as a key to economic development. I should add that it is a key likewise to the even more important, though less easily identifiable and measurable, processes of political and social development.

An allocation problem implies that a resource is scarce, in the sense that the more we apply to one use the less we can apply to others. If we define the intellectual resource in terms of the learning process, it is clear that it is scarce in the above sense and that an allocation problem arises. An individual cannot know everything and cannot learn everything in the course of his lifetime. In any particular year, if he learns one thing there are things that he cannot learn as a result. A society as a whole has to cope with the consumption of knowledge as a result of old age, incapacity, and death. A large part of the educational activity of a society consists in the replacement of knowledge which is lost in this way. The ability of a society to expand its stock of knowledge—what Adam Smith himself calls the "quantity of science"—depends on its having an intellectual resource which is greater than that needed for the mere maintenance of the knowledge which is lost by death and other means. One reason why primitive societies are apt to be stable is that it takes their whole intellectual resource merely to replace the loss of knowledge by death, and hence there is nothing to spare for an increase in the stock of knowledge. The fewer intellectual resources are necessary, therefore, to maintain the existing knowledge structure, the more can be spared for increase and improvement. This is why, for instance, an increase in the expectation of life introduces a dynamic process into almost any society. If the expectation of life at birth is only thirty years, a much larger proportion of resources will have to be devoted to simple maintenance of the knowledge stock than if the expectation of life is sixty years. There is even something, though not much, in Bernard Shaw's suggestion that we shall have to go back to Methuselah before we can spare enough intellectual resource for improvement.

Perhaps the most important question that any society can ask itself, therefore, is: what are the signs of misallocation of the intellectual resource, and, if these signals are flying, what can be done to correct the situation? We have no simple measure here in the shape of a rate of return, as we have in the case of allocation of financial capital. The same general principle applies, however, that, if the rates of return on the investment of intellectual resources are much larger in one employment than in another, this is a sign that the resources are being misallocated and there should be a transfer out of the low-return employment into the high-return employment. We would have to define the returns to intellectual investment in terms of the relevance of knowledge to the "problems" of the society. The definition of "problems" presents real difficulty, as a definition in terms of *perceived* problems is not always satisfactory. A society may have unperceived problems which are of great importance to its survival and ultimate success. The best we can do, perhaps, is to start off with the perceived problems and then inquire into the reality testing to see whether there are unperceived problems which are important and whether the perceived problems are not real ones.

For any particular society, therefore, we could visualize a process of self-examination which might go something as follows. We first of all would examine the whole learning process in the society, including not only the institutions of formal education and research but also the less formal learning which goes on in the field, the shop, the factory, the family, the church, and so on. We then look at how much of this total process can properly be ascribed to mere replacement and how much is *net* in the sense of a net addition to the total stock of knowledge. We then look at whether there are unused intellectual resources. There is a problem in the use of intellectual resources somewhat akin to the problem of underemployment as a result of deficient social organization. In most societies the underemployment of intellectual resources is likely to be massive, for the biological capacity of the human organism for learning is usually much larger than the actual performance. We need to look therefore at the blocks to learning and particularly for the points at which social organization can improve the learning performance. We must also look at the distinction between useful knowledge and useless knowledge, difficult as this may be. A society in which knowledge of an elaborate ceremonial structure unrelated to real problems has to be maintained, generation after generation, is clearly wasting its intellectual resources. Finally, we must look at the extent of redundancy in the information system, and the absence of significant communication channels.

We then ask whether that proportion of the intellectual resource which is devoted to development and the increase in knowledge is in fact being directed along the right lines. This is a delicate question, because it is part of the mythology of science that this should not be a problem—knowledge is supposed to grow by a spontaneous process by which there is a gradual division of labor into specialized disciplines and by which the problems on which people work are determined by the growing-points of the structure of knowledge itself. That is, the questions which science asks of nature are supposed to be determined by what we already know. Unfortunately this myth becomes more and more divorced from reality, especially in an age in which research and development has become such big business. Knowledge always grows towards payoffs, like any other growth structure, and the payoffs in this case consist not merely of the rewards of disinterested curiosity; they consist of very tangible economic rewards which are determined by the structure of the society. We need to look at these economic rewards, therefore, to see whether they are introducing any malfunctioning into the growth of knowledge, and particularly whether they are directing intellectual resources towards the solution of unreal, unimportant, or insoluble problems.

Even the most cursory inspection of the allocation of intellectual resources in the United States according to the above criterion suggests that we are, in fact, suffering from a massive misallocation of current intellectual resources. There are two aspects of this problem. In the first place, we are not increasing the stock of already known, useful knowledge in the population as a whole to an adequate extent. The image of the world held by the mass of the people is now unrealistic to the point where this constitutes a grave danger. This is because the folk knowledge on which we mostly rely for our image of society is not adequate in a period of rapid change in the social system, and especially in the basic parameters of that system. An even more basic problem concerns the allocation of resources to research, that is, to the development of knowledge that nobody knew before. The problem may be summed up by saying that, whereas our major problems lie in the field of social systems, our major intellectual resource is still being devoted towards physical and biological systems. As a result of this, the growth of knowledge has become so one-sided that it actively threatens us. The change in the parameters of the social system which results from increased knowledge of physical and biological systems is so great that we are threatened all along the line with a collapse in social systems as a result of our inability to understand them and to operate them successfully. In a brief paper of this kind one can do no more than outline a few cases where this principle is at work.

(1) After spending four billion dollars on flood control in this country, we are more in danger of major disasters than before, because we have treated floods as a problem of the river, not as a problem of people, and we have attempted to deal with the problem in engineering terms instead of in terms of social institutions such as zoning and architectural design. Transportation policy is not much better, because of the strong prejudice in favor of cement.

(2) The health revolution in the tropics, made possible as a result

of our increasing knowledge of biological systems, is threatening the world with a major social disaster in terms of unmanageable rates of population increase, a shift in the age composition of these societies out of the labor force groups into both the young and the old, and the consequent imposition on these societies of a problem in education and knowledge formation which may be beyond their powers to solve.

(3) In agricultural policy we have created an almost insoluble problem in the misallocation of agricultural resources, because again our capacity to solve biological problems has run so far in advance of our capacity to solve social problems.

(4) Lest we should think that these problems are confined to Western society, we should note that China is facing a major disaster in terms both of agriculture and of industrial development, because of the application of a premature and inadequate knowledge of social systems, as enshrined in an unrealistic quasi-Marxist ideology.

(5) In regard to war and peace, we are all traveling on the edge of almost irretrievable disaster because of our attempt to achieve national security by concentrating almost exclusively in physical systems, in terms of weaponry. Because of this we have changed the parameters of the international system so radically that the concept of national defense as an international system has collapsed. Specifically, we put billions of dollars' worth of intellectual resources into attempting to operate an unworkable system, and we put practically nothing into the study and operation of conflict resolution in the international social system, which is where the problem really lies.

(6) Above all, we are putting quite inadequate resources into the study of the learning process itself, which seems to be the key to all the other problems. An improvement in the efficiency of the learning process would have a tremendous leverage; it would not only enable us to replace depreciating knowledge with a smaller expenditure of intellectual resources, because of increased efficiency in the educational process, but it would also increase the efficiency of intellectual resources expended in the production of new knowledge. For the processes by which old knowledge is disseminated and new knowledge is acquired are not essentially different.

The basic difficulty seems to be that whereas in the area of physical and biological systems we have accepted long ago the inadequacy of folk knowledge and the necessity of scientific knowledge, in the field of social systems we have not yet reached this point. Consequently in the operation of the political, social, economic, and educational systems we are still operating to a large extent with "wisdom"— that is, folk knowledge rising out of the ordinary experience of life.

No one will deny that wisdom is better than folly, that is, good folk knowledge is better than bad folk knowledge. We have now reached a point in the development of man, however, where wisdom is inadequate to operate the increased complexity of his social systems. We must improve both our theoretical structures and our information-processing apparatus. We live in the day when even the best wisdom is not far from folly, and a major intellectual effort in the field of social systems is going to be necessary if our trust in wisdom in the face of a lack of knowledge is not to betray us.

Expecting the Unexpected: The Uncertain Future of Knowledge and Technology[*]

How Is Prediction Possible?

One thing we can say about man's future with a great deal of confidence is that it will be more or less surprising. This phenomenon of surprise is not something which arises merely out of man's ignorance, though ignorance can contribute to what might be called unnecessary surprises. There is, however, something fundamental in the nature of an evolutionary system which makes exact foreknowledge about it impossible, and as social systems are in a large measure evolutionary in character, they participate in the property of containing ineradicable surprise.

Mechanical Systems. In *mechanical* systems which have no surprise in them, we can hardly say that there is a future or a past at all, as the present is a purely arbitrary point. The best example of a system of this kind is the solar system, at least before the advent of political astronomy in the shape of man-made satellites. In the Newtonian system in which the planets are moved by angels, that is, differential equations of the second degree, the system can be moved backwards or forwards in time simply by turning the crank of an orrery. Time is reversible, and what we have is a wholly predictable succession of

* In: *Prospective Changes in Society by 1980 Including Some Implications for Education.* Reports Prepared for the First Area Conference Designing Education for the Future: An Eight-State Project, Edgar L. Morphet and Charles O. Ryan, eds. (Denver, Colo.: July 1966), pp. 199–215.

This paper was prepared for a conference on Prospective Changes in Society by 1980 on June 29, 1966 in Denver, Colorado. I was unable to be present and the paper was read by my colleague, Daniel R. Fusfeld, whose excellent additional comments will be found in the original volume.

states of the system. The fact that such a system takes place in time is quite accidental to it. We could just as well set it out as a succession in space, as we do, for instance, when we express it as a graph.

We can express the same thing in another way. If we use the familiar sequence of Monday, Tuesday, Wednesday, etc., to denote successive states of a system, then if the state of the system on any one day depends only on its state of the day before, we say that the system is of the first degree, and it can be expressed by a difference or differential equation of the first degree. If we know, then, the constant relation between today and tomorrow, and we know what the state of the system is on Monday, we can predict its state on Tuesday. Knowing its state on Tuesday we can predict its state on Wednesday, and so on indefinitely into the future. This is how we calculate compound interest or exponential growth. If a system is of the second order, then the state today depends not only on the state yesterday but also on the state the day before yesterday. In that case we have to know both Monday and Tuesday independently before we can predict Wednesday. If we know Monday and Tuesday, however, we know Wednesday; then we know Tuesday and Wednesday and hence we know Thursday; then we know Wednesday and Thursday and hence we know Friday, and so on indefinitely. The greater part of the solar system can be predicted with equations as simple as this, though comets, I understand, require equations of the third degree, in which case we need to know Monday, Tuesday, and Wednesday before we can predict Thursday. Having Thursday, however, Tuesday, Wednesday, and Thursday gives us Friday, and so on again. As the degree of the system increases, we need more and more initial information about it before the total description of the system and therefore prediction about it becomes possible. As we move towards evolutionary systems, we shall find that the degree of the system increases eventually to the point where mechanical predictions simply break down. If the system, for instance, has an infinite degree, which human history probably has for all practical purposes, exact prediction becomes theoretically impossible; for we could never put enough information into the system to describe it exactly. Even if we knew everything that had happened before the present, a sufficient pattern would not emerge.

Pattern Systems. There are many systems which do not possess the hundred percent predictability of mechanical systems like the solar system, but which nevertheless exhibit partial predictability in greater or less degree. If we put a chicken egg to hatch, we should be extremely surprised if it hatched into an alligator. When we see a kitten, we have a great deal of confidence that it will grow up into a cat, not a dog, if it grows up at all. Similarly, little boys almost invariably grow up into men and little girls into women, though there are a few exceptions to this rule. Similarly, when we see a skeleton steel structure, we expect to come back in a few months and see a finished building; when we see a keel in a shipyard we would later expect to find a ship, and so on over a very large range of human experiences. Probably the most respectable name for systems of this kind would be pattern-systems, as their predictability depends on the perception and recognition of a pattern which has been experienced in the past. We have watched our parents aging, so we predict that we will age ourselves in much the same way. There is a pattern of all human life from the fertilized egg to the grave, even though this pattern may be sliced off at any time by death. In a more frivolous mood I am tempted to call these systems wallpaper systems. Once we have perceived a pattern on wallpaper, we have great confidence in predicting it beyond the corner of the room that we cannot see, even though here too it might be cut off by an unexpected system break such as a door.

Just as astronomy and physics are the principal domain of mechanical systems, so the biological world is the principal domain of the pattern systems. In the fertilized egg there is a genetic blueprint for the creature that will emerge (if the process is not stopped by death), which charts within very narrow limits the growth of the phenotype, and in a very real sense creates the creature. Even if the growth of the creature is interrupted at some point by a nonfatal illness or temporary deficiencies in the food supply, the growth pattern often catches up again once the deficiency is restored. We have a great deal of confidence, therefore, in the stability of these patterns, a confidence which is rarely misplaced. The main uncertainties involved are those relating to the limits of the system, beyond which it cannot recover, for every system of this kind is subject to certain random processes which may lead to death at any time. In the mythology of the Fates, Clotho spins the pattern with great regularity; Atropos snips it at the moment of death (she is clearly the goddess of system break); and Lachesis, who measures it, is a fairly random number. Her measure is a roulette wheel with one mark on it that gives the sign to Atropos, and then— snip!

Equilibrium Systems.   A third broad class of systems which admit of predictability may be identified as *equilibrium systems*. These are systems in which the dynamic processes produce a succession of states, all of which are virtually identical. Whatever sense we have of stability in the world is derived from our perception of equilibrium processes. In the short run at any rate, people stay much the same from day to day; the field, the forest, the swamp and the lake reproduce themselves season after season, year after year, in an ecological equilibrium. The stores are always full of commodities, the gas stations full of gas. Cities contain streets, public buildings, churches, schools, and houses, year after year. The university has freshmen, sophomores, professors, deans, and a president; when one goes, another takes his place. When an equilibrium is stable, we have a good deal of confidence that a disturbance will be followed by a movement toward equilibrium again. The sick man recovers, the burned city is rebuilt, the forest comes back after a fire.

An increasingly important class of equilibrium systems is what may be called *control systems*, that is, equilibria which have been deliberately contrived by man. In a house with a furnace and a thermostat we can predict the inside temperature with a great deal of confidence, even though the outside temperature cannot be predicted with any great degree of confidence. In this case we predict the future not because we know it but because we make it. Thus modern economists are not merely interested in predicting the business cycle but in controlling it, and in setting up social "thermostats" which will counteract the random and perverse processes which operate on the economy, just as a thermostatically controlled furnace counteracts changes in outside temperature. Control systems must have what is called "equilibrating feedback." When outside disturbances threaten the equilibrium of the system, it must be capable of detecting and interpreting this information and of setting in motion dynamic processes which will counteract the disturbances. Thus if we want a stable rate of growth in the economy, we must be able to perceive when the rate of growth is slowing down and be able to speed it up, or when the rate of growth is getting too large and be able to slow it down. Similarly, if we want stable peace, we have to have a control apparatus which will perceive the movement towards war and set in motion counteracting dynamic processes.

In the biological world and also in social systems, we often get patterns of succession of short-run equilibrium states, which are generally described as ecological succession. The lake fills up and becomes a swamp, finally a prairie, and then a forest. Many philosophers of history have tried to interpret human history likewise in terms of a succcession of states or stages, hunting, pastoral, agricultural, and industrial, though the pattern of human history is not as clear and precise as those we find in the biological world. Insofar as we can detect these patterns of succession, however, we gain some powers of prediction.

Evolutionary Systems.   The patterns of ecological succession, however, do not help us very much when it comes to the great processes of evolution. These involve the processes of genetic mutation and ecological selection in the biological field, and parallel phenomena involving the growth of knowledge and organizations, cultures and societies, techniques and commodities, in the social field. Evolutionary theory is all hindsight; it has practically no predictive power at all. In evolutionary systems, time is not reversible nor is it arbitrary. There are indeed two systems in which time is not reversible; one is thermodynamics and the other is evolution. In thermodynamics, time's arrow points "down," according to the famous and dismal Second Law, by which entropy, that is, disorganization, continually increases, the availability of energy continually declines, potential is continuously used up, and what's done cannot be undone and can never be done again. Thermodynamics postulates a universe which starts off, as it were, with a capital and potential which it is inexorably squandering; and the end of the process is a kind of thin uniform soup in which all things are equally distributed, all at the same temperature, and chaos and old night have returned again.

By contrast, in the evolutionary process time's arrow points "up," towards the development of ever more complex and more improbable forms. Thermodynamically, it may be true that evolution is only just the segregation of entropy, that is, the building of more and more complex little castles of order at the cost of increasing chaos elsewhere. Nevertheless, the castles of order do get more and more complex, from hydrogen to carbon to uranium, from small molecules to big molecules, to viruses, to cells, to multi-celled organisms, to vertebrates and mammals, to man, to families, to tribes, to nations, and perhaps to a world. If the evolutionary process continues, therefore, it is pretty safe to predict an increase in complexity. The nature of that complexity, however, because it is itself an information system, cannot be known in advance, at least by an organism with a merely human capacity for knowing things.

In practice, the main cause for failures in prediction is a sudden change in the characteristics of the system itself. Such a change has been called a "system break." Death, bankruptcy, and conquest are extreme forms of a system break, in which a complex system at some point simply ceases to exhibit any kind of equilibrium or homeostasis, and disintegrates. Less dramatic system breaks, however, are also common—graduation, a new job, or marriage in the case of an individual, turning points in the economy, the outbreak of war or peace in the international system, sudden changes in birth or death rates in demographic systems, and so on. The growth of knowledge and technology is as much subject to system breaks as other systems. Sometimes, for instance, there is what I have elsewhere described as an "acceleration," that is, a sudden change in the rate of growth of knowledge or productivity. Such an acceleration occurred in Europe about 1600 with the rise of science. It took place in Japan around 1868, at the time of the Meiji Restoration. As we shall see, a system break of this kind seems to have occurred in American agriculture about 1935.

System breaks, unfortunately, are very hard to detect. They are virtually impossible to predict in advance; they are even difficult to detect after they have happened for some time, because in the short run it is virtually impossible to distinguish the beginning of a new long-term trend from a strictly temporary fluctuation. Thus suppose we had a sudden increase in the birth rate which persisted for four or five years; it could still be argued (and was!) that this was only temporary. A change has to be established for a considerable time before we decide that it is permanent, and even then it can fool us.

Predicting Knowledge and Technology

The Problem of Predicting Knowledge. The growth of knowledge is one of the most persistent and significant movements in the history of man, and, one might almost say, in the history of the universe. It is perhaps stretching the word to regard the whole evolutionary process as essentially a process of growth of knowledge, but if we think of knowledge as a capital structure of information, that is, as an improbable arrangement or structure, we see that it is this increasing improbability of structure which characterizes the whole evolutionary process. Even the chemical atoms have "know-how" in the form of valency—carbon knows how to hitch onto four hydrogens, but not onto five. The gene unquestionably represents know-how in the form of a blueprint for the creature which it builds, and human and social development is ineradicably bound up with the growth of human knowledge, that is, with images inside the organism which correspond in some way to the world without.

Of the various processes which we have identified as permitting prediction, the growth of knowledge is least like a mechanical process and most like an evolutionary process. Mechanical projections of trends in growth rates in a system as complex as this are to be treated with the utmost reserve, though the concept of a rate of growth of knowledge which has some stability, at least in short periods, is by no means absurd. We can perceive also a certain acceleration in the growth of knowledge, that is, the rate of growth increases all the time. Thus knowledge is like a sum of capital which accumulates at continually rising interest rates. Even though the absence of any measure of the total stock of knowledge makes quantitative statements about it more akin to poetry than to mathematics, in a poetical sort of way we can hazard a guess that human knowledge perhaps doubled in a hundred thousand years in the paleolithic, in five thousand years in the neolithic, and perhaps every thousand years in the age of civilization until the rise of science. In many fields of science now knowledge seems to double about every fifteen years. It is this enormous increase in the rate of growth of knowledge which has dominated the history of the last two or three hundred years, in all aspects of human life, politically, economically, and in all forms of human organization. The domination of the world by European culture, for instance, is almost a by-product of what may have been an accident, the fact that the mutation into science first took place in Europe.

The growth of knowledge, however, has been a subject of many interruptions and even reversals, and it would be very unwise to predict that just because knowledge has been growing at a certain rate in the past, it will continue to grow at the same rate in the future. It would be still more unwise to predict a constant rate of acceleration. We could say pretty safely, however, that the probability of growth is greater than that of decline, and that of acceleration is greater than that of deceleration.

A number of pattern systems can be detected in the growth of knowledge, especially in the spread of knowledge through education. The growth of knowledge has two aspects which can be summarized by the words education and research. Education is the spread of knowledge from one mind to another by means of communication processes between them. The communication may be one way, as when a person reads a book or sees a TV program, or it many be two way as in classroom teaching, conversation and dialogue. Thus education is a process by which what somebody knows or knew is transmitted to others. Research by contrast, is a process by which somebody gets to know something which nobody knew before. The two processes are highly intertwined. In the very act of transmitting knowledge, new knowledge is often created, which is one reason why universities combine the research and education processes. Knowledge is also lost in transmission, which is a kind of negative research, through noise and misunderstanding, which incidentally points up the great importance of dialogue and two-way transmissions if the body of knowledge is not to deteriorate in transmission.

The growth of knowledge in the individual follows a pattern which is closely related to the life pattern itself, and we hopefully suppose that knowledge increases with age. Formal education is an important part of this pattern, though it is not the only source of increase of knowledge. The growth of knowledge even in the individual is not a simple cumulative process by which information is pumped into the head and remains in a reservoir. Knowledge is a structure, and its present form always limits its possibilities of growth. Hence we get the phenomenon of "readiness" for certain kinds of knowledge at different stages of life. We get the phenomenon of wasted information input, which goes in at one ear and out the other, because it cannot latch onto anything in the existing knowledge structure. We get the phenomenon of superstition, or the development of false knowledge, as a result of the acceptance of authoritarian pronouncements and the failure of feedback; and we get the process of mutation through the imagination and testing through experience which is strikingly parallel to the evolutionary process itself, by which true knowledge grows.

The fact that the growth of knowledge has so many parallels to the evolutionary process renders it incapable of exact prediction. We can predict with some confidence that if the present system continues, knowledge will increase, not only because it has increased in the past but because we have a very large apparatus for increasing it. On the other hand, we run into a fundamental dilemma in attempting to predict the content of future knowledge, because if we knew the content of future knowledge, we would know it now, not in the future. That is, if we knew what we were going to know in twenty-five years, we would not have to wait twenty-five years for it. Consequently the growth of knowledge must always contain surprises, simply because the process itself represents the growth of improbable structures, and improbability always implies potential surprise. The whole idea of knowledge as a capital stock of information implies, therefore, that in detail its growth cannot be predicted. The difficulty is compounded by the fact that we know very little about the physiological structure which carries human knowledge. This difficulty, however, is less important than it might seem, for the carriers of an information structure are important only insofar as their properties limit the amount and complexity of the information that can be carried. We seem to be so far from the physical limits of the information content of the human nervous system that its physical properties can almost be neglected as a limit on the growth of knowledge.

Even though we cannot predict the specific content of future knowledge, what we know about the pattern of inputs and outputs enables us to venture at least on some probabilities. The distribution of new knowledge among the various fields and disciplines is at least likely to have some relation to the current distribution of research funds among these disciplines. Similarly the spread of knowledge in the world population is going to be related to some extent to the size of the educational industry and the funds allocated to it. I have argued elsewhere[1] that our research resources in particular are poorly allocated in the light of the importance for human welfare of the problems to which they are addressed. I have argued more particularly that the resources devoted to social systems are absurdly small in the light of the practical importance of these systems, and that whereas a failure of knowledge to advance in the physical and biological sciences for the next twenty-five years would not present mankind with any serious problems, the failure of knowledge to advance in the social sciences could well be fatal. Nevertheless we continue to devote our major effort to the physical, biological, and medical sciences and unless there is a change in this we can expect a continuation of the present imbalance in the growth of knowledge.

Predicting Technology.   Many of the considerations which apply to the growth of knowledge also apply to the growth of technology. We can predict with a great deal of confidence that technology will change. In a society like ours, where a good deal of resources are devoted to improving technology, it will be very surprising if technology does not improve in the sense that it increases human productivity. On the other hand, we cannot predict the exact forms which this improvement will take, simply because again, if we could predict it we would have it now. The proposition perhaps is a little less true in regard to the spread of already known technologies to places and societies which do not yet possess them. We have already noted the distinction between education, consisting in the spread of old knowledge to people who did not have it before from people who did have it before, and research, as the development of new knowledge that nobody had before. A similar distinction can be made in regard

---

[1] K.E. Boulding, "The Misallocation of Intellectual Resources," pp. 151–57.

to technology between the spread of an old technology and the creation of a new one. Strictly speaking, it is only the creation of a new technology which has to contain these elements of fundamental surprise. One might perhaps modify this proposition in the light of the fact that the transfer of technology, like the transfer of knowledge in the educational process, is itself a technology, and this too can be subject to technological change. The great problem of economic development of the poorer countries at the moment seems to be much dependent on an inability to produce an adequate technology for the transfer of technology, and of education for the transfer of knowledge. There may, therefore, be unexpected changes in the technology of transferring technology, and even this, therefore, may be subject to fundamental surprise.

While always preparing to be surprised, however, we can at least make some projections according to the simpler modes of prediction. As in the case of the growth of knowledge, even simple mechanical projections of rates of growth of technology are not meaningless. Perhaps the best general measure of the overall level of technology, in society is the index of output per man-hour. The accompanying chart from *Technology and the American Economy,* (Report of the National Commission on Technology, Automation, and Economic Progress, February 1966), page 3, shows the changes in output per man-hour for the last fifty years or so for agriculture, the private non-farm economy, and the total private economy. It is clear that we have been in a process of rapid technological advance. Output per man-hour has quadrupled in agriculture, tripled in the non-farm economy, in little over forty years. If this process continues to 1980, we might expect the output per man-hour in agriculture to be almost eight times what it was around 1920, and in the private non-farm sector to be perhaps four and a half times what it was in 1920. There are no great signs of any acceleration in this process, contrary to some of the pronouncements which have been made by the more excitable writers on automation. In agriculture, indeed, we seem to have something like a system break in the mid-thirties, which could well correspond to the development of large inputs into agriculture, not only for research and development but also in price supports. It is somewhat sobering to project the index of output per man-hour in agriculture as I have done in the wavy line in the figure (which is not in the original). If agricultural productivity had continued to increase from the mid-thirties at the rate which it had followed in the preceeding twenty-five years, in the early 1960s the index would have been barely 135 or 140, by comparison with the nearly 400 which it actually reached.

FIGURE 1.   Indexes of Output Per Man-Hour
Total Private, Farm, and Private Nonfarm Economy, 1909-65*

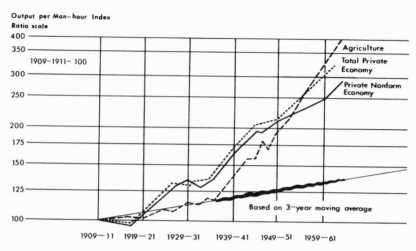

Adapted from *Technology and The American Economy*, Feb. 1966 (National Commission on Technology, Automation, and Economic Progress).

Nothing could illustrate better the dangers of projection, especially projection of trends, even trends which seem to have been established for quite a long period of time. Systems of this kind are always subject to system breaks, and hence the projection of existing trends should be treated with extreme reservations. Just because a boy doubles his height between the age of 8 and 18 does not mean he is going to double it again between 18 and 28, and in growth processes of any kind we have to be on the lookout for exhaustion of the original impetus which gave rise to the growth or the development of new impulses, such as the one we have just noticed in the case of agriculture.

The Qualitative Impact of Technology.   We may be somewhat hesitant about the projection of quantitative trends and at the same time we may be more confident about certain qualitative and structural changes which these movements are introducing into the social system and which are likely to continue. We must first notice a phenomenon which is beginning to be of considerable importance in the American and other developed economies. This is that the more progressive sectors of the economy tend to shrink in regard to the proportion of

* Compiled from information provided by the U.S. Department of Commerce and Bureau of Labor Statistics, U.S. Department of Labor.

the GNP which they generate or the amount of labor force which they absorb, relative to the technologically unprogressive sectors. This phenomenon is most striking in agriculture, where between 1930 and 1964 the proportion of civilian employment in agriculture fell from 25 percent to 7.6 percent in a little over a generation. We have managed to produce a small increase in agricultural output while reducing the absolute labor force to little more than a third of what it had been in 1929. This is an astonishing technological—and social—achievement. Even if it is repeated, however, and we continue to release people from agriculture, it is clear that the absolute numbers which can now be released are relatively small, and that though agriculture will almost certainly continue to shrink as a function of the economy, the resources released from it will not make the very large contribution to the non-agricultural labor force which they have made in the past, simply because there are not very many people left in it.

There is a question in many people's minds as to whether manufacturing is now about to suffer the fate of agriculture, thanks to cybernation. Manufacturing itself, however, is now not much more than 25 percent of the total labor force, so that even if the rate of technological change in manufacturing accelerates in the next fifteen years, and there are no immediate signs that it is doing this, it would be surprising if the proportion in manufacturing dropped to as little as, say, 20 percent of the total labor force. I am inclined to the view, therefore, that the great adjustment has already been made, the great adjustment, that is, out of agriculture. What has been displaced from agriculture has been absorbed largely in government, the professions, the service trades; and those who will continue to be displaced from agriculture and manufacturing will continue to be absorbed on balance in these expanding—because unprogressive—sectors. I will be a little surprised, therefore, if any spectacular change is observed in the structure of the labor force or the industrial structure of the economy in the next fifteen years, though, as I warned earlier, I am always prepared to be surprised.

Some further considerations of a qualitative kind might make the rather optimistic tone of the foregoing paragraphs seem like a very clouded crystal ball indeed by 1980 or still more by 2000. The crucial problem here is whether the development of electronics, automation, cybernation, and the whole complex of control systems does not introduce as it were a new gear into the evolutionary process, the implications of which are as yet only barely apparent. The computer is an extension of the human mind in the way that a tool or even an automobile is an extension of the human body. The automobile left practically no human institution unchanged as a result of the increase in human mobility which it permitted. The impact of the computer is likely to be just as great, and indeed of the whole world electronic network, which represents, as McLuhan has pointed out, an extension of the human nervous system and what is perhaps even more important, a linkage of our different nervous systems. It seems probable that all existing political and economic institutions will suffer some modifications as a result of this new technology; in what directions, however, it is hard to predict. That the ultimate results of this development will be benign can hardly be doubted except by those extreme pessimists who regard original sin as genetic in character and hence regard any extension of man's power as a mere increase in the opportunity to do harm. The faith that an increase in human power will be benign does depend, it is true, on certain assumptions about human teachability in ethics as well as in everything else. The very character of men's nervous system, however, assures us of his teachability, though it does not assure us that we can find ways of teaching him. At least, then, there is no theorem which drives us to a necessity for despair, even though there are plenty of occasions for a very reasonable disquiet.

We see the possible impacts of this new mode of human operation in a number of different fields. It has made the present international system, for instance, enormously threatening and so potentially destructive that it is hard to see how it can survive a generation. The day of national sovereignty and of unilateral national defense seems to be clearly over, though it may take a major catastrophe to convince us of this. As I have put it elsewhere, the world is rapidly becoming a very small crowded space ship in which men on horseback, even cowboys, cannot be tolerated. *The network of electronic communication is inevitably producing a world superculture, and the relations between this superculture and the more traditional national and regional cultures of the past remains the great question mark of the next fifty years.* For regions in which the defense industry is heavily concentrated, this question mark is particularly large, not only because of the economic adjustments which may be necessary, but because they represent prime target areas.

Another possible consequence of the qualitative changes in technology which seem to be under way is what I have sometimes called the "milk and cream" problem. Will the world separate out into two cultures, both within countries and between countries, in which a certain proportion of the people adapt through education to the world of modern technology and hence enjoy its fruits, while another proportion fail to adapt and perhaps become not only relatively worse off but even absolutely so, in the sense that what they have had in the past of traditional culture collapses under the impact of the technical super-culture and leaves them disorganized, delinquent, anomic, and poor? In "creamy" societies like the United States, the "cream" may be 70 or 80 percent of the population, and the "skim milk" may be only 20 or 30 percent. The depressed sector, however, may be large enough to be threatening not only to the consciences of the rich sector but even to its security, as frustration and anger lead to violence.

On the world scale, the outlook is even darker. At the moment the separation-out phenomenon is proceeding at an alarming pace. The rich countries are getting richer at an unprecedented pace, many of the poor countries are stagnating or even retrogressing; and the differ-ence between the rich and the poor gets larger every year. This situa-tion can easily create dangerous instability in the international system, though perhaps because of the very poverty and impotence of the poor countries, the threat to the rich is not very great. The greater danger may be that of a stable divided world with perhaps less than 50 percent of the people having made the transition into the modern world and at least half sunk into utter misery and degradation. Such a situation could hardly persist without corrupting the cultures of both the rich and the poor, and the stability of such a system could certainly not continue forever.

Technology is an offshoot of knowledge. Hence we might expect to find something of a stable pattern between the growth of knowledge and the improvement of technology with perhaps a certain lag to ac-count for the application of new knowledge to productive processes and also the spread of these processes throughout the economy. There is some evidence that the diffusion of knowledge into technology is taking place a little more rapidly than it used to.[2] What is difficult to identify, however, is exactly what new knowledge is going to be rele-vant, for a great deal of new knowledge is created in the progress of the sciences which is not relevant to technology in the immediate future and which may even never become relevant. The plain fact is that if a prediction of future technology were at all easy, there would be no money to be made in growth stocks, for the growth of the right ones would all be anticipated. The fact that fortunes are made as well as lost in new technologies suggests that the uncertainties of prediction here are very great, and that the relation between present knowledge

---

[2] See, for instance, the report of the National Commission on Tech-nology, Automation, and Economic Progress, *Technology in the American Economy*, February 1966, pages 4 and 5.

and future technology is not really stable enough to admit of any very secure predictions.

When we add to the general uncertainties of the technological future an attempt to predict the impact on particular regions, the uncertainties become even greater. It would be even more unwise to project, for instance, constant rates of growth for a particular region than it would be for the economy as a whole. A region which is heavily devoted to, say, mining and agriculture, might expect to share in the relative decline of these industries. A region which is heavily involved in government, especially in defense, might be expected to share in the extreme uncertainty of this sector.

The Implications for Education

Perhaps the most important conclusion which emerges from this discussion for the educational system is that it should plan for surprise. This is not to say, of course, that its policies should not be based on predictions or projections, for all policies have to be directed towards the future and we must have some idea of what the future is going to be like, otherwise all rational decision is impossible. Wherever it is possible to project into the future simple dynamic systems which have had reasonably stable parameters in the past, this, of course, should be done. We do this, for instance, in population projections, which are perhaps one of the most fundamental tools of the educational planner and which are covered in other papers. We should remember even here that the population projections of the mid-1940s turned out to be completely erroneous because of a sudden change in the parameters of the system, particularly in regard to quite unexpectedly large birth rates which persisted until the mid-1960s. One would very much like to see a study of the impact of these erroneous projections of the 1940s, particularly in regard to the failure to plan for educational expansion. It would be interesting to see at what moment school systems became aware of the fact that they were going to have to provide for much larger numbers of children than they had previously expected, and how they made adjustments to these new images of the future.

In regard to the more quantitative aspects of technology, a sudden change in the rate of growth of productivity might not be felt appreciably for a few years, but in ten or twenty years the effects might be very noticeable, either in unexpected gains or unexpected declines in the growth of income.

On the qualitative side, it could well be that the most important area of possible technological change is in the field of social inventions, and it is these which might have the greatest impact on the environment of the educational system. The very strains which modern technology puts on society create a demand for social invention which did not perhaps exist before. When material technology is only advancing slowly, social invention may keep pace with it fairly easily. Thus in the course of the last three hundred years we have had such social inventions as banking, insurance, the corporation, the income tax, universal public education, conscription, social security, and even socialist states, all of which represent in a sense a response on the part of the social system to challenges presented by the growth of material technology. With the qualitative changes that seem to be taking place in material technology, new demands are placed on social invention. Certainly at some point, as per capita incomes rise, we may reach something of a watershed after which the traditional values and organizations become rapidly less capable of organizing society, and rapid social invention will be necessary. As suggested earlier, we cannot predict what these inventions will be, we can only suggest a few challenges to which some response will have to be made. We can conclude, therefore, by outlining some suggestions of possible future challenges.

1. The American educational system in the past has been quite successful in preparing people to be middle class, to the point indeed where middle-class values permeate perhaps 80 percent of our population. The system has not succeeded in preparing people to live useful and cheerful lives at the lower end of the income scale, mainly because educators are themselves middle class and hence are unsympathetic to the values of a lower-class culture. Maybe a social invention is needed here in the shape of an educational subsystem which will give the culture of the poor a status of its own.

2. American society up to now has stressed the idea of a "melting pot" and has sought to create through public education a uniform culture. With increased affluence and increased political skill, this ideal can now be called into question. Can we now invent a "mosaic" society, composed of many small subcultures, each of which gives to its participants a sense of community and identity which is so desperately needed in a mass world, and which can at the same time remain at peace with its neighbors and not threaten to pull the society apart? An educational system designed for this purpose would look enormously different from what we have today. Private education would compete on equal terms with public; we might have something like the "voucher" scheme proposed by certain British economists by which each child would be given a voucher which would be exchanged for education in any school, public or private. This would not exclude the

possibility of imposing certain legal minimum standards, but it would open up an enormous possibility for experimentation in education, which is something we severely lack under the present system.

3. It would not surprise me to see the educational system head for a major financial crisis within the next few years. The tax systems by which public education is supported tend to be regressive and inequitable, and they only seem to be tolerable as long as the total tax collections for these purposes are smaller than the needs of this sector of the economy. The contrast in this regard between the public and the private sectors of the economy is very striking, as Galbraith has pointed out so eloquently. A great many studies have indicated that in terms of sheer rate of return on investment, investment in education probably brings a higher rate of return than that of any competitive industry, and when we add the intangible benefits, which are considerable, the argument that we are underinvesting in education as a whole and grossly underinvesting in certain aspects of the system becomes almost irresistible. We do not need to go as far as Dr. West[3] and propose turning the whole educational system back to private enterprise, for there are good reasons to suppose there would be underinvestment under these circumstances too, even more serious than what we have at present. The fact remains, however, that access to capital is much easier for material technology than it is for human investment, and we need social inventions to correct this. It may well be that a major problem here is that we have not so much supplemented the operations of the price system in this area as destroyed it, and there is a strong case for taking a hard look at the principle that education should be universally free. Public education at all levels can easily result in the subsidization of the rich, and in view of the regressive nature of so many state and local tax systems, the public school system may even result in a redistribution of income from the poor to the rich, or at least from the poor to the middle class. If this is so, it is not surprising that taxpayers become increasingly resistant to any expansion of the educational system, and that the system operates in an atmosphere of increasing financial crisis.

4. The final problem is subtle and hard to put one's finger on; nevertheless it may be the most important problem of all. This is the problem of the role of the educational system in creating what might be called a moral identity. The obsolescence of older moral identities in the face of enormous technological change is a problem which

---

[3] E. G. West, *Education and the State: A Study in Political Economy*, London: The Institute of Economic Affairs, 1965.

underlies almost all others in the social system. We see this in the so-called sexual revolution; we see it in the inappropriateness of belligerent nationalist emotions in a nuclear world; and we see it also in what may be the most serious social byproduct of automation, a loss of self-respect and "manhood" on the part of those whose skills are being displaced. The greatest human tragedy is to feel useless and not wanted, and with the rise in the intelligence of machines, we may face a period in which the human race divides into two parts, those who feel themselves to be more intelligent than machines and those who feel themselves to be less. This could signalize the beginnings of a widening human tragedy which would require the utmost exercise of our skill and knowledge. I am by no means sure that this is a problem which is really upon us. It is one, however, for which we should be prepared, and in its solution the educational system would play an absolutely crucial role. It would be precisely indeed in the things which our conservatives despise as "frills" that the development of satisfying human identities might have to be found. It must never be forgotten that the ultimate thing which any society is producing is people. All other things are intermediate goods, and all organizations are intermediate organizations. No matter how rich we are or how powerful we are, if we do not produce people who can at least begin to expand into the enormous potential of man, the society must be adjudged a failure. The educational system is peculiarly specialized in the production of people, and it must never lose sight of the fact that it is producing people as ends, not as means. It is producing men, not manpower; people, not biologically generated nonlinear computers. If this principle is stamped firmly in the minds of these who guide and operate our educational system, we can afford to make a great many mistakes, we can afford to be surprised by the future, we can even afford to make some bad educational investments, because we will be protected against the ultimate mistake, which would be to make the educational system a means, not an end, serving purposes other than man himself.

Religion and Ethics

Religious Perspectives in Economics[*]

I

The economist—or any other specialist—differs from his fellow-teachers mainly by reason of the subject matter which he teaches. It may be, of course, that there is some relation between the nature of a subject and the nature of its practitioners: the social sciences are perhaps more likely to attract those of reforming temperament, the experimental sciences those of a mechanical temperament, and the humanities those of an artistic temperament. But by and large these differences are small, and there is not much reason to suppose that economists are either more or less religious than biologists or musicians. Religion is a matter for the whole man and the full man, not for the specialized part of him. It is for this reason perhaps that specialization is in itself somewhat inimical to religion; the man who throws his whole being into the narrow channel of a single specialty, be it chemistry or economics, is quite apt to be hostile, or at least indifferent, to the great generalities of the spiritual and moral life. The Love of God escapes both the test tube and the formula. In this matter the economist is not much different from other men: and such differences as there are arise from the peculiarities of the subject which he teaches and investigates. I shall begin my argument, therefore, by considering religion and economics as subject matter, that is, as two great fields of human experience and study: and ask to what extent are they adjoining, overlapping, or quite independent; to what extent are they enemies or friends, do they compete with or complete each other in the vast ecology of ideas.

We shall consider first the impact of religion on economic life and history. The impact on economic life seems to have been much greater

[*] New Haven: Hazen Foundation, 1950, p. 24.

This paper was prepared for a symposium volume on Religious Perspectives of College Teaching sponsored by the Hazen Foundation. It was originally published as a pamphlet in 1950 and reprinted two years later in a volume: *Religious Perspectives of College Teaching*, Hoxie N. Fairchild, ed., (New York: Ronald Press, 1952), pp. 360–83.

than the impact on economic thought. From its very beginning religion has strongly affected not only the nature of the commodities which form the main subject matter of economic life, but also the economic institutions and practices which so largely determine the course of economic development. Religion built the pyramids, the temples, the cathedrals. It draws resources into the manufacture of vestments, incense, images, prayer rugs, and prayers. More important than this, however, from the point of view of the economist, is its impact upon the minds of men, its shaping of their beliefs, customs, and practices. It is not the physical resources so much as the human resources of a society which determine the course of its economic development, if any, whether towards riches or towards poverty. Men have languished in utter poverty in the midst of great natural resources, and have wrung comfort and even luxury from stern and unfriendly physical environments. It is what lies in the minds of men that determines, for the most part, whether a society shall grow in productive power; it is only this growth that has carried man from a pitiful, half-starved savagery to the splendor, comfort and dangers of civilization, and this growth is closely connected with the nature of this dominant religion.

The exact conditions of economic progress are very complex and imperfectly understood. Certain physical conditions seem to be necessary—e.g., the absence of extreme pressure of population. Given these conditions, however, the most apparent determining factor seems to be the character of the religion of the period—particularly whether it is "prophetic" or "priestly." This distinction corresponds roughly to the "early" or "late" stages of any particular religion or any phase within the history of a particular religion. In its early or prophetic phase religion acts as a revolutionary force, stirring the minds and hearts of men out of their routines, changing them and making them receptive to change. It is in this stage that economic progress is most likely to be rapid, for progress cannot take place without change, and the willingness to change, to try new methods of production, new commodities, and new techniques, and the willingness to tolerate others who are making such changes is likely to be greater in an age of "conversion," when there is also a willingness to try new ideas, new faiths, and new patterns of life. When on the other hand religion settles down into its "priestly" stage it becomes a conservative force making for the persistence of established routines and the satisfaction of creative energies through repetitive ritual rather than through innovation. In this stage religion is likely to be inimical to economic progress, simply because it creates a general disapproval of change of any kind.[1]

Besides its influence in affecting attitudes towards change, religion, through its theology and its ethical systems, also influences the attitudes of men towards various forms of economic behavior. Thus a very "otherworldly" religion is likely to lead to a low social status for merchants, shopkeepers, artisans, businessmen and other "money-changers" whose activities seem to be centered on "this world," and a correspondingly high status for monks, nuns, fakirs, contemplatives and mendicants whose contribution to the economic order is that of consumption rather than of production, however great their contributions to spiritual welfare. Such a religion is also likely to discourage accumulation of capital—not so much because of its encouragement of consumption—there is great frugality among the otherworldly—but because of its discouragement of the production of tangible objects of desire. On the other hand a more "this-worldly" type of religion, stressing, for instance, some concept such as the "Kingdom of God on earth" and emphasizing the attainment of some degree of perfection and satisfaction in this world, is likely to place a higher value on those engaged in the more humdrum tasks of life, and consequently to be favorable to economic progress. A this-worldly religion is also likely to encourage capital accumulation, by its emphasis on productive work, and when this is combined with ideals of frugality and simplicity in living the favorable effect on accumulation is thereby reinforced.

We cannot, in an essay of this length, do more than illustrate these propositions. The most famous illustration is Max Weber's thesis regarding the influence of the Protestant Reformation on the development of capitalism. The Protestant Reformation (not only in itself, but also in the Counter-Reformation which it induced) represents a great upsurge of religion of a more prophetic, and also more this-worldly type than the medieval Catholicism which preceded it. New ideas, ferment and change in the realm of faith and morals, paved the way for new adventures in trade, agriculture, and industry. The puritan

---

[1] I do not mean to imply, of course, that there is any rigid separation between the prophetic and the priestly stages, nor that each is necessarily embodied in a particular form of organization. Thus the Catholic Church, while priestly in its general organization, has produced a number of "prophetic" movements such as that of the Franciscans; and the Protestant churches, while generally ostensibly "prophetic" in their form of organization, have passed through many periods of "priestliness."

morality, with its emphasis on work, "vocation," and activity on the side of production, and its emphasis on simplicity of life, temperance and frugality on the side of consumption, greatly favored that rise of production above consumption which is necessary for capital accumulation. In a sense also the simplification of religion itself which Protestantism represented enabled men to satisfy their religious requirements with a smaller expenditure of time and energy than before, and hence left more for other pursuits. Instead of the great apparatus of masses, feasts, fasts, confessions, penances, retreats, novenas and so on of Catholicism, we now have a stripped sabbatarianism fed by once-a-week calls to action from the pulpit rather than by constant daily meditation in the cloister. I shall not debate in these pages whether the spiritual product of the new religious technique was as good as the old; but there can be no doubt that it was obtained much more cheaply in terms of time and effort, and that therefore human energy which in the middle ages was channeled into vast ritual or religious practices and "works" was now available for trade, industry, and economic development. These "worldly" activities moreover were themselves sanctified by the idea of "vocation," according to which all things could be done to God's glory and in obedience to His will.

Just as the Lutheran,[2] Reformed, and Episcopal church movements of the sixteenth and seventeenth centuries influenced the so-called "commercial revolution" of this time in England, Holland and to a less extent in Germany and Scandinavia, so the even more "prophetic" Protestantism of the Quakers and Methodists influenced the "industrial revolution" of the eighteenth and nineteenth centuries. It is astonishing how many of the basic technical discoveries of the early industrial revolution in England are associated with the members of nonconformist sects. This can hardly be an accident. These groups emphasized a "lay," non-priestly religion, stressing conversion and change in the individual, and emphasizing the this-worldly aspects of the Christian gospel in terms of disciplined daily living. They were, moreover, barred from higher education and hence delivered both from intellectual conformity and from easy professional ways of life. They had a deserved reputation for honesty and integrity. It is not surprising, therefore, that they developed iron-smelting, textiles, railroads, insurance, banking, retailing, and were deeply involved in all the technological changes of the period. Nor were these involvements

---

[2] It is significant that Lutheranism—by far the most "priestly" of the Protestant movements—exercised a much smaller effect on economic life than did the other Protestant movements.

merely of a material nature. The "social inventions" which are equally part of the same revolution in human affairs were also inspired in no small measure by nonconformists and evangelicals. Social legislation, beginning with the abolition of slavery and the development of the factory acts, was in its beginnings largely the work of nonconformists or evangelicals like Wilberforce, Clarkson, and Lord Shaftesbury and their coteries. Even more important is the influence of nonconformity on the growth of science: a wholly disproportionate number of members of the Royal Society, for instance, were nonconformists: it was men like Priestley the Unitarian and Dalton the Quaker who were most active in scientific inquiry. It was British nonconformity which set the moral and intellectual tone of American society, and the progressive nature of American economic life is closely connected with the prophetic, evangelical, individualistic and this-worldly character of American religion. In America we are all Methodists now!

These two examples are sufficient to illustrate the intimate connection between religious and economic history; the historically minded reader will think of many others. The great economic development in Europe of the tenth and eleventh centuries—embodied in the Romanesque cathedrals and castles—is closely connected with the earlier conversion of the barbarian tribes to Christianity. The flowering of Arab civilization after the rise of Mohammed is another striking example of the impact of a "prophetic" religion, just as its rapid withering is an example of the corrupting effects of a rigid orthodoxy.

II

So far we have looked at the relationship mainly from the point of view of the impact of religion on economic life: we do not have to be a Marxist to admit that this connection is reciprocal, and that in their turn economic institutions and conditions affect the form and content of religion. The economic interpretation of history is little help in explaining the *genesis* of religions, which arise as a result of certain *mutations*—to borrow a word from genetics—in human personality and experience. Where the economic interpretation is useful is in explaining the survival of such mutations as occur. There are many prophets, but few of them are founders of living religions. A religion cannot survive unless it is accepted among men, and its acceptance depends largely on its ability to satisfy human wants and needs. This is not to say that only those religions survive which enhance material prosperity. To a considerable degree the Bread of Life is a substitute, if not for the bread at least for the cake of this world, and the fire of Charity may warm as effectively as fine clothes and central heating.

Indeed, one may say with some confidence that when the tide of religion runs strongly in the minds of men it draws them away from worldly power, wealth and security, and offers them in return a power, a wealth and a security which are not of this world, not dependent on the favor of other men, but are secured by a secret inward covenant between the soul and its heavenly Lord. Taking no thought for the morrow, carrying neither scrip nor staff, the heaven-intoxicated pilgrim "walks cheerfully over the world, answering that of God in every man" unencumbered by worldly cares or worldly goods. There have been many such golden dawns of Gospel purity, and one and all they fade into the plain light of a workaday world. As the early enthusiasm recedes substitute satisfactions must be found, and when manna no longer falls we must devote ourselves to husbandry. But a religion cannot survive unless it increases men's satisfactions, however compounded these may be of earth and heaven: this is the "economic test." A religion which makes men miserable will scarcely survive its first generation.

The nature of the dominant religion, therefore, is determined in an appreciable degree by the economic opportunities which are open. In some societies, for instance, the pressure of population makes any economic progress almost impossible, and Malthus' "dismal science" is operating at its most dismal. Any improvement in techniques is immediately swallowed up by the flood of population, and the final result of such improvements is not to improve the lot of individuals, but to enable more people to live in the old misery! In such a situation religion is likely to be otherworldly, ritualistic, and mystical, offering to man hopes of the hereafter and the present consolations of inward experience. On the other hand in a situation where a rapid increase in the economic welfare of a society is possible through the improvement of techniques and the accumulation of capital, a religion which is this-worldly, economical of resources, and practical in its applications is more likely to meet human needs. Thus the religions of the over-crowded East have laid great stress on salvation by withdrawal from the world: in such a society the monk, the contemplative, and the fakir flourish, and the appeal of religion to the mass of men is either that of propitiation of fortune or of hope for a better life elsewhere, whether in a reincarnation or in a heaven. In bustling America on the other hand the world has seemed too good to withdraw from, and economic opportunity too great to be spurned: religion has adapted itself accordingly and has become more secular, more "lay," more "practical."

If wealth consists in the satisfaction of wants there are two roads to riches: one is the diminution of wants, the other is the increase in the means of satisfaction. Which road we take depends on their relative roughness. If the increase in the means of satisfaction is denied us by the rigor of economic circumstance, we are more likely to take the *via negativa* towards a nirvana of wantlessness. This is the way that we associate with the congested and hopeless East. The West, on the other hand, came later to civilization and had opportunities for geographical expansion northward and westward which the East did not have. Here the increase in the means of satisfaction has always seemed more possible and the *via negativa* has been less attractive, except in periods of recession and collapse. It is not surprising therefore that it was Macedonia (that America of ancient Greece!) that gave the call to the apostle Paul, and that Christianity became the religion of the West, for Jesus gave Christianity a stamp of this-worldliness which it can never quite escape. At the heart of Eastern religions is a Way from Man to God: at the heart of Christianity is an incarnation of God in Man and a dream of a Kingdom of Heaven on Earth.

It is clear that the causative relationship between religious and secular life in the stream of history is a complex mutual one of a hen-and-egg nature, and that attempts to interpret history solely in terms of one or the other, as in the Marxian economic interpretation, is like trying to develop an egg theory of hens or a hen theory of eggs. A satisfactory theory of history must consist of two elements: an understanding of the principles of ecological equilibrium and succession, and an ability to recognize mutations when they occur. History is the record of the growth and decline of populations, whether of the flora and fauna of a forest or of the characteristics, ideas and institutions of men. The rise and fall of states, empires, churches, religions and philosophies is a similar process to the rise and decline of species in the world of nature, and is determined mainly by the competitive or complementary relationships of the various forms of life or organization. The succession of cultures in human history is not unlike the succession of complexes of plant and animal life in the pond or the forest: each culture provides the breeding ground for ideas, institutions, and patterns of behavior which will eventually supplant it. This ecological succession, however, is not confined to any one aspect of life, but covers the whole of it: material and spiritual species interact upon each other ceaselessly and with endless complexity: religions breed civilizations, and civilizations breed and spread religions in a continuous pattern.

Every "ecosystem" (as the biologists call a complete system of mutually interacting populations of different species) is subject from time to time to incursions from without. These may be invasions of

new species from other ecosystems, as when Japanese beetles invade
the United States or Marxist ideology invades the labor movement. Or
they may be "mutations"—changes in the genetic constitution, coming
from we know not where or whom. Were it not for these invasions
and mutations every society would soon settle down to a position of
equilibrium: it is these which keep history perpetually on the move.
Both the economic and the religious aspects of society are subject to
invasions and mutations. The invention of a new technique in production, or of a new commodity, represents a "mutation" in economic life.
The founders of religions likewise represent mutations in the spiritual
life. The spread of new techniques, or of new religions, is a process
analogous to "invasion." It must not be thought, of course, that mutations are arbitrary. They can only take place within narrow limits set
by the existing state of affairs. A mutation from a mouse never turns
out to be an elephant. The automobile could not have been invented
in the seventeenth century: it could hardly help being invented at the
end of the nineteenth. Given the invention of the rudder the discovery
of America was almost inevitable—as someone has well said, how
could Columbus miss it! It is easy to find these connections in history;
they are never, however, as certain or as definite as they look after
the event. It is not always easy to recognize true mutations, but it can
hardly be doubted that they occur, and that they occur as much, if
not more, in the world of belief and ideas[3] as they do in the world of
techniques and commodities. We cannot, therefore, understand economic processes in time without reference to the whole universe of
social phenomena, of which religion is a vital and significant part.

III

I have sketched very briefly some of the interactions of religious
and economic life in history, and while the details of the interconnectedness may be open to some question, the fact of interconnectedness is abundantly evident. Nevertheless the student of economics
in our universities can easily get through his course, and can be turned
out as a full-fledged teacher of the subject, without any awareness
of this interconnectedness penetrating his consciousness. It is no
exaggeration to say that unless a student happens to come into contact
with a teacher whose specialized interests lie, say, towards Max
Weber's type of interpretation of history, he can pass through his

---

[3] To Christians, of course, Jesus represents the most significant "mutation" in history: with him a new spiritual species—the "new man in Christ
Jesus" enters the world of time.

whole formal instruction without any sense of contact between economics and religion, as realms of discourse. Religion, like liquor, is something which he can take or not, according to taste, but unless indulged in to excess it will in no way affect the world of ideas which he inhabits as an economist. The conceptual framework of economics and the practical questions on which it impinges—whether new or old—supply and demand, prices, savings, investment, trade, tariffs, taxes, output, employment—are concepts which inhabit a self-sufficient realm of their own, and seem to have nothing whatever to do with the realm of discourse in which we discuss God, prayer, worship, grace, salvation, communion, justification, and the like.

This is quite understandable, and even up to a point, proper. Although in life and history religion and economics are inseparably intertwined in the great web of reality, in thought and theory they are quite distinct, and have very little contact. Both theology and economics—along with all other theoretical frameworks—represent *abstractions* from reality, and hence we should not expect them to cover much of the same material. It is as if economic theory looks only at the black threads, and religious theory (i.e., theology, in its broad sense) only at the gold threads of a great and complex tapestry: the picture that each presented would be very different, yet each might be part of a single reality. Moreover, to him that concentrated on the black, the gold might appear to be simply a meaningless irruption of unnecessary spendor in the chaste material of reality, while to the specialist on gold the black might appear as completely beneath his notice, an insignificant background to the real splendors of the creation. Other specialists similarly may concentrate only on other threads, to their similar gain and loss.

The economist, by reason of the peculiar history of economic thought, is especially in danger of being *indifferent* to religion. It is difficult for a student of history, or literature, or ethics, or art, to be *unaware* of the intimate connection in life and history of his own speciality and religious life. Some of the natural sciences, perhaps even medicine, have a certain history of hostility on the part of the church which may lead to a conflict with religion. Economics, however, sprang at least half grown from the head of Adam Smith, who may very properly be regarded as the founder of economics as a *unified* abstract realm of discourse, and it still, almost without knowing it, breathes a good deal of the air of eighteenth-century rationalism and Deism. Adam Smith, it will be remembered, was an intimate friend of David Hume; between them they almost personify the eighteenth century at its most urbane, like the elegant New Town of Edinburgh that was building around them. They both led blameless lives in a quiet way; they both express the amused tolerance and sweet reasonableness of an age whose fires are banked. Both regarded religious enthusiasm as a serious break of good taste, yet both are saved from dullness by a good touch of Scottish wit and moral indignation.

Adam Smith's observations on religion are worth mention at this point, even at the cost of some digression, not only because of their intrinsic interest, but because they represent almost everything that economists, *qua* economists, have said on this subject. It is indeed curious that no economist since Adam Smith seems to have dealt at any length with the economics of religion[4]—perhaps it was felt that Adam Smith had said the last word on the subject! His observations are found, oddly enough, in that chapter of Book 5 of the *Wealth of Nations* headed "Of the Expenses of the Sovereign or Commonwealth," under Article III, "Of the Expense of Institutions for the Instruction of People of All Ages." In the previous section ("Of the Expense of Institutions for the Education of Youth") he has applied his principle of the free market to education, denounced educational monopolies and endowed professors, and pointed out that the best teaching is usually done by those whose rewards are related in some manner to the success of their efforts— hence he advocates what is essentially the "elective system." He then goes on to apply the same principles to the church, and to point out how the endowment and establishment of a monopolistic state church leads to a diminution of religious zeal, which flourishes most among those whose support depends upon it. "The advantage in point of learning and good writing may sometimes be on the side of the established church. But the arts of popularity, all the arts of gaining proselytes, are constantly on the side of its adversaries. In England those arts have long been neglected by the well-endowed clergy of the established church, and are at present chiefly cultivated by the Dissenters and by the Methodists. The independent provisions, however, which in many places have been made for dissenting teachers by means of voluntary subscriptions, of trust right, and other evasions of the law, seem very much to have abated the zeal and activity of those teachers. They have many of them become very learned, in-

---

[4] A possible exception is found in the writings of a group of American economists in the generation before the first World War, especially T. N. Carver, S. N. Patten, and Richard T. Ely. None of them, however, made particularly significant contributions to economic theory; their works are little read nowadays, and the American Economic Association which they helped to found today exhibits practically no marks of their influence.

genious, and respectable men; but they have in general ceased to be very popular preachers. The Methodists, without half the learning of the Dissenters, are very much more in vogue." One is tempted to continue the quotation, but the *Wealth of Nations* is easily available, and the reader can continue for himself.

In spite of the fact that he agrees with Hume that an excess of religious enthusiasm, when it manifests itself in violent factionalism, is a grave danger to society, he does not follow Hume in what would seem to be the obvious conclusion, that the remedy is to moderate religion by the establishment of a monopolistic state church. Monopoly in religion as in everything else is distasteful to him, and consequently he comes out in favor of free competition in religion, the separation of church and state, and the consequent multiplication of sects, for, he says, "the concessions which they would mutually find it both convenient and agreeable to make to one another, might in time reduce the doctrine of the greater part of them to that pure and rational religion, free from every mixture of absurdity, imposture, or fanaticism, such as wise men have in all ages of the world wished to see established; but such as positive law has perhaps never yet established—because, with regard to religion, positive law always has been, and probably always will be, more or less influenced by popular superstition and enthusiasm." If the enthusiasm of competing sects leads society into too "unsocial or disagreeably rigorous" a moral code, this can easily be remedied by the State promoting first the study of science and philosophy and secondly frequent and gay public diversions. Then, as a good Scot should, he comes out in favor of the equality, but not the democracy, of the Presbyterian form of government, and urges that the clergy should not be too well paid, because "nothing but the most exemplary of morals can give dignity to a man of small fortune."

I doubt if anything so witty and penetrating has ever been written on the economic sociology of religion. Yet nowhere do we find any deep understanding of the *content* of religion. Neither the transports nor the dark night of the soul have any place in this pellucid eighteenth century air. Adam Smith could never have had any real knowledge of the mind of the Wesleys. Mystical experience of any kind he would have dismissed as "fanaticism and enthusiasm." He is in some sense almost the ideal of the "good" intellectual; a very good, very moral, admirable, almost one might say a pious man. Yet there is clearly a realm of experience into which he does not penetrate. He can tell us a great deal about the forces that make for decay in religion as it becomes entangled with the world; he can tell us very little about the ultimate sources of its life and power. The world and its corruption are much easier to observe and describe than heaven and its purity; the cooling of zeal takes place in public, but it is kindled inwardly. Only those who have in some measure walked the road to Emmaus know how far it stretches through history, and how the heart that is "strangely warmed," whether of a Paul, a Francis, a Fox, a Wesley or a Booth can set great movements in motion and change the whole temper of an age. The followers of these movements, it is true, become in their turn "learned, ingenious, and respectable"; but instead of competition reducing all to the stationary equilibrium of a "pure and rational religion" the status quo is perpetually disturbed by the invasion of new enthusiasts and a fresh outpouring of the Holy Spirit—a Spirit neither learned, nor ingenious, nor respectable, but bearing unmistakable marks of heavenly origin.

IV

It is evident that the economist, and especially the teacher of economics, who is at the same time a man of religion—more specifically, let us say, a practicing Christian—will be exposed to certain rather special temptations and dangers because of the craft which he follows, and it may be well to examine these in further detail. We may note first, briefly, some problems which arise because the economist is of necessity an intellectual by profession, and therefore in common with other intellectuals may be particularly subject to those "higher vices, that have to be paid for at higher prices." Pride, envy, self-love, self-deceit, self-righteousness, cynicism, frivolousness and cowardice are common diseases in intellectual circles, and of these the most to be feared is pride, a disease utterly devastating in its ultimate effects, yet so subtle that there seems to be no remedy for it save a simple-hearted daily dependence upon God. The teacher also, in general, has certain problems which arise from the nature of his occupation—the temptation to a misuse of authority, or to gain authority over his students by a mere display of wit or erudition rather than by devotion to truth—how much easier it is to say a clever thing than a true one! These problems however are not peculiar to the economist, and I merely mention them here. One problem which is especially likely to trouble the social scientist is that of preventing his moral and religious concerns from undermining the scientific integrity of his specialized discipline. Many people are attracted into the social sciences, and especially perhaps to economics, because they feel a concern for the ills of society or wish to learn how to reform them. This is a most proper motivation, yet it needs to be disciplined by a strong sense of scientific integrity and by a willingness to acquire real skill in the abstract disciplines before venturing to make applications. Our notions of what *ought to be* must not be allowed to prejudice our painstaking inquiry into what *is*, and goodwill is in no sense a substitute for scientific competence—nor, of course, is scientific competence a substitute for goodwill.

On the whole, however, the atmosphere of our institutions of higher learning is so overwhelmingly favorable to scientific competence that the professional—as opposed perhaps to the amateur—economist is not in much danger of sacrificing his scientific integrity to moral fervor. It is the opposite danger which threatens him—that of becoming so engrossed in the refinements of scientific abstraction—and in the substantial rewards, which in these days often accompany proficiency in such abstractions—that he forgets the ills of society and becomes deaf to the cry of the hungry and blind to the misery of the oppressed. It may be true that a man does not understand the laws of demand and supply any better for being a member of the Communion of Saints. It may be, even, that the clamorous realities of the Communion of Saints actually unfit a man for performing the delicate and beautiful abstractions of economic theory. It is also true, however, that it is possible to retreat into abstraction from the demands which the real world is making upon us, and to take refuge from the demands of the moral law behind a screen of scientific indifference. The prolonged contemplation of abstract systems may also lead to a certain cynicism and weariness: a paralysis of the will-to-good sets in because of a sense of the immense complexity of social life and the ill effects of a rash do-good-ism. It was not the economists who liberated the slaves or who passed the Factory Acts, but the rash and ignorant Christians! Those who have knowledge have a peculiar responsibility to be sensitive to the ills of the world, for if they are not, then it will be the ignorant who will be the movers of events, and the value of knowledge will be lost.

v

I turn now to the problems which are likely to be encountered in the actual teaching of economics. There are perhaps four main divisions of the subject matter: (i) pure theory, (ii) the description of present-day economic institutions, (iii) the study of economic history and (iv) the study of economic policy. This division does not correspond to any division of courses—indeed, the courses given are likely to include something of all four aspects. A course on Money and Banking, for instance, is likely to include some theory of money, some description of financial institutions, some history, and some policy discussion. Pure theory is essentially a branch of mathematics or logic: religion may therefore be expected to make very little impact on it. There is no more reason to suppose a "Christian" economic theory, for instance, than there is to suppose a "Christian" mathematics. Theory is essentially a tool, and should not be even a highly specialized tool. Tools or instruments can only be given moral or religious attributes as they are specialized. There is no such thing as a Christian screwdriver, for screwdrivers may be used either for good or for evil ends quite indiscriminately. It is true, of course, that historically economic theory developed as a rather specialized instrument for the interpretation of early industrial capitalism. This limitation however has been steadily relaxed, and the progress of theory is towards greater and greater generality: the most significant techniques of economic theory, for instance, are as applicable to socialist or to primitive economies as they are to capitalism. This is particularly true of what may be called "equilibrium economics"; it is less true of the theory of economic change and development, where purely economic abstractions are less useful and a broad interpretation of history is necessary.

Similarly in the description of economic institutions there is not much contact with religion, though it may be relevant to point out how certain institutions, such as commercial or bank credit, depend on the existence of standards of individual honesty and integrity which are themselves in part a product of religion. It is when we come to the study and interpretation of economic history, however, that the contact between religious and economic life becomes clear and significant, as we have shown earlier. In consideration of economic policy also the *ends* of society cannot be left out of the picture, and the abstractions of pure economics can only carry us a small part of the way. We may say, in fact, that in any field which involves the *application* of economic principles there is great danger among specialists of confounding abstraction with reality, and of drawing unwarranted conclusions from abstract logic.

The nature—and dangers—of the economic abstraction are so little understood, even among economists, that a brief digression on this topic may be in order. The focus of interest of economics is the *commodity*—that is, something which can be exchanged, produced, and consumed. Exchange, production, consumption, and accumulation are the main human activities on which economics concentrates. Economics is not however primarily interested in human behavior as such: it is interested in the "behavior of commodities." The world of commodities is something which is regarded as following its own laws of motion, like the planets of the solar system; the men who move them are not the focus of interest, any more than the angels, if any, who move the planets are a focus of interest of the astronomer. We know, of course, that in reality it is not commodities that behave, but men, and that commodity prices, outputs, accumulations, exchanges, and so on are ultimately the result of human behavior. But if human behavior is regular enough it can be neglected, just as astronomers can neglect angels. And *in the mass* human behavior is fairly regular—which explains, incidentally, why so much of economics assumes the mass-interactions of perfect competition and why indeterminacy appears in the theory of oligopoly—i.e. in the interaction of *few* exchangers. It may be noticed incidentally that the same difficulty crops up in physics, where the law of behavior of gases, being a statistical law involving enormous numbers of molecules ("perfect competition") is nicely determinate, but where much less is known about the behavior of individual molecules, and where the strangest indeterminacies crop up in the oligopolistic interactions of the few in the atom. This remoteness from human behavior is seen most clearly perhaps in the Keynesian economics, which consists of "models" (solar systems!) whose component variables (national income, consumption, investment) are vast statistical aggregates which enjoy cozy relationships among themselves but which are only distantly related to the millions of flesh-and-blood people of whose experiences these aggregate variables are in some sense a sum.

The economist is quite falsely accused of creating an "economic man"—that revolting creature of popular imagination who knows, in the words of Oscar Wilde, the price of everything and the value of nothing. If ever there was an economic man (which I doubt) he certainly died at the hands of Philip Wicksteed, a Unitarian minister, and perhaps the greatest economist of the late nineteenth century. In his *Common Sense of Political Economy* Wicksteed established economics firmly as a general theory of choice under conditions of limited resources, and the student who has read his illustrations of the theory of value in terms of how much one should shorten family prayers in order to speed a parting guest to the train, or how high a cliff one should jump off to save a mother-in-law will have little doubt of the generality of economic principles. It is evident from the above also that economics cannot be accused of being materialistic. Economics clearly recognizes that all material objects are intermediate goods, mere means which serve the end of increasing that ultimate spiritual product known technically as "Utility." The economist does not know what utility is, any more than the physicist knows what electricity is, but he certainly could not do without it.

The danger in the economic abstraction lies in its very success. I am not attacking abstraction as such—it is absolutely necessary if the huge complexity of human life-experience is to be reduced to manageable terms. Moreover the economic abstraction is reasonably coherent and is very illuminating in the interpretation of history, both in the large and in the small. But because of its coherence, its beauty and its success, its practitioners—especially those skilled in mathematics—are apt to forget that it is an abstraction, and that it is men and not commodities that are the ultimate social reality. A good example of both the necessity and the danger of economic abstraction is found in the study of labor: unless we understand clearly that labor *is* a commodity, in spite of all pious pronouncements to the contrary, we shall never understand the phenomena of industrial relations. But we shall also not understand industrial relations unless we realize that labor is much *more* than a commodity, and that the labor-bargain involves a complex set of psychological, sociological, even theological relationships out of which the commodity aspect is abstracted.

It is at this point, I think, that the teacher whose acquaintance with religion is something more than secondhand can be of great help to his students, not only as persons but also as economists. To seek God is to find man. To live deeply with the life of Jesus, as revealed in the Gospels, is to know the glory, wonder, folly, and depravity of man in his fullness. Unless the economist has something of this sense of the fullness of man he will be in constant danger of misusing his abstraction, particularly as applied to the interpretation of history and in developing an appraisal of economic policy. It is not, of course, the business of a teacher to interlard his teaching with sermons, and there are, of course, the familiar dangers; the danger of using a position of authority in one field to give weight to opinions or indoctrinations in another; the danger of insensitivity to the religious susceptibilities of students of differing faiths on the one hand, or of tampering with truth to avoid giving offense on the other. A teacher who makes clear, however, when he is speaking as a specialist and when as a whole person, and who approaches his task with a proper humility, can avoid these dangers and give his students a sense of the significance and setting of his specialized knowledge in a way that is impossible for one who never transgressed the narrow limits of his own discipline.

VI

It remains to consider some of the responsibilities of the economist towards the church—not so much towards the religious organization of which he is a member, as towards the "Church Invisible" of which the visible churches are manifestations. It is none the less true for being almost a cliché that the crisis of our age is at bottom a religious crisis. Religion, we feel, should be the Center of Town, the integrating factor in the welter of life, experience, and knowledge. There is sting in the remark of a Roman Catholic friend of mine that a State University is a "City of God that is all suburbs"; our innumerable specialties spread around the intellectual map in formless clusters, with only the most congested trickles of communication between them, and there seems to be no center which can relate one to the other. Because of this the increase of knowledge actually threatens to destroy us, and we are faced with the nightmare of infinite power in the hands of unregenerate man. The trouble is, of course, that the town has grown so big! The little medieval center, with its quaint narrow streets and lovely cathedral, is quite inadequate to handle the traffic of the vast suburbs that have grown up in the past three centuries. The highways that could handle the traffic from Ptolemy and Aristotle with comfort have hardly adjusted themselves to Copernicus and Darwin, and are hopelessly congested by Freud, Keynes, and Einstein! Consequently the true center is by-passed, rival centers of nationalism, fascism, communism and so on are set up, and the whole vast city threatens to disintegrate. And so we long for a new and greater Aquinas, to bring together once again Grace and Truth, Wisdom and Power, Faith and Knowledge in blessed union.

In any such synthesis the social sciences must find a place. We are apt today to think of the natural sciences, with their ominous threat of atomic or bacteriological destruction, as the greatest danger to mankind. It may well be however that the social sciences, all of which seem to be on the threshhold of a vast expansion of knowledge, ultimately constitute an even greater threat to human dignity, welfare, or even existence. In the sciences knowledge inevitably leads to power and power is of itself neutral—it can be power for evil just as for good. Indeed, it may not even be neutral, for the existence of power may even predispose to evil. But whereas the natural sciences lead mainly to power over nature, the social sciences lead directly to power over man. The horrors of psychological and sociological warfare may exceed those of atomic warfare, for the physicist can merely kill and maim men's bodies, where the social psychologist may be able to kill and maim their souls. A greater nightmare than that of atomic destruction is that of a world tyranny resting on the unshakable foundation of social-scientific knowledge of the manipulation of men— the "Brave New Worlds" of Aldous Huxley or George Orwell. Between us and this triumph of learning, ingenuity and respectability there stands that strange force in history which can only be called the Holy Spirit: the foolishness of God, the naïveté of children, and the disreputability of saints, this spirit of Christ, of Divine Love. Unless men—including scientists, social or natural—can be brought under the gentle domination of this spirit, all science is dismal, and leads to the damnation of man and not to his salvation, for knowledge leads to power, and power without holiness—i.e., the right will—is damnation.

To say that there is danger in knowledge and power does not mean, however, that there is virtue in ignorance and impotence. And even if there were, there seems to be no way short of catastrophe by which knowledge and power can be lost, any more than innocence can be regained. There is no way of uneating the Apple, no way back to the Garden of Eden, and the only way out of the City of Destruction leads to the City of God, to the redemption and not the suppression of knowledge.

The economist, along with others who are gifted with specialized knowledge, has a responsibility here to bring his knowledge to the service of the church and to keep the channels of communication open between his own speciality and the "center of town." This task has its own special dangers. In a subject like economics which deals with the commonplaces of life and which for the most part uses the language of ordinary life the specialist finds it difficult to be patient with the amateur, and is apt to pretend to a greater degree of certainty of knowledge than he possesses in order to impress the unspecialized. The professional economist is apt to be impatient with the "easy answers" of the preachers, such as prohibition, "sentimental unionism," and the "cooperative commonwealth." He faces on the one hand the naïve conservatism of fundamentalist Protestantism, with its limitation of interest to the grossly identifiable sins and its narrow concept of regeneration, and on the other hand the almost equally naïve liberalism of the "social gospel," with its emphasis on social sins which are not identifiable enough to trouble the individual conscience and its undue optimism in regard to regeneration by legislation. He is apt to be equally impatient with the millenialist crudities of Marxism, with its subtle substitution of moral judgments for intellectual analysis. On the other hand his knowledge of the infinite complexities of social life is apt to paralyze his will-to-action and to breed a kind of sophisticated conservatism of hopelessness. For the sake of his own spiritual and intellectual health the economist must face the challenge of prophetic indignation: on the other hand the prophet also must be prepared to submit his moral insights to the rigorous discipline of intellectual analysis when it comes to translating these insights into policies.

Religious Foundations of Economic Progress*

One of the most challenging—and tantalizing—propositions of what may be called the "larger economics" is that the success of economic institutions depends to a large extent on the nature of the whole culture in which they are embedded, and not on the nature of these institutions in themselves. This proposition is of particular importance in two current fields of economic inquiry: (a) the study of the complex forces which underlie economic development and (b) the study of the stability and survival power of the characteristic institutions of capitalism.

Indeed, it is only a slight exaggeration to say that the wealth of a nation is a by-product of certain elements in its culture, cumulated through the years. Over a broad range of human societies within the extremes of the Eskimo and the desert nomad, if one area is rich and another poor, it is not because of anything inherent in the natural resources or in the genetic make-up of the people, but because of the cumulative effect of certain familial, educational, and religious practices. Thus the forbidding soil and climate of New England provided a comfortable—if not opulent—homeland for the Puritan, while under the Turk, in his unspeakable days, the ancient cradles of civilization became barren and starveling deserts.

Of all the elements of culture which shape economic institutions, religious practices particularly play a key role—a doubly important one because many other elements of the pattern of life, such as sex, child rearing, work habits, agricultural and industrial practices, are themselves profoundly affected by the prevailing religious beliefs. That religion plays such an important role is not, however, sufficiently recognized by most people, and it is my purpose here to throw more light on it. More specifically, I shall attempt to survey certain aspects

* *Harvard Bus. Rev.* 30, 3 (May–June 1952): 33–40. © 1952 by the President and Fellows of Harvard College; all rights reserved.
This paper was written especially for the *Harvard Business Review*.

of our own society in the light of the contribution which religious ideas, practices, and institutions have made to its economic development and to its power of survival.

Process of Economic Development

To appraise the role of religion in economic development, we must understand the process by which economic change takes place. All change may not be for the better, but it is clear that there can be no betterment without some change.

Essential Features of Improvement.   There are, then, three essential features of any process of economic development in a society—innovation, imitation, and displacement; and two further features which, though conceivably not indispensable, are almost certain to be present in any kind of economic improvement process of which we have knowledge—accumulation of capital and limitation of population. Let us look more closely at these five features:

(1) There must be an *innovator*, who first makes the change. He can be divided, as was done by Schumpeter, into an inventor and an entrepreneur. But the point here is that whether the function is specialized or not, or whether it is performed by a single individual or by a number, the function itself is necessary. If we are to have progress, somebody, somewhere, must do something in a way that has never been done before.

(2) If, however, there is no freedom to *imitate* a change—still more, if the innovator himself is suppressed by the conservative institutions of his society—there can be no testing out of the innovation to see whether it in fact constitutes a "betterment" or not. It would be rash to say that all innovations which are widely imitated are in fact "betterments," for even the mass may be wrong. But we can say that unless there is opportunity for imitation, an innovation *cannot* be tested, and nobody can ever find out whether it is in fact a "good" innovation, that is, a "better" way of doing things.

(3) Imitation cannot take place, in turns, unless there is *displacement* of the old methods. It is the resistance to displacement (that is, to "competition") on the part of those whose interests are bound up with the old ways, and who are not flexible enough in their habits or opportunities to change, which is likely to be one of the main obstacles to change.

(4) Next, practically all economic innovation of which we have knowledge involves the *accumulation of capital*, in the broad sense of

the increase in "valuable objects." The objects so accumulated are not only material; the acquisition of skills, traits, and abilities constitutes capital accumulation just as much as does the stockpiling of materials and material equipment.

If capital is to be accumulated, production must exceed consumption—production being gross additions to the total stock of capital, and consumption being subtractions from it. Such accumulation is far from automatic. In poor societies it is difficult because the minimum needs of consumption press daily on the meager and hard-won product; most of the activity of the society is concerned with more maintenance, and little is left for accumulation. In rich societies the threat may be from more subtle sources—from unwillingness to accumulate (i.e., to invest) leading to unemployment and from levels of production below the society's capacity.

(5) Even if there is an increase in the total capital or income of a society, however, economic progress will not necessarily result. Economic well-being must rise on a per-capita basis. Hence the accumulation of capital will not constitute "improvement" unless capital increases, in some sense, faster than population. And hence a permanent high-level economy is not possible unless there is *limitation of population*—that is, unless population is checked by methods other than starvation and poverty (according to the familiar "dismal theorem" of Malthus that if nothing checks the growth of population but misery and starvation, then the population will grow until it is miserable and starves).

Even if a society starts on the road of economic improvement, then, there are many elements in its culture which may prevent the improvement in techniques from resulting in an actual improvement in welfare. The newly won powers may be used merely for the support of larger populations at the old level of poverty, or they may also be squandered in the luxury of a foolish ruling class or in the waste of total war. The pyramids of Egypt and the endless wars of Rome are good examples of the waste of resources liberated by technical improvement.

Influence of the Protestant Ethic

The past three centuries have witnessed a rate of economic development in the "western world" which, measured by any standard we choose, almost certainly exceeds the achievement of any other period of equal length in human history. We are so much accustomed to this rapid progress, both in techniques and in general levels of income, that we are likely to take it for granted. Nevertheless, looking over the whole range of human history and prehistory, we can clearly see that these last 300 years represent an episode in human development which has no parallel, except perhaps in that dim period when settled agriculture was invented and gave rise to the first civilizations.

The unique nature of the achievement makes it all the more important that we should not take it for granted, but should inquire very carefully into its sources in the culture of the western world. The history of civilizations reveals that it is perfectly possible, indeed easy, to dry up the springs of progress in a society, and that virtually all past civilizations have eventually done so. Therefore, unless we are aware of the nature of those elements in our total pattern of life which are responsible for this rapid rate of development, we may run into grave danger of changing that pattern, without knowing it, in a way that destroys those peculiar elements in the culture from which development springs.

Important among the elements in our complex culture having favorable influence on the rate of economic development are certain religious ideas and practices which comprise the so-called "Protestant ethic."

The thesis of Max Weber and his school that the Protestant ethic has influenced the development of capitalism is now well accepted. Though one's estimate of the quantitative importance of this influence will depend to a great extent on the interpretation of history which one favors, the direction of the influence can hardly be in doubt.

What has not, I think, been pointed out with sufficient force is that the Protestant ethic has contributed to the *success* of capitalist institutions, particularly in regard to their fostering a high rate of economic progress. Economic sociologists like Weber, Sombart, and Tawney, who have emphasized the close connection between religious and economic ideas, have been on the whole unfriendly to capitalist institutions and have consequently tended to lay stress on their failures rather than their successes. This is perhaps because the ethical systems of these writers were conceived in fairly static terms—in terms, for instance, of the problem of justice in the distribution of a given total income, rather than in terms of the encouragement of a growing total income.

It has now become clear, however, that the consequence of even a small rate of economic progress, persistently raising average incomes, is so enormous over even a few decades that from the point of view of long-run human welfare the capacity of a system to generate economic development has come to overshadow all other criteria in judging it "good" or "bad." (Curiously enough, this has also become true of

Communism; in the interest of inducing a rapid rate of economic development the rulers of Russia have thrown overboard practically every other ideal of their ethical system, and have developed degrees of inequality which even the most uncontrolled period of capitalist development could hardly rival.)

In other words, we see now that in practice the abolition of poverty can come only from development—not from redistribution, not from taking from the rich to give to the poor, but by making everybody richer. And it is on this score that the Protestant ethic, which was born with the Reformation, has been so influential.

Innovation in Religion. Innovation, imitation, and displacement in economic life have their counterparts in religious life. Thus the Reformation marked the beginning of a series of innovations in religion. Men like Luther, Calvin, Menno Simons, George Fox, John Wesley, General Booth, and even in our own day Frank Buchman, represent a disturbance of the previously established equilibrium, with a new form of religious enterprise and new arrangements of human time and spiritual energy. They are widely imitated, and the spread of the new technique forces profound adjustments even in those older institutions which do not go over completely to the new ideas.

It generally seems to be true that these innovations in religion have preceded and in some sense paved the way for innovations in economic life. Indeed, the most important innovation in any society is the *idea* of innovation itself, for this represents the Rubicon between the traditional stationary type of society, in which each generation repeats the pattern of its elders, and the "economic," dynamic society, in which innovation becomes an accepted and profitable role. A strong case can be made out for the claim that the principal historical agency bringing about this critical change is a reformation (or revolution) in religion, that this liberates the society from its previous equilibrium and exposes it to all the terrors and delights of dynamics. Once iconoclasm has succeeded in the most traditional and "sacred" area of life, once "free enterprise" has been successful in religion, the spirit of innovation seizes upon all other areas of life.

What in our western society we call *the* Reformation is of course only one among many. The period of rapid innovation which followed the rise of Mohammedanism is another and spectacular example. Within Christianity itself the monastic reformations—especially of the Benedictines and Cistercians—paved the way for the economic development of medieval Europe. Again—if only to remind us that Protestantism is not the whole story—the Counter-Reformation within the Catholic Church also represents a period of "innovation," though of a less dramatic and less iconoclastic nature.

Individual Responsibility and Perfectionism. The fact remains that the Protestant Reformation has certain specific features of its own which have increased its importance for economic development. I am not referring to the sanctification of economic activity through the extension of the concept of "vocation," as emphasized by earlier writers. The concept of vocation is not peculiar to Protestantism, nor is it so important as what I have in mind.

First of all, there is the "unmediated" character of Protestant religion, that is, the emphasis on the individual's own responsibility for his religious life and salvation without the intermediary of priest or prescribed ritualistic "works." It is this unmediated quality of Protestant religion which underlies the sociological significance of the doctrine of justification by faith. Protestantism, that is to say, represents private enterprise in religion, as opposed to the great organized collectivism of the Catholic Church.

It is not surprising that private enterprise in religion carried over into the economic field. The full effect of this is seen in the eighteenth century, where the immense economic innovations which constituted the beginnings of the technical revolution in banking, trade, and industry were to an astonishing extent the work of the British nonconformists, and especially of the Quakers, who had developed the most unmediated of all Protestant varieties of religion.

Another aspect of Protestantism which relates closely to economic development is its perfectionism. Like the earlier monastic reformations, Protestantism reflects a discontent with compromise with the "world" and a serious attempt to return to the pristine revelation of perfection implied in the Christian vision of perfect love. Unlike the monastic reformation, however, the Protestant Reformation—because one of the things against which it was protesting was the corruption of the monastery and nunnery prevalent in the time of Luther—rejected the monastic solution and became an attempt to lead the life of Christian perfection in the workaday world rather than in cloistered separation.

Such an attempt, however, is almost doomed to fail, and the difficulty of practicing the major virtue of charity will lead to an insensible substitution of the "minor virtues" as attainable ends of the religious group. So the perfectionist subsides into the Puritan, and groups of people arise practicing, with some success, the minor virtues of thrift, hard work, sobriety, punctuality, honesty, fulfillment of promises, devotion to family, and so on. The minor virtues, however, lead almost inevitably to accumulation and increased productivity, and eventually therefore to an escape from poverty.

The Lost Economic Gospel

This all adds up to what I call the "lost economic gospel" of Protestantism. Poverty is the result of "sin," sin being defined in terms of intemperance, loose living, prodigality, laziness, dishonesty, and so on (that is, in terms of violation of the "minor virtues").[1] On yielding to the power of Christ and the discipline of the congregation the individual is converted, gives up his evil ways, and becomes temperate, frugal, thrifty, hard working, honest, and so on; as a result of which he begins to accumulate skill and other capital and raises his standard of life. Thus he becomes respectable, and incidentally, but only incidentally, he may become rich by hitting on a successful innovation.

In the process of the individual's becoming richer, society also becomes richer. Indeed, the improvement of society is nothing more than the sum of the improvements of individuals. In a dynamic and improving society, therefore, the increase in riches of the individual is not thought of as a redistribution of wealth (one individual gaining at the expense of others) but rather as a creation of wealth (the gains of one individual representing net additions to the total and being taken from no man). Economic life is not a "zero sum" poker game in which a fixed volume of wealth is circulated around among the players, but a "positive sum" enterprise in which the accumulation of each person represents something which he brings to the "pot" rather than something which he takes out.

Another doctrine which Protestantism shares with other forms of Christianity has combined with the "lost gospel" to contribute to the success of capitalist institutions: the doctrine of stewardship, of charity in the narrower sense of the word. Those whose virtue, energy, or plain good fortune have brought them material success are expected to regard their riches as in some sense a trust, to be used for the benefit of the less fortunate. Over the long pull, this aspect of Christian culture has proved of great importance in modifying the inequalities of capitalism. As in the middle ages the establishment of monasteries was an important agency in the redistribution of wealth and income, so in the nineteenth and twentieth centuries the establishment of uni-

---

[1] Kenneth E. Boulding, "Our Lost Economic Gospel," *The Christian Century*, August 16, 1950, pp. 970–972.

versities and foundations has provided a means whereby private accumulations have found their way into public uses.

The habit of mind engendered by the doctrine of stewardship has also been important in removing obstacles to legislative methods of correcting inequalities, such as progressive income and inheritance taxation. It is quite possible that this factor may have something to do with the different impact of capitalist institutions in the West and, say, in China, where the acquisitive opportunities have been less likely to be modified by the sense of responsibility for the welfare of those outside the circle of kinship.

It can hardly be doubted, then, that the "lost gospel"—the old gospel of individualism, of self-help—is in many respects a sound one. Indeed, the middle-class nature of Protestantism is a testimony to its long-run success. If Protestants are middle-class, it is largely because their Protestantism has made them so—has developed a culture in which hard work, thrift, family limitation, productivity, and frugality have been important values. There is hardly any better over-all recipe for economic development, whether for the individual or for a society.

Decline of the Old Doctrines. Nevertheless to a considerable degree the old doctrines are discredited in the churches today, especially, oddly enough, in the more prosperous ones. The old gospel of self-help flourishes among the little rising sects, the pentecostal people, and the store-front churches, it is actually the poor who seem to be least aware of the new "social gospel" and who cling to the old-time individual virtues. In the large Protestant denominations, as represented by the National Council of Churches, it is not perhaps unfair to say that there is more awareness of the weakness of the individualist gospel than of its strength, and that even where the older gospel is preached, it is often the result of the momentum of tradition rather than of any continuing spiritual insight.

There are significant reasons for the decline of the gospel of self-help and the rise of the "social gospel." Part of the cause lies in sheer misunderstanding, stemming from failure to appreciate the ethical significance of economic progress, and a resultant economic ethic based on static assumptions, in which an undue stress is laid on distributing a fixed sum of wealth fairly rather than on increasing the total to be distributed.

More fundamental is a certain inevitable tension between the ethic of the New Testament and the ethic of Samuel Smiles (the old Scottish biographer of industrialists and extoller of thrift and self-reliance). There is an anti-economic strain in the teaching of almost all the prophets and poets. The careful, calculating, economizing way of life is neither prophetic nor poetic. It counts the cost; it asks for reward; it has no fine frenzies; it is humdrum, commonplace, even a little sordid. The stimulus to economic progress, therefore, is not in the ethic of the New Testament itself; rather it is in the "Puritan" substitute-ethic, the product of the impact of the ethic of love on the iron laws of the world.

The substitute-ethic, however, is itself somewhat unstable, because it is always subject to criticism by the pure ethic which generates it. Hybrids are vigorous but can generally only be reproduced from pure stock! Thus when the New Testament makes a fresh impact on a sensitive and vigorous mind—as it is likely to do at least once in a generation—the gospel of "be righteous and grow rich," for all its truth and practicality, looks cheap and pharisaical beside the poetic vision of "sell all thou hast and give to the poor"; and radical forms of Christianity tend to appear. There is something in Toynbee's suggestion that Communism is a Christian heresy!

Technical Weaknesses of Capitalism. Perhaps a still more fundamental reason for the failure of capitalism to sustain the ethic which supports its most characteristic institutions is to be found in certain technical failures of these institutions themselves.

The ethic of capitalism is based firmly on the proposition that wealth is produced by saving and that saving is accomplished by producing much and consuming little. That is why the principal recipe for riches includes hard work and thrift and the other Protestant virtues. Under some circumstances, however, wealth is not produced by saving. Hard work works the worker out of a job, parsimony produces unemployment, and the fluctuations of the price system redistribute wealth without regard to any of the soberer virtues. The thrifty and hard-working find their net worth disappearing in deflation and their hard-earned interest and pensions evaporating in inflation, while the speculator and the manipulator reap what others have sown.

In conditions of general price and output instability the poker-game aspects of capitalism come to the fore. Instead of wealth being accumulated by carefully contributing to the physical stock more than one takes from it, it is accumulated by taking advantage of the shifting structure of relative values, by buying cheap and selling dear. Every economist will recognize, of course, that there is a legitimate function of speculation, and that some flexibility of the price structure is necessary to reflect changing structures of productivity and tastes. In fact, however, the characteristic institutions of capitalism—especially the organized commodity and security markets and the real estate market —have lent themselves to fluctuations far beyond what the flexibility of the system requires, and have therefore been the instrument of redistributions of wealth which have created a gap between economic virtue (in the sense of contribution to the progress of real wealth) and reward.

The phenomenon of depression has been particularly destructive to the capitalist ethic, because the misery which it has entailed has seemed to be so meaningless: why work and save when the end result is the foreclosure of a mortgage and selling apples in the street! The whole technical weakness of an ungoverned market economy can be summed up in two concepts: (a) speculative instability in price levels due to the dynamics of self-justified expectations and (b) the limited or imperfect market resulting either from monopolistic imperfections in the market structure or from general deflation. Speculative insta-bility leads to essentially meaningless redistributions of wealth. The limited market leads to an undue shift of emphasis away from pro-duction, to wasteful advertising and selling costs, to restrictions of output, to featherbedding, and to other familiar devices by which individuals or segments of the economy seek to protect themselves from the impact of general deflations or seek to enhance their own particular power position at the expense of others.

The all-important question is whether these defects are to be regarded as diseases of the free economy, potentially curable within the general framework of market institutions, or whether they are to be regarded as essential genetic characteristics of it, quite incurable without a radical overthrow of the whole market economy itself.

Chances of Survival

It is in this connection that the contribution of Keynes to the survival of capitalism is so important, for it is the essence of the Keynesian view that the defects of capitalism are curable diseases rather than incurable deformities. While the actual cures may be a matter still in considerable dispute, it is the great virtue of the Keynesian analysis that it gives us a clearer picture than we have ever had before of the nature of the disease, and it has consequently engendered the hope that institutions can be devised within the general framework of a free market economy which will prevent deflation and unemployment, on the one hand, and inflation, on the other.

If such a "governor" can insure the over-all stability of the econ-omy (and it is not the purpose of this article to say how this should be done), most of the ethical objections to a market economy fall to the ground. Given a reasonable degree of stability of the over-all price and output system, the old-fashioned virtues of hard work, thrift, honesty, and so on come into their own.

The Problem of Underdeveloped Areas. Perhaps the crucial test of the capitalist system will turn on its ability to solve what is by far the greatest single economic problem facing the world today: the development of the so-called underdeveloped areas—inhabited by about three-quarters of the world's population—to the point where at least the grim consequences of extreme poverty (malnutrition, early death, constant ill health, superstition, squalor, and misery) are mitigated.

There are, roughly speaking, two kinds of society in the world today. The "high-level" societies have low birth and death rates, an expectation of life at birth rising up toward 60 or 70 years, disease well under control, malnutrition rare, literacy universal, education widespread, a high status and much freedom for women, complex economic and political institutions, and so on. The "low-level" societies, on the other hand, have high birth and death rates, an expectation of life around 30 years, disease and malnutrition rampant, literacy and education confined to a small upper class, a low status for women among the mass of the people, burdensome and exploitative financial institutions, often a colonial status, and so on.

The crux of the problem is how to raise the three-quarters of the world that live on a low level to the high level of the other quarter, for it is precisely this wide disparity that makes our world so unstable. American-Russian relations, for instance, would not constitute the apparently insoluble problem which they now pose if the relationship were simply one of America and Russia; in that event they could perfectly well leave each other alone! The relationship is complicated almost unbearably by the fact that each power is competing for the support of the vast fringe of underdeveloped countries which divide them on the globe, from Poland to Korea. These countries are dissatisfied with their present state and are hovering between the two cultures, wondering which offers them the best chance of shifting from their present low-level to a high-level economy.

In this whole difficult situation it is of vital importance to appreciate the relation of economic institutions and economic development to the *whole* culture pattern, and to realize that the success of any set of economic institutions depends on the total culture setting in which they are placed. The success, even of modern technology, therefore, may depend quite as much upon the missionary as upon the engineer.

One of the tasks of human inquiry is to discover exactly what the elements are in any culture which perpetuate poverty—whether in family life, in religious life, in education, in politics, or in economic and financial institutions—and then to effect a *minimum* change in the culture which is necessary to eradicate these germs of poverty.

We do not want, of course, the kind of cultural imperialism that insists on giving the Fiji Islanders Coca-Cola and Christmas trees whether these things are meaningful extensions of their present culture or not. Cultural change and cultural impact, however, there must be. Such impact is immensely dangerous and may result in disaster to both cultures; yet with the collapse of isolation such impact is inevitable. If it is to be ultimately fruitful, it must be understood much better than we understand it now; the marriage of economics and cultural anthropology must be accomplished, even at the point of a shotgun!

Inadequacy of Social Sciences. It must not be thought, however, that all that is needed for world salvation is a stiff dose of social science, no matter how well documented empirically and no matter how well integrated analytically. The rise of social science presents man with problems of an ethical and spiritual nature of which he is still for the most part not aware. The spectacular "success" of the physical sciences in expanding the power of man, both for good and for evil, is dramatically symbolized in the atom bomb. The worst that a physicist can do for anybody, however, is to cause pain and death. The social scientist, when he knows a little more, may be able to destroy the soul, that inner core of freedom and integrity which constitutes at once the humanity and the divinity of man.

The nightmare of the "manipulative society"—the brave new world of Aldous Huxley or George Orwell—is not too far from reality. We see it foreshadowed in the crudely manipulative society of Soviet Russia, and it is this aspect of Communism which rightly fills us with disgust and fear. In its very conflict with Communism, however, the West may find itself sliding imperceptibly into a manipulative society more horrible, because more efficient, than the Soviet counterpart.

A world of unseen dictatorship is conceivable, still using the forms of democratic government, in which education has been replaced by training, in which government creates artificially the public opinion which keeps it in power, in which "loyalty" investigations corrupt the whole system of communications, in which only "safe" ideas are expressed, in which love of country is corroded by conscription and integrity is swallowed up in expediency, and in which the springs of technical, as well as of moral, progress are eventually dried up. The cleverer we are and the more we know, the more thoroughly we may damn ourselves.

Increased Significance of Religion

When the final history of the human race comes to be written, therefore, the part played by religion and religious experience may be even more significant than I have suggested earlier. I have argued that religion is an important autonomous force in the development of the technical revolution. It may turn out to be even more important in the control of this revolution.

We do not yet realize, I believe, what a portentous watershed in human history we are now treading. Civilization is a product of the increase in human control over environment which resulted from the invention of settled agriculture. All past civilizations, however, have proved to be unstable; the "iron laws" of social dynamics have eventually caught up with them and destroyed them. It is by no means improbable that our own civilization will suffer the same fate.

Yet there is reason for hope. As our knowledge not only of nature but of man and society expands, we may get to the point where man comes not to be ruled by history but to rule it. He may be able to take the iron laws and fashion them into an instrument for his own purposes, to mold the unconscious dynamic which drives him to destroy his civilizations into a conscious dynamic which will empower him to perpetuate them indefinitely.

The possibility of permanent and universal civilization therefore rises before us, though the prospect is not necessarily one to be approached without fear. It might be the kingdom of heaven on earth, but it might also be an indestructible and universal tyranny, securely based on the power of both physical and social science. A world of refugees is bad enough, but a world in which there is no place of refuge would be worse.

An increase in human power, therefore, makes all the more urgent the question of the discipline of the human will. Economic development means an increase in our ability to get what we want. Religion, however, raises the question of whether we want the right things. As long as we are impotent, it does not perhaps matter so much in regard to externals whether we want the right things or the wrong things. We cannot get what we want in any case. But if we can get what we want, the question of whether we want the right things becomes acutely important.

There are those who think that as economic development comes to fruition in a humanistic heaven on earth where war, poverty, and disease are abolished, religion will wither away. In that millennium faith will be swallowed up in knowledge, hope in fulfillment, and love in psychoanalysis and group dynamics! Such a belief seems to be naïve. As power and knowledge increase, the question of the *truth* of religion —of what is the "will of God," and how it is discovered and incorporated into the human will—becomes all-important. The feather of religious experience may then tip the great scales toward either heaven or hell on earth.

The Principle of
Personal Responsibility*

If we were to seek the one thing on which all those who count themselves Christians agree, it is that the greatest of the Christian virtues
is love. Love is the heart of the Gospel, the essence of salvation, the
most precious attribute of God. It is when we come to interpret the
meaning of love in daily life, however, that we run into the dilemmas
and the disagreements. For Christian love is not merely an emotion,
an agreeable warmness or liking for people and things, even though its
emotional attributes must not be neglected. We are commanded to
love all men, even our enemies, but we clearly cannot feel the same
depth of emotion towards all the two billion inhabitants of the earth
that we feel to those who are near to us. Even in terms of intimate
relationships the meaning of love is not always clear—where, for instance, in our relationships with our children, between total permis-
siveness and authoritarianism is the best expression of parental love?
When we come to consider the less intimate relationships of economic
life—our relationships with the butcher and baker, the sales clerk and
cleaning lady, the employee and the boss, the income tax collector and
the far-away state, the problem of the right expression of love in action
becomes even more difficult. Still more difficult is the question of our
relationship with those millions of the unseen who serve us and whom
we serve in the vast web of commercial relations—the coffee grower
of Brazil, the sheep rancher of Australia, the tin miner of Bolivia. In
a simpler day one's "neighbor" was literally someone who was "near"
and most economic connections involved personal contact. Today the
world has become a neighborhood, thanks to improvements in communications; but in very consequence of this the simple ethics of
neighborhoodliness have become less adequate to deal with its prob-

---

* *Rev. Soc. Economy* 12, 1 (Mar. 1954): 1–8.
This paper was presented at a meeting of the Catholic Economic
Association in December, 1953.

lems. We affect, and are affected by, the actions of people we neither see nor know. Under these circumstances not only is it difficult to *feel* love for these blank faces; but even if we persuaded ourselves to feel, what *difference* would this feeling make to our actions? This is a critical and indeed an embarrassing question for those of us who profess to be moved by Christian love, for if there is no way of expressing this love in action, and if it makes no difference to our behavior, then it is a false emotion hardly removed from self-deception.

One attempt to reduce the unmanageable claims of love to reasonable dimensions is through attempts to define and limit responsibility. The idea of responsibility is certainly not to be identified with love, but perhaps it is a reasonable first approximation, especially in dealing with the complex relationships of economic life. Or if we look at the matter from the point of view of different levels of abstraction we may say that responsibility implies a certain extension of self, in that we are concerned for the welfare of others as well as for ourselves; and it is precisely this extension of self which is implied in the concept of love. Love and responsibility do not imply, it should be observed, pure altruism. We are not commanded to love our neighbor and hate ourselves, but to love our neighbor *as* ourselves. Indeed one sometimes suspects that the love of these miserable selves of ours, whose ugliness and weakness we know all too well, is much harder than the love of our superficially attractive neighbors!

We must beware, however, of two different meanings of the term "responsibility." Responsibility *to* someone is a very different thing from responsibility *for* someone. The latter might be called *internal* responsibility. It rests on an inner sense of concern for the other person and at least a partial identification of his interest with ours, a sharing of his joys and sorrows. Responsibility *to* someone is a very different matter. We might call it *external* responsibility. This concerns the ultimate locus of power and the structure of organization. We are responsible *to* the people who can put us out of our job if we don't satisfy them!

Responsibility *to* may be thought of in both formal and real terms. Confusion of thought frequently arises because the real power relationships in society do not correspond very closely to the formal structure of organization. Thus in an American university the formal power relationships generally flow from the trustees or governors to the president to the deans to the department heads to the faculty. The president is formally responsible to the trustees, the deans to the president, and so on. Formally, therefore, the president is not responsible to the faculty, as he is, say, in an Oxford college. Nevertheless one suspects that the informal power structures do not differ very greatly in widely differing formal types of institutions, and that in fact an American university president has little more power over, and is almost as much subject to opinion of his faculty as, say, the Warden of All Souls. If I may venture an even more delicate example, if we compare the actual power structures in episcopal and congregational forms of church organization, which formally are so different, we might find them much more similar than the formal difference would suggest. Authority, Chester Barnard has argued, is granted from below and not from above. The cynic might argue that advancement in episcopal churches comes by pleasing the Bishop and in congregation churches by pleasing the people; but in fact the parish priest who outrages his congregation is likely to find himself unpopular with the Bishop, and the congregational minister who outrages the leaders of his denomination is likely to find himself in trouble with his congregation.

I do not want to suggest, however, that formal responsibility is unimportant. Indeed, the central point of my argument is that one of the principal objectives of political structures, customs, and organizations is to identify the various forms of responsibility. That is to say, it is desirable that we should be responsible *to*, in both a formal and an informal sense, those whom we are responsible *for*. I do not put this forward as a single absolute objective, for there may be other objectives of social and political organization which compete with it, and a due balance must be struck. Nevertheless I suggest that this is one objective which must be considered in the evaluation of organizational structures, and one which has a high ethical content. If we are responsible for, but not responsible to any group of people the relationship is both difficult and dangerous. Even if we are men of the utmost good will the relationship can easily degenerate into an insensitive parternalism which either corrupts or drives to revolt those in subordinate positions. If we are not men of good will the relationship can easily descend into the blackest tyranny. But the important point is that good will itself is not necessarily enough to protect us from the dangers of inadequate or improper organization. In the highest sense love can only exist between equals, and when we attempt to exercise love towards inferiors, or towards those who are unreservedly in our power, or towards those in whose power we are, the relationship falls short of the highest ideal, and becomes at best pity or submissiveness, and at worst sentimentality and toadying. And while I would not want for a moment to deny that there are real virtues which are less than love, it is important not to mistake them for love.

The implications and ramifications of the theory of responsibility outlined above would carry us into all spheres of human life, and cannot be developed in a short paper. It leads clearly in the direction of non-authoritarianism in family life, and towards democratic institutions in political life. The main concern of this paper, however, is with economic life. What, especially, is the significance of the institution of the market in regard to the responsibility of the individual both to and for the people who are affected by his decisions, and what is the relation of the structure of economic responsibility to the structure of economic power?

I shall argue, perhaps with some appearance of paradox, that the market under conditions approaching pure competition is an institution of high ethical value, in that it provides a check on concentrations of economic power and goes a long way towards accomplishing that union of responsibility and power which I have put forward as a prime object of human organization. I shall also argue, however, that the institutions of the market, and the kind of behavior which is involved in commercial life, are inadequate to generate the *motivations* of responsibility and of concern for others which are both desirable in themselves and necessary as a cement of the social fabric.

Consider for a moment the difference between an institution like a business enterprise which exists primarily in a market environment, and an institution like a state, an army, or an established national church which does not. The prime difference between them is that the former must depend for its survival on the voluntary cooperation of the individuals who are related to it, whether as workers, capitalists, suppliers, or customers, whereas the latter depends for its survival on its power to coerce individuals into cooperating with it. This is the old controversy between the carrot and the stick. The "market" organization survives, if it does, because of its power to persuade those related to it that it "pays" them to continue the relationship. It must attract workers by offering them at least as good wages and conditions of work as they can get elsewhere. It must attract customers by offering them goods or services as good and cheap as they can get elsewhere. It must attract investors by offering them a rate of return at least as good as they can get in comparable occupations. And in a well-operating free market there is always an "elsewhere"—this is the essence of the concept of pure competition as the economist understands it, and this is how competition limits the power of the organizer or the entrepreneur. In a very real sense, therefore, the business man is responsible *to* those persons who are affected by his actions, in the sense that he is in their power as much as they are in his. If he cannot offer workers the "going wage" or consumers the "going price" he will not be able to attract them to his shop. A market-determined organization therefore can only survive by satisfying human wants—at least those wants which can be expressed through the market. The organization must be *serviceable*, at least in this restricted sense, if it is to survive.

There are, of course, important qualifications of this too-optimistic view of the market, with which most economists are familiar. Monopoly (or monopsony) represents a kind of knot, kink, or distortion in the general field of economic relationships, or a toll-gate in the network of economic communications which enables some individuals to capture and exploit power-positions which otherwise competitive forces would erode away. Furthermore needs are not quite the same thing as wants, especially those wants which can be expressed in the market. There are collective needs which are unsuited to market expression, and for this reason government—and a tax system—is necessary in spite of the inevitable element of coercion involved. Indeed Baumol[1] has suggested that there might be a species of "voluntary coercion," where we have something (like paying taxes) which we are all willing to do if everybody does it but are not willing to do *unless* everybody does it.

It is also true that there are substitutes for the market environment in the case of political organization like states, and that political democracy can best be understood in these terms. There is a world of difference between the absolute state, whether of Louis XIV or of Malenkov, in which the citizen has virtually no choice of rulers and no say in decisions, and the democratic state in which the citizen can lawfully depose his rulers and can write indignant, and frequently effective letters to his congressman. The vote of the citizenry is the "market" for the product of the democratic state, and it plays much the same role in modifying the power of the state that the consumers or the labor market does in modifying the power of the businessman. The congressman is "responsible to" his constituents because they have the power to throw him out of office at the next election. Similarly the businessman is in a sense "responsible to" his workers and his customers because they likewise have the power to throw him out of office by shopping elsewhere. In the latter case the power is not so visible, and hence not so well understood, as it results in a removal of the office from the businessman rather than the removal of the businessman from office; but it comes to the same sort of thing.

---

[1] W. J. Baumol, *Welfare Economics and the Theory of the State*, Harvard, 1952.

One value of this way of looking at things is that it points to the "politicising" of business through the rise of labor unions, collective bargaining, "co-determination" and so on as in a sense a *substitute* for the market. These things are most likely to arise therefore in periods when the market as an institution is functioning poorly, either because of monopoly or because of deflation and depression. If the worker *cannot* get a job elsewhere he feels acutely his inferior power position and is strongly motivated towards unionism as a "countervailing power." Thus unionism can be regarded as an attempt to make employers responsible *to* their workers, or in other words to put the workers in a better power position *vis a vis* the employer. It must be pointed out however that an active labor market does much the same thing, and that if it had not been for the inability of capitalist economies to maintain continuous active labor markets over the past hundred years or so the motivation for the rise of the labor movement would have been much weaker. One interesting and difficult question in this regard is whether in the dynamic processes of society the attempts to provide political substitutes for the market do not themselves weaken the ability of the market to function properly, and so set up a social dynamic process which will eventually eliminate the market. This is the basis of the "Schumpetrian pessimism" about the future of capitalism. All one can say I think is that the pessimistic view is at least not proven, and that we still have opportunities to find a set of institutions which will stabilize the market as an institution by remedying its vices without leading to its destruction.

There is yet another, and perhaps more fundamental reason, for qualifying the optimistic view of the market as a spreader of power and allocator of responsibility. It is that market behavior and market institutions—that is, commercial life—frequently leads to the development of a type of personality which mistakes the abstractions of commerce for the realities of existence, and hence loses much of the richness of full human relationship. The exchange relationship is by its very nature abstract, and indeed it owes its success to its very power of being abstract. When we make a purchase from a store clerk we do not enter into a full and intimate relationship with him. Even the relationship of employee to employer, though it is richer and more complex than that of simple commodity exchange, is still exchange, and still falls far short of the richness and complexity, say of the marital relationship. And this is as it should be: the worker-employer relationship is not the same as the son-father relationship, and any attempt to make it so will create frustration and resentment on both sides. There must be economy in human relationship if *large* fabrics of society are to exist at all, because if we are to have relationships with *many* people these relationships must be limited and abstract rather than full. There is danger, however, in a predominantly commercial society, that people will take economic behavior as the measure of all things and will confine their relationships to those which can be conducted on the level of the commercial abstraction. To do this is to lose almost all richness or purpose in human life. He who has never loved, has never felt the call of a heroic ethic—to give and not to count the cost, to labor and not to ask for any reward—has lived far below the peak levels of human experience. Economic man dwells in Limbo—he is not good enough for Heaven or bad enough for Hell. His virtues are minor virtues: he is punctual, courteous, honest, truthful, painstaking, thrifty, hardworking. His vices are minor vices—niggardliness, parsimoniousness, chicanery. Even the covetousness of which he is often accused is a playful and innocent thing compared with the dreadful covetousness of the proud. On the whole he escapes the deadly sins, for his very vulgarity saves him from pride (how much better, for instance, is the commercial vulgarity of Coca Cola than the heroic diabolism of Hitler). But he misses also the Great Virtue, and in that he is less than Man, for God has made man for himself, and he has an ineradicable hunger for the Divine, the heroic, the sanctified and the uneconomic.

What this means, I think, is that if the market is to be a stable and fruitful institution in society it must be hedged around with other institutions of a non-market character—the home and the school and the church. For here and only here can the *motive* of responsibility develop. It is only as we are ourselves loved—by our parents, our mentors, and by our God—that we gain the capacity to love. "We love Him because He first loved us" is no pious platitude; it is one of the deepest truths of life and existence. It is the great task of economic and political institutions to place limitations on power, that we may be checked when we are moved to evil. But these institutions are not adequate to move us towards good. We must achieve the right distribution of power, so that power does not corrupt the will. But we must also grow towards the right will, which is His Will. This I conceive to be the great earthly task of religion; not so much to prevent us from doing wrong as to make us eager to will the good.

Some Contributions of Economics to Theology and Religion*

It might surprise, and even annoy, a good many economists to contemplate the possibility that economics might have something to contribute to theology or religion. Economics grew up in the essentially secular atmosphere of eighteenth century rationalism. Adam Smith, the unquestioned founder of the discipline, was a close friend of David Hume, and shared most of his rationalistic prejudices. On the other side, Mammon has never had much of a reputation among the religious, and the pursuit of wealth has generally been regarded as somewhat dangerous to spiritual virtue. As economics has developed it has tended to become more abstract, more mathematical, more remote from the higher as well as from the lower passions of mankind, more concerned with an abstract system of commodities and less with the rich complexities of human personality. What then, we might ask, can a highly abstract system of thought regarding the relationships of commodities have to do with religion, which deals with human life, history and experience in its fullest height, depth, concreteness, and confusion?

Nevertheless no person, and no discipline, is too lofty to learn. Economics, grubbing around at the roots of the tree of knowledge, brings up insights within the framework of its narrow world which are of the same stuff as the brave questions which make the fine flowers of ethics, philosophy, and religion. Many of the concepts which economics has developed within its little universe—exchange, production, consumption, distribution, and above all, *value*, are little clear shadows, as it were of great, vague, universal concepts which lie above them. And by clarifying the relationships of his narrow abstract world, the economist may at the same time—often unknown even to himself—be clarifying the larger, vaguer, and more difficult relationships of the great world of universal concepts.

---

* Reprinted from the Nov.–Dec. 1957 issue (pp. 446–50) of *Religious Education* by permission of the publishers, The Religious Education Association, New York City.

This paper was written especially for the journal in which it appeared.

Consider, for example, the concept of Value. Adam Smith worried about the paradox of Value in Use and Value in Exchange—why did water, which was absolutely necessary to existence and of enormous value in use, have so little value in exchange, and why did diamonds, so obviously a piece of vanity and feminine foolishness, with so little value in use, have so great a value in exchange? It took a hundred years to answer the question clearly, though the answer is simple; water being plentiful, a little more means little to us, and it is on the significance of the little more (marginal utility) that value in exchange rests, not on the significance of the total stock or supply (total utility). Diamonds, on the other hand, being scarce relative to the demand for them, have little total utility but a high marginal utility. What this means is that it is not the basic *preference* system which determines values-in-exchange, or relative values, as much as the relative *scarcities* of the things valued. As W. S. Gilbert sings "His wise remarks, like precious stones, derive their value from their scarcity!" The economist simply points out that all things derive their (relative) values from their scarcities, not merely from people's preferences. We cannot therefore deduce the basic preference system merely from relative values, without knowing something about the relative scarcities of the things valued.

This principle holds as well for abstract virtues and vices and for the more profound and holy objects of value as it does for more humble commodities. We may hold some ideals or principles high in our scale of relative values not so much because we have a great preference for these things as because they are scarce in our culture. Thus the harsh, cruel cultures of Europe, which through history have been ruthless, vindictive, and loveless, repressing domestic affection and treating children with brutal punishment and discipline, have responded avidly to Christianity as a religion of love, not so much perhaps out of the love of love as out of its scarcity. In the gentler, more easygoing and permissive culture of Asia, on the other hand, where love, at least in childhood is plentiful but where goods are scarce and families large and crowded and living in very close quarters, a religion of love has had less appeal and a religion of courtesy like Confucianism, or a religion of withdrawal into an inward world like Buddhism appeals to qualities which again derive high value from their natural scarcity in the culture.

The economist thus sees relative values as established by relative scarcity, and relative scarcity in turn established by the relative ease of difficulty with which the quantity of the valued object can be increased. From this arises the extremely important concept of *alterna-*

tive cost, which may be defined as the amount of one thing which must be sacrificed in order to obtain a unit of another. Alternative cost is itself a result of some basic scarcity in "resources." If there were no limitation in resources we could have all our cakes and eat them too, and we could have more of one thing without giving up anything of another. Where resources are limited, however, as in this life at least they always are, alternative cost inevitably raises its dismal head. More guns means less butter, more butter means less cheese, more churches means less schools, and more piety means (perhaps) less art. The fact that we have only twenty-four hours a day to spend, and only one earth to exploit, and only so much knowledge to draw on, and only so much equipment and stocks of goods previously accumulated, imposes on all our activities, from the lowest to the highest, the iron law of alternative cost. It is a law all the more important because of its golden exceptions. Sometimes we move in a realm of blessed complementarity in which more of this means not less but more of that! After an hour in the classroom the students (we hope) know more, but—strange miracle—the teacher knows more too! An expression of love increases love all around, both of the giver and of the receiver. Cells multiply by dividing in the magical mathematics of life, genes print their images on the chaos around them and organize inert matter into organisms of vast complexity. It is as we ride these waves of complementarity that we break through the grim laws of conservation and scarcity, and emerge with evolution and with economic development, with knowledge and civilization and organization.

Over the short run however scarcity and alternative cost hold sway. We value highly what we must sacrifice a lot to get, or high costs mean high prices. The relationship however is a curiously indirect one. High costs do not *cause* high prices. I might make a solid gold Cadillac at a cost of a million dollars, but I might then have to dispose of it for a paltry hundred thousand. High costs however beget scarcity, and scarcity begets high prices. One interesting conclusion follows from this analysis. It is that if unit costs are unaffected by the quantities of goods produced, then relative values are quite unaffected by any change in "demand" or preferences. A change in preferences changes the relative *quantities produced* but not the relative *values* of the goods. If there is a switch in demand from tea to coffee, for instance, there will of course be an eventual decline in tea production and an increase in coffee production. If these changes however produce no change in relative costs, so that no matter how much is produced the sacrifice of a pound of tea releases resources which can then produce, say, three quarters of a pound of coffee, then the shift in outputs will go on until the relative prices have returned to what they were before the switch in demand. Thus though the first impact of the switch in demand will be a fall in the price of tea and a rise in the price of coffee, the effect of this price change is to discourage tea production and to encourage coffee production, and as the output of tea diminishes its price will rise, and as the output of coffee increases, *its* price will fall. This process will go on until the relative prices are equal to the relative costs, at which point it will not pay to switch resources from tea to coffee any longer.

Tea and Coffee may seem to be a long way from the Great Values —Freedom and Justice; Goodness, Truth and Beauty; Courage, Patience, Modesty, Serenity, Vigor, Sensitivity; Faith, Hope, and Charity. The principles which govern the relative evaluation of the great values however are not essentially different from those which govern the evaluation of the small. In spite of the difficulties in measurement the great values are all at least capable of degree. It makes sense to say that this person has more patience, but less vigor than that person, or that this culture has more freedom but less justice than that culture. We are not really much better off than this in the measurement of the quantities of the goods of commerce; there is a deceptive appearance of accuracy in the pound of tea, as there is also in an accountants' figures, but this is appearance only; behind the figures lie a morass of quality differences for which no objective measurement is possible. It is just about as hard to say whether there is more automobile in a Volkswagen Microbus than there is in a Plymouth station wagon as it is to say whether there is more freedom in Russia than in Spain.

In the Great Values as well as in the small, therefore, the economist will look for certain fundamental relationships. What are the relations of complementarity and competitiveness? What are the alternative costs? How much freedom must we give up in order to achieve a certain increase in social justice? Must a certain amount of truth be sacrificed on occasion in the interests of love? Are there some values the pursuit of which actually *increases* the others? These are important questions, for the moral philosopher if not for the theologian. They are questions however which come directly out of the mode of thought of the economist. They relate to what an economist would call the opportunity functions of the Great Values. The Great Values as well as the small are subject to the basic laws of scarcity; we cannot have enough of them all. So with these as with others we face a problem of *choice*. And the theory of choice is the peculiar concern of the economist.

If the economist, then, has anything special to say in the area of the Great Values it is that values, whether great or small, are always the result of acts of choice. Values do not "exist" independently of the actions of a valuer; they are quantities which are conveniently descriptive of acts of evaluation. It is these acts which exist, not the values. The "price" of a commodity is not a physical quantity like its weight; it is a quantity descriptive of an act, either of exchange or of evaluation, and is meaningless without the actor. The economist, therefore shifts the discussion of value from the value as a "thing" to the evaluation as an act.

Let us look for a moment then at the economist's concept of the "act"—that is, of "economic behavior." The actor is seen in the midst of a "field of choice," or a set of alternatives. Action always involves the selection of one among a number (perhaps a very large number, perhaps not) of *possibilities*. One of the economist's great interests is the exact description of the field of choice, and the delineation of the boundaries between the possible and the impossible. Most of the functions or curves which are the stock in trade of the economist—demand curves, cost curves, and the like—are "possibility boundaries" which divide a certain field into two parts—a possible set and an impossible set. Over the whole field of choice (or at least over its most relevant parts) the economist postulates a *value ordering*. This simply means that if we have a set of possible situations, A,B,C—etc., then we can *rank* these in an order of "betterness and worseness," just as a teacher, for instance, may rank a class of students in a class list "first," "second," "third" and so on. Economic behavior then consists simply in the selection of the "best"—that is the "number one" selection in the value ordering of the relevant field of choice.

Ethical behavior, however, is not essentially different from economic behavior, for ethical behavior too involves choice among selections according to some value ordering. When we distinguish ethical from "unethical" behavior, or "higher" from "lower" standards of behavior we are in effect *evaluating the value orderings* themselves. *All* behavior involves value orderings; the murderer decides that the elimination of his victim is the "best" out of all the possible states of the world which are open to him, the martyr decides that his own death is the best of the possible states which are open to him. It is the ethical judgment which argues that the first value ordering is "low" and the second is "high." An individual usually is faced with a hierarchy of value orderings. Thus I may say that A is better than B for "me" but that B is better than A for my family, or that C is better than D for my family but D is better than C for the nation, or that E is better than F for the nation but that F is better than E for the world at large. Each of these value orderings is characteristised by a frame of reference (the self, the family, the nation, the world). Generally speaking ethical theory argues that the larger the frame of reference the "higher" the ethic and the better the value ordering. This rule is not without conceivable exception, however, and the choice of the appropriate frame of reference presents real and difficult problems.

The apparatus of economic analysis, especially the use of opportunity function and indifference curves, can be used to clear up many cases of ethical confusion. Ethical confusion arises when many different points of the field of choice are "bracketed" at the top of the value ordering, or are very close together at the top, so that a very slight shift in preferences or in opportunities may produce large shifts in the decision. The shifts in the communist party line, or the shifts in behavior on the outbreak of war, are examples of dramatic shifts in the *position* chosen because a relatively slight shift in the nature of the opportunities may bring a radically different set of positions to the top of the value ordering. This further emphasizes the proposition that what is actually *selected* as best is apt to depend more on the opportunities than on the preferences. The same set of basic preferences may produce widely differing behavior as opportunities change.

Besides its contribution to ethical theory economics also has an important contribution to make to the sociology of religion and the study of the church as an institution. The economist's basic abstraction of the social institution is that of the "firm," which derives revenue from the sale of a product and is able to produce the product because out of the revenue it can reward the factors of production sufficiently to induce them to make this particular product and not some other. The church as an institution has many of the aspects of a firm. It produces a spiritual rather than a material product (church buildings and furniture come under the heading of plant and equipment rather than of product) nevertheless it is not unreasonable to suppose that the financial contributions which give the organization its revenue are paid "for something" which the contributor receives. Out of these revenues the church must pay what is necessary to attract resources over and above those which are attracted by the purely internal rewards of service. The "success" of the church as measured by the worldly standards of size, membership and income depend on its power to attract revenue on the one hand, and its power to attract resources on the other.

The question what is the "spiritual product" of the church is one of great interest not only to the sociologist of religion but also to the theologian. The truth seems to be that there are many such products; the church is not a single-product firm, but it produces many different products, some of which do not appear in its official prospectuses! People may contribute to the church out of a sheer desire for sociability, or respectability, or acceptability. They may go to church for spiritual entertainment from the minister and the choir, much as they would go to a concert or a play. They may support the church because it is a symbol of a larger culture—for instance of a national or a language group within a larger cosmopolitan culture. They may support the church because they think it is good for their children in some ill-defined way. Or they may support the church because it provides for specifically religious needs—for religious instruction, for salvation, for personal spiritual help. Or the church may be the expression of an individual discipleship and commitment to a person or an ideal. One suspects that the purely "religious" product of the church is a fairly small part of its total social product, even though this may be the ostensible excuse for its existence as an institution.

The question of the organization of the church to supply spiritual products is also somewhat within the purview of the economist. Are there increasing returns to scale—that is, can large churches supply spiritual products (and attract support) more easily, and with less unit expenditure of resources, than small churches? The answer here seems to depend on the nature of the product; churches which give their members respectability, acceptance, emotional security and so on probably have increasing returns to scale and easily become large: churches which appeal to highly special needs or exceptional devotion have diminishing returns to scale and tend to stay small. This is of course the difference between the "church" and the "sect." The ecological competition of churches is thus not very dissimilar from that of firms. Thus in the transportation system we have the railroads, which are something like the Catholic Church (hierarchical, ritualistic): we have the large automobile firms, General Motors, Ford, Chrysler which may perhaps be compared to the great Protestant denominations—Presbyterians, Methodists, Baptists. But we also have sectarian modes of transport (Volkswagens, Renaults, down to three wheelers, motor bikes, bicycles and electric wheel-chairs) which correspond to the smaller and more specialized sects from the Quakers to Jehovah's Witnesses. If theologians are offended by these comparisons I must remind them that even the greatest spirit must inhabit a body, and that bodies are all subject to the laws of the body!

When it comes to questions of high theology, to the great concepts of salvation and redemption, the work of the Living God in history, the nature of Christ and the Holy Spirit, the theological nature of the Church, and so on we would hardly expect a discipline as earthy as economics to make any great contribution. Nevertheless there may be insights from economics which are valuable even here. One reflects, for instance, that all creativity—in art, in music, in architecture, in literature—involves *economizing*—that is making the most of a set of limitations, allocating scarce resources, equating marginal gains to marginal losses. It is *because* the artist is limited by his material that art exists; all creativity is making the best of a bad job, and if there is no bad job to be made the best of—that is, no scarcity, no limitation —there is no art, only formless and cancerous growth. Even when art seeks to escape from one set of limitations (as for instance in modern painting) it must accept another set; otherwise it is mere random dabbling. In contemplating the mystery of the Creation of all things, then, and of their Creator, we may not be surprised to see the same principle at work, and to find the Infinite, in the interests of creation, take on finitude, and the Immortal take on mortality.

Ethics and Business:
An Economist's View[*]

It would be presumptuous for a mere economist to attempt to set forward a complete theory of ethics. However, one cannot talk about this subject at all without outlining a tentative ethical theory. It is not necessary to assume that a single set of ethical principles will guide conduct in all spheres of social life and in all the roles which an individual may play. Nevertheless, if we are to talk about the ethical principles of a part of a society and of an aspect of human behavior, we must be able to see these in the framework of a larger ethical system. Even though I can claim only amateur status as a moral philosopher, I feel it is necessary to say something about ethical principles in general before I can begin to apply them to a business society.

The first principle of my ethical theory is that all individual human behavior of any kind is guided by a value system; that is, by some system of preferences. In this sense everybody has a personal ethical system. No one could live, move, or act without one. We can distinguish between what might be called the "real" personal ethic, which might be deduced from a person's actual behavior, and the "verbal" ethic, which would be derived from his statements. We find it a common—indeed, almost a universal—phenomenon that a person will give lip service to one set of ethical principles, but that in his behavior he will follow another set of values. Without a set of values of some kind, however, his behavior is inexplicable. Even if his behavior is random and irrational it is presumably because he sets a high value on randomness and irrationality. This is a view of human behavior which is derived mainly from economic theory. The economist thinks of behavior in terms of choice. He envisions the individual at any mo-

* *Ethics and Business, Three Lectures* (University Park, Pa.: Penn State Univ. College of Business Administration, 1962), pp. 1–14.

This paper was originally presented at a seminar sponsored by the College of Business Administration of Pennsylvania State University in State College, Pa. on March 19, 1962.

ment faced with a number of alternative images of possible futures, out of which one is selected. The fact that it is selected is a demonstration that it has a higher value for the individual than any of the alternative choices. For the economist, a value system is simply a system of rank order. We look at the field of possible futures and we rank them first, second, third, and so on, which is what the economist means by a utility or welfare function. And having performed this complicated and arduous act, we then behave in such a way that the future which we have ranked first has, we believe, the best chance of being realized. In these terms, of course, even the worst of men has an ethic of his own. If a person prefers to be cruel, mean, and treacherous, he is expressing a value system which ranks these types of behavior high.

It is clear that merely to say that everyone behaves according to a personal ethic or value system does not solve the problem of ethical theory, the major perplexity of which is to develop a rule of choice among possible personal value systems. The individual is faced not only with images of the world which are ranked according to a particular value system, he is faced with a number of different value systems according to which the world may be ranked. Just as there is a problem of choice among alternative futures, so there is a problem of choice among ways of choosing these alternative futures. It is assumed that out of all possible ways of choosing—that is, out of all possible value systems—only one is "right" or "best." This is the ethical value system.

By way of illustration, let us imagine an individual who is at a point of time where he faces three possible futures: A, B, and C. Let us suppose, to simplify matters, that he visualizes the effects of his actions on himself and on others in terms of a single variable which we will call "riches." If he chooses A, he will be a little richer, and other people will be richer too. If he chooses B, he will be greatly richer, and nobody else will be worse off. If he chooses C, he will be a little poorer, but other people will be a lot poorer. Which he chooses, of course, depends on his value system; that is, on his personal ethic. If he has an altruistic personal ethic, in which he enjoys the riches of others as if they were his own, he will probably choose A. If he has a selfish personal ethic, in which he places a high value on his own riches but is indifferent to the condition of others, he is likely to choose B. If he has a malevolent personal ethic, in which he takes a positive satisfaction in the misfortunes of others, he is likely to choose C. Thus, any choice is possible depending on the personal ethic of the individual making the choice.

The ethical problem, however, is the problem of what my personal ethic shall be. Some may wish to argue that this choice is not really open to the individual, that his personal ethic is simply a result of his life experience and of the various punishing or rewarding consequences of various acts. If we admit the possibility of choice at all, however, it seems to me that we must admit the possibility of choice among value systems as well as among possible futures; a determinism which excludes the ethical problem also excludes the possibility of any rational behavior at all.

My third principle is that no a priori proof is possible in any proposition of ethical theory; that is, we cannot arrive at a rule of choice which will always give us the best personal ethic by a process involving pure logic, without reference to the world of experience. This does not mean, however, that ethical problems are in principle insoluble. The problem here is essentially one of limiting the field of choice among personal ethical systems. We may not by pure reasoning alone be able to limit the choice to a single system. This does not mean, however, that no limitation of this choice is possible. In the first place some limitation of choice can be made by a *reductio ad absurdum* argument. Suppose we had a society in which the prevailing personal ethic involved killing all children at birth. It is clear that a society of this kind would not persist beyond a generation and its prevailing personal ethic would die with it. Thus, even though we may not wish to set up survival value as an absolute standard for the choice of personal ethical systems, it is clear that survival value strongly limits the choices which may in practice be made. The history of personal value systems can be regarded as something like an evolutionary process in which there is constant mutation as charismatic individuals are able to impose a personal value system on a society or are able to initiate a subculture within a society. In all societies groups are constantly arising which proclaim new ethical standards and which seek to obtain adherents to these standards. Each mutation, however, encounters the selective process, and in the biological world some mutations have survival value and some do not. Some may have survival value in the short run but not in the long. For example, the Shakers developed a personal value system which excluded sexual intercourse. Whatever its merits (and these were, no doubt, for some individuals considerable, or the Shakers would never have come into being), the system proved fatal to the subculture in the long run.

I am not suggesting that survival is the only test of validity. I am suggesting that it narrows the field of choice. It does not necessarily narrow the field to a single position. Within cultures that have survival value there are still better or worse cultures by other criteria. A culture, for instance, may have survival value and yet be extremely disagreeable for the individuals to live in. On the other hand, if it is agreeable but does not have survival value, we must exclude it from our system of possible choices simply because it excludes itself. Thus, even though an ultimate and final answer to the question as to whether any particular value system is "right" may not be possible, the question as to its rightness is meaningful simply because it is possible, by taking careful thought and by knowing more about the world, to limit the field of choice. The more we limit the field of choice, however, the harder it becomes to resolve the arguments about how to limit it further. Some, for instance, may not wish to exclude those value systems which lead to unhappiness if by excluding them we also exclude certain aspects of nobility and creativity. The solution which seems to be working itself out is one in which we have a number of different cultures, each embodying a different ethical principle. These differences, however, may correspond to deep differences in human nature, which may even have a genetic base. Within a complex society there is room for many such subcultures and many ethical systems, ranging from the Amish to the Zoroastrians. It is one of the great virtues of the division of labor, as Durkheim pointed out, that it permits a diversity of subcultures and therefore a diversity of ethical systems within the framework of a larger society; it is not necessary to impose a single ethical system on the whole society.

My fourth proposition is that corresponding to every culture or subculture there is an ethical system which both creates it and is created by it. In other words, any ethical system is embodied in a social system of which it is an essential part. Changes in ethical systems inevitably produce changes in the social system, and changes in the social system likewise react upon the ethical system. Sometimes a change in the ethical system is embodied in explicit form, in the shape, for instance, of a Bible, a Koran, or a Book of Mormon, around which a subculture is then built. Sometimes the ethical system exists in an almost unconscious set of rules of behavior and norms of conduct (as in the development of mercantile capitalism) which never become embodied in sacred writings or achieve any charismatic power, yet which profoundly affect human conduct and are transmitted from generation to generation. The relationships here are complex in the extreme. Where an overt ethical system, such as the Christian ethic, contains elements which are inappropriate to the social system in which it is embedded, it may remain the overt system because the covert system by which people really act is different. On the other hand, the overt system exercises a constant pressure on the society in which it is recognized. The dynamic character of a society, in fact, often depends on there being a certain tension between its overt and its covert ethical systems. A culture in which the overt and covert ethic coincide and in which there is no hypocrisy is likely to be deplorably stable. Where there is hypocrisy, there is a force within the culture itself making for change. A good example of this is the constant pressure in the American society towards a better integration of the Negro community: a pressure which is imposed upon us by the fact that our overt ideals and our actual behavior do not correspond. Because the overt ideals have a sacred character about them, they are not easy to change. Therefore, they exercise a constant pressure on the society to bring its practice closer to its professions. Where there are no overt ideals, a gap between ideals and practice is easily closed by changing the ideals. This is why a society with impossible ideals is likely to be highly dynamic, whereas a society with possible ideals is likely to stagnate.

I am arguing then that we must reject the type of ethical relativism which says that all ethical answers are equally valid, just as we must reject the cultural relativism which refuses to raise the question about the value of a culture. Even though we cannot regard ethical norms as absolute in the sense that they are independent of the cultural milieu, the ethical problem in any culture is a meaningful problem because it is usually fruitful to raise the question as to whether better solutions than the one currently in vogue are possible. Once a society ceases to raise this kind of question, once it ceases to examine itself in ethical terms, that society is very likely doomed to stagnation and to eventual decay.

Before going on to apply these principles to the ethical problems of a business society, we must take a brief look at the nature of social systems in general, for we must be able to see a business society as a special case among possible social systems. I define a business society as a social system which is organized primarily through the institution of exchange. Exchange, however, is not the only organizer of social systems and is not the only organizer even in a business society. A social system consists essentially of relationships among persons. If we want to be more exact we might even define it as a system of relationships among roles, for very often it is not the whole person that is significant but the person acting in a role, and one person may occupy many roles in the course of a lifetime. The conflict of roles within the person would then be regarded as essentially a problem of the social system. There are, of course, a great many relationships which are possible between persons and among roles. However, most of these can be classified into three major categories. The first of these is the threat system, in which one says to another, "You do something nice to me or I will do something nasty to you." Almost all prebusiness civilizations were based primarily on threats, from Sumeria and Egypt to ancient Rome. Civilization was founded first, on the development of a food surplus from the food producer, more than he needed to eat himself, and, second, on the ability of coercive organization of the society to take this surplus away from the food producer and use it for the purposes of the elite, whether these were art, architecture, religion, or war. Slavery is the typical institution of a threat-based civilization. A threat system, however, is intrinsically unstable. It tends to pass over from the unilateral threat system, which is a powerful organizer if unchallenged, into a bilateral threat system or deterrence: "If you do something nasty to me I will do something nasty to you." Deterrence is an inherently unstable social system because of the fact that the threat is only capable of being an organizer as long as it is credible, and it is only credible if it is occasionally carried out. A system of deterrence, therefore, always involves the eventual carrying out of mutual threats, and when this happens everybody is worse off. The threat system then becomes a negative-sum game, like the "prisoners' dilemma" of game theory, in which the dynamics of the system leads everybody into positions where everybody is worse off.

By contrast, the exchange system, which may be regarded as peculiarly characteristic of a business society, is a positive-sum game and is a much more successful organizer. Exchange is the relationship whereby one says to another, "You do something nice to me and I will do something nice to you." An exchange system, therefore, is based upon promises rather than threats, and a business society especially is built upon what Harry Scherman once called "the promises men live by." The great advantage of a promise system over a threat system is that when the promises are carried out, as they have to be if they are to be effective in organizing behavior, everybody is better off rather than worse off. Accordingly, a promise system is a positive-sum game. It is not surprising, therefore, that in the long run the exchange system has been a more powerful organizer than the threat system and that, for instance, a slave economy has never been able to compete on the free market successfully with a free labor economy.

In addition to the threat system and the exchange system, there is another set of relationships among persons and roles which may be called generally the integrative system. This is a rather heterogeneous category which includes persuasion, teaching, and love: "What you want, I want." All social systems and subsystems are based on mixtures of these three major elements, in varying proportions. Thus, in an authoritarian state or in a military organization, the threat system is dominant, but exchange is still present. The member of the organization gets something for what he puts into it. The integrative system likewise must be present; otherwise generals and dictators would not have to make speeches. No organization can be successful unless its members identify in some degree with the purpose of the organization as such. At the other extreme we have the family or the larger utopian community, in which the integrative system is dominant, and in which people do what they do because of persuasion, teaching, or love. Even in the family or the integrative community, however, there must be some exchange; there must be some sense in which the individual gets something for what he gives up, and there is likewise at least the remains of the threat system, for even in the most loving community there is the underlying threat of expulsion or of the withdrawal of love. One suspects that the stability of a social system depends upon the proportion in which the three main organizers are employed. A system which tries to rely too much on any single one of them is likely to be unstable. A pure system of coercion without any elements of exchange or integration is likely to arouse such opposition against itself as to be unstable. The history of utopian communities is a sad commentary on the difficulty of organizing communities beyond the size of the natural family on a basis of the integrative system. Love, where there is no exchange, easily passes over into threats, and there is a very real sense in which exchange is the food of love. A system of pure exchange, however, is also likely to be unstable. On the one side, it may find itself incapable of dealing with incipient threat systems which arise outside it, for we cannot always buy off the threatener, and tribute has a way of getting more and more expensive. At the other side, an exchange system does not satisfy adequately the basic desire of man for rich interpersonal relationships. Prostitution, which is a solution to the problem of sex at the level of exchange, is seldom regarded as wholly satisfactory simply because it does not satisfy the demand for richness in relationships. Thus, while exchange systems may reinforce the integrative system, it also follows that without an integrative system, the exchange system itself is likely to be unstable and is likely to disintegrate toward a threat system.

It is now high time to get past the preliminaries and begin to apply these principles to the ethics of a business society. We should notice first that no society is a pure business society. No society, that is, has ever organized itself around the institutions of exchange alone. Every society has a government which organizes the threat system and every society has integrative institutions in the family, the church, the school, the club, and so on. Furthermore, business institutions themselves, such as the corporation, the bank, the organized commodity or security exchanges, and the labor union, are not organized solely by exchange even though we can properly regard exchange—that is, buying and selling and the transformations of inputs and outputs that go on in the process of production—as being the major organizer of the system. There remain, however, coercive or threat system elements in the threat of cutting off exchange, the withdrawal of custom, quitting, firing, and so on. There may be internal threat systems in the shape of industrial discipline, and there are also extensive integrative systems in the attempt to build morale, loyalty, the corporate image, systems of authority and instruction, and so on. Nevertheless, we shall not go far wrong if we suppose that anything which undermines the institutions of exchange and the organizing power of exchange undermines the business system.

Again the first thing to note is that there are certain individual value systems which undermine the institutions of exchange and are, therefore, extremely threatening to a business system. An exchange system, for instance, cannot flourish in the absence of a minimum of simple honesty because an exchange system is an exchange of promises, and honesty is the fulfillment of promises. If we extend the concept of honesty a little further into the fulfillment of role expectations, we see this also is essential for the successful operation of a system based on exchange. This is why the institutions of capitalism cannot operate successfully in the total absence of what might be called the puritan virtues. Thus, if capitalism is to work successfully, there must be defenses in the society against dishonesty. These defenses may lie in part in the threat system; that is, in the system of law and police. But I suspect that a good part of the burden must be carried by the integrative system in the internalization of these moral standards in the individual. This is done in the home, in the church, and in the school, but it is also done, of course, by the example of those around the individual and especially the example of his peer group. For this reason, the building of honesty into a culture in which it does not already exist is a difficult matter, for dishonesty tends to perpetuate itself through the teaching process which it develops. Here again there is a constant struggle between the overt and the covert elements in the value system; however, if this results in a collapse of the overt system—in a general lapse into cynicism and the overt acceptance of a dishonest covert system—a society is doomed.

The second set of problems relates to the political images, value systems, and institutions which provide the framework for a market-oriented economy. Because exchange is not sufficient to organize society by itself, even in a society which is organized mainly by exchange, there must be a minimum governmental framework. The success of the market economy of the United States, for instance, can be attributed in large part to the fact that there has been no hesitation in using the instruments of government for economic purposes where this has seemed to be desirable. An exchange economy, for instance, may pass over into a degree of monopolistic organization which undermines it. Hence, we have antitrust and related legislation, which may not always carry out its intent but which profoundly affects the structure of the economy and the norms of business behavior. As it has been well said, the ghost of Senator Sherman sits at every board of directors' table in America. Similarly, because a pure market economy is susceptible to meaningless fluctuations of inflation or of unemployment, there must be a cybernetic machinery in government to stabilize the general level of the economy. Political images and value systems which are hostile to this necessary governmental framework, even though they may be derived from a moral commitment to the exchange economy, are in fact inimical to it.

The third ethical problem of a business society arises out of the fact that the institutions of exchange in themselves do not develop enough of the integrative system. Exchange is a highly abstract relationship. It is something, indeed, which can be done just as well by a machine as by a person in many cases, as the rise of vending machines indicates. It is precisely because exchange is an abstract relationship that it is capable of creating organizations on such a large scale. A large organization would be impossible if every member had to have a rich personal relationship with every other. This, indeed, is the rock on which all utopian communities have foundered. At some points in the society, however, there must be personal relationships which are richer than those of the excange relationship if the society and its activities are to have meaning and significance for the individuals. The poets, preachers, and philosophers have, on the whole, taken a rather dim view of trade ("all is seared with trade," says Gerard Manley Hopkins, "bleared, smeared with toil"). In spite of the success of a business society in increasing productivity and in providing for human wants, it has a tendency to undermine itself because of its inability to generate affection. It is a positive-sum game in which everybody benefits, but in which the game itself is apparently so lacking in emotional effect that it does not produce loyalty, love, and self-sacrifice. Very few people have ever died for a Federal Reserve Bank, and nobody suggests that they should. Consequently when the institutions of a business society come under attack from those who are emotionally committed to another way of organizing economic life, they often fail to generate in their own supporters the same degree of emotional commitment. The situation is, indeed, even worse than I have suggested, for when business institutions, such as corporations, attempt to develop emotional commitment and try to develop welfare capitalism, baseball teams, company songs, and the school spirit, the overall effect is likely to be slightly ridiculous, like that of a good solid workhorse putting on wings and trying to set up in business as a Pegasus.

Thus, we face this dilemma: if a business society is to survive it must develop an integrative system and integrative institutions, but the peculiar institutions of a business society (such as markets, corporations, banks, and so on), because they are essentially instrumental in character, are not capable of developing a powerful integrative system in themselves. If market institutions are to survive, therefore, they must be supplemented by a matrix of integrative institutions, such as the family, the church, the school, and the nation, which develop individual value systems based on love, self-sacrifice, identification with goals outside the person, and altruism.

Unless these integrative institutions exist, there is grave danger that the market institutions may develop a personal ethic which is inimical to their survival in the individuals who operate them. The man whose life is lived wholly within the pages of account books and who devotes all his attention to the minutiae of economic life and organization may find that the internalization of the essential virtues of probity and honesty gradually weakens. The exchange system almost inevitably provides opportunities for individuals to make personal gains by the sacrifice of moral principles because the institutions of exchange, in themselves, provide neither the policing nor the internalization—that is, neither the threat system nor the integrative system—by which these moral values can be sustained. A society which devotes a disproportionate amount of its life and energy to the exchange system may find this system eventually undermined. On the other hand it is equally true that when coercive systems, such as the state or the military, or integrative institutions, such as the church or the school, attempt to go into trade—that is, into the exchange system—they are apt to be very unsuccessful. The problem of society, like so many other problems, is a problem of finding the right proportions. Disproportionate emphasis on either the coercive systems, the market system, or the integrative system is likely to result in a corruption of the moral life and the eventual disintegration of the society. These considerations may help to illuminate what is undoubtedly one of the most complex problems of our day: the ideological struggle between socialism and capitalism. The ethical appeal of socialism is primarily to the integrative system. The exchange system is despised as being somehow a low and unworthy form of human activity, and in a sense the ultimate ideal of the socialist is a society in which all things are done for love and not for money. In practice, unfortunately, the attempt to abolish exchange as a major organizer of society and in particular to abolish the institution of private property in commodities (which is, of course, an essential condition of exchange, for we cannot exchange what we do not have) results not in the replacement of exchange by love as the major organizer of the system but rather in the replacement of exchange by coercion and by threats. In the mild socialisms of Western Europe private property and the exchange system still remain as the principal organizers of economic life, and the threat system is, therefore, not so much in evidence. However, in the thoroughgoing socialism of the communist countries, which have become "one-firm states," the threat system pervades the whole society and even gobbles up, as it did under Stalin, the originators of the revolution themselves. It is this coercive element in a socialist society which makes it so unacceptable to the developed societies of the West and which makes it seem almost like an industrial feudalism.

Nevertheless, the threat system is not the whole story, and the strength of communism lies not in its coercive power but in its ability to develop an integrative system of organizing economic life. I know of no better illustration of this than an amusing misunderstanding which took place in a seminar of Russian and American young people at which I was a consultant. An American student made an excellent little speech in which he said that one of the great values of American society which we prize very highly was that a man should "think for himself." A young Russian then got up and said that he did not think a man ought to think for himself, he thought a man ought to think for others! The Americans were amused at this remarkable misunderstanding and then had to explain why they were amused. Eventually some sort of communication was established, and some of the Russians, I hope, appreciated that independence of mind and altruism are not incompatible values.

Much of the moral appeal of communism, however, rests precisely on its appeal to the altruism of the individual and to the desire we all have, in greater or lesser degrees, to identify ourselves with a larger body and to work for "others." We must make it quite clear to ourselves and to the world that altruism is in no way inconsistent with the institutions of the market or with the organization of society through exchange. There is nothing in a profit system which requires a narrow selfishness and a lack of identification with mankind on the part of the profit maker. This confusion between the profit system, as an organizer of economic life, and the "profit motive," in the bad sense of unadulterated lust for selfish gain, is responsible for a great deal of confusion in social thought. We can, indeed, argue that the profit system will operate successfully only if the profit motive is constantly tempered by altruism, by a sense of public responsibility, and by the sense of identification of the individual with the larger community. Here again, however, the problem of balance is crucial. Pure altruism is no more desirable than pure selfishness. It is one of the great advantages of a system of private property that it clearly limits the responsibilities of the individual to that which is immediate to him. Protestations of general love for mankind are apt to sound hollow from a person who neglects his immediate responsibility to his own children, his own neighbors, and those who are his partners in the complex of exchange relationships.

The challenge of socialism to an absolutely pure market economy, unrestrained by coercion and unmodified by love, would be a very servere one. We can, however, assert with some confidence that in what might be called the North Atlantic Community the challenge of socialism has been profitably met. We need not hesitate to admit that in large part it has been the socialist challenge which has enabled us to modify the market economy in the direction of a better balance among the three organizing elements. If we admit this, we can challenge the socialist world also to achieve a better balance, to make more use of the market as an organizer where this is more effective, and to abandon its undue reliance on the coercive system without abandoning its very proper appeal to the integrative system and to the identification, at some levels, of the individual with the great society of mankind.

IV

Towards Politics

Social Justice in Social Dynamics[*]

I propose to approach the problem of social justice as an economist and social scientist in a manner somewhat different from that which is customary among the philosophers. The philosopher treats the concept of justice as essentially a normative concept. He is concerned with abstract notions of what is right, good, and just. He is concerned with what ought to be, not necessarily with what is. These normative discussions are important and I would not for a moment wish to decry their value. There is, however, another point of view from which the problem of social justice can be examined. This might be called the *positive* or *operational* point of view in which social justice—or at least the image of social justice as it exists in the minds of the members of society—is an essential variable in determining the dynamic processes and the evolution of that society.

By "social dynamics," I mean neither more nor less than social evolution; that is, the whole great process by which a society moves from Monday to Tuesday to Wednesday and so on. Social evolution is, of course, a process of extreme complexity. It can be illuminated, however, by theoretical models which are drawn essentially from the processes of biological evolution. Although there are great differences between biological evolution and social evolution, there are important similarities as well. The most important point of similarity is the fact that the notion of ecological succession and of a dynamic based on mutation and selection applies to both. Biological evolution can be regarded as a succession of short-run biological equilibria of the ecosystem. A pond, for instance, can be regarded as an equilibrium system of interacting populations of different chemical and biological species. This equilibrium is likely to survive small disturbances. If, for instance, ten per cent of one kind of fish are taken out of a pond, the proportions among the populations of the different species in the

---

[*] In: *Social Justice*, Richard B. Brandt, ed., © 1962. (New York: Prentice-Hall (Spectrum S-38), 1962), pp. 73–92. Reprinted by permission of Prentice-Hall, Inc. Englewood Cliffs, N.J.

This paper was originally presented as part of a lecture series at Swarthmore College, Swarthmore, Pennsylvania, on March 19, 1961.

pond will be upset, but it is likely that in a year or two they will be re-established. Yet even in the absence of external forces, the equilibrium will gradually change over the long run because of certain irreversible factors in the very processes by which the equilibrium is maintained. The metabolic processes of life, for instance, absorb carbon from the air and the pond gradually will fill up and become a swamp. Mutations occur in the genetic materials of the different organic species. Most of these disturb the equilibrium for a while and disappear. Occasionally, however, one appears which gives the organism—and eventually the species—an advantage so great that a *new* and lasting population equilibrium takes the place of the old. Sometimes the ecological revolution is swift and dramatic: a small change in the environment produces a drastic change in the population of species. The precarious equilibrium of the forest and the prairie in the Middle West before the advent of civilization was an interesting example of this point.

Society, likewise, may be thought of as a large pond filled with interacting populations. In addition to biological and inorganic species, there are social species such as automobiles, schools, gas stations, teachers, clubs, philosophers, corporations, states, missiles, and ideas. It is the last of these which constitutes the essential difference between a social system and a biological system and between social evolution and biological evolution. Below the level of the human species, ideas or images are present only in a very rudimentary form: there are instincts that are genetically determined and behavior patterns which may properly be attributed to images—that is, to cognitive structures within the organisms concerned. These images, however, are not learned from experience, but are built into the organism by the growth process which is guided by the genes. The bird builds its nest and the spider spins its web because in some sense it "knows" how to do this, but this knowledge has not been created by a learning process and has not been erected by experience. The image, the instinct, is built into the organism itself by its genetic processes of growth.

The principle of learning from experience begins to appear in the evolutionary process only with the higher animals. A cat, for instance, behaves like a cat not only because of its genetic constitution but also because it has learned things from its mother as a kitten. In a very real sense, cats have a culture in a way that insects do not. In the development of the human species, however, still another principle comes onto the evolutionary stage. The human nervous system is capable of creating symbolic images and modifying and transmitting these images through speech. Cats teach through signs; humans teach through symbols. This seemingly small change has resulted in an enormous acceleration of the pace of evolution. Under the impact of man, the face of the earth and the composition of its species changes at a pace a hundred or even a thousand times greater than it had done previously. This pace accelerates all the time as social evolution produces more and more complex social forms.

One may be tempted to ask, "But what does this have to do with social justice?" The answer is that the images that men have of themselves and of the society around them—because of their impact on human behavior—are an important, indeed, almost a dominant element in the course of social evolution. In these images the idea of social justice plays a significant role. In an earlier work,[1] I developed a theory of human behavior (or at least a way of looking at it) as consisting essentially of setting in motion a course of events which is intended to carry the person into the most highly valued of his images of potential futures. This is, of course, an economist's way of looking at the matter: to regard behavior as being fundamentally subject to choice. Choice is a process by which we scan a number of possible futures and allot some ordinal numbers such as first, second, third, etc., to elements of this set, and pick out the element which is labeled first. All that is strictly necessary for this process is that we divide the set of possible futures into two sub-sets, one of which we label first and the other second. If the set labeled first contains only one element, this constitutes the chosen future and we behave accordingly.

The future, of course, does not always turn out as we expect, for the choice of a future does not necessarily guarantee it. The future, however, is determined by the choices that we make. That is, there will exist a set function relating the chosen future to the actual future. Thus suppose that F_1, F_2, ... F_n is the set of images of the possible future, and G_1, G_2, ... G_n is the set of actual futures. The choice of, say, F_1, does not necessarily mean that we shall proceed into the identically corresponding actual future G_1; it does mean, however, that for any F_1 that we select, there is some G_j which corresponds to it. For many choices, there is a high probability that G_j will, in fact, be the same as G_1, but this is not necessarily true.

If, for instance, I find myself lecturing at Swarthmore on March 19 of a certain year, it is because at some earlier time I had an image of time and space in which, out of all possible futures, my lecturing in Swarthmore on March 19 was labeled first in my value system. Because

---

[1] *The Image* (Ann Arbor: The University of Michigan Press, 1956).

of this value preference, the formation of which is irrelevant here, I performed certain acts—such as telephoning a travel agency, picking up a plane ticket, driving to an airport, getting on a plane, and so on—all of which were designed in my image of cause and effect to make the image of the future correspond with the actuality. Without having formed and selected the image "in Swarthmore on March the 19th," I would certainly not be there. But the mere fact of my having the image, and of setting in motion certain behavior to realize it, did not guarantee that the image and the actual future would correspond. As I write this on March the 9th I must recognize a certain possibility that I will not be at Swarthmore on March the 19th. I may be taken ill; trains and planes may be immobilized by strikes, or Swarthmore may be hit by a nuclear bomb before that date. In the absence of extraordinary events, however, I shall be somewhat surprised if the actual future does not correspond to my image.

How does the image of social justice fit into this pattern of human behavior? My visit to Swarthmore is clearly—in my own eyes—good, or I would not go. I am not sure, however, that I have thought of this particular activity as being just or unjust either socially or individually. I might feel, I suppose, that it is unjust that I should be asked to give this lecture when Professor X obviously would have given a much better one. On the other hand, Professor X may have already been asked and refused, in which case the injustice is lessened. It may even be that the organizers of this lecture believed that, in fact, I am the best person to give it. In this they may be unwise and mistaken, but error, or lack of wisdom, does not constitute injustice. It may be also that the reward which I will get for the lecture, both the honorarium and the pleasure I will receive at being among old friends at Swarthmore, is more than I deserve. On the other hand, I am not sure that I can provide an operational definition of the concept of desert. If we all get our deserts, as Hamlet said, "Who should 'scape whipping?"

It may be that my total reward for giving this lecture is larger than the smallest amount for which I would have consented to come. In this case, I am getting what the economist calls *economic rent* or *economic surplus*, and this is perhaps in some sense unjust. If it is unjust, I must confess, it is a burden that I will bear with some equanimity. It is clear from this that my concept of social justice played a very small part in making the decision to come and give a lecture about it. This fact demonstrates that the image of social justice is not a universal element in that valuation process by which men come to decisions. There are, however, some choices in which the image of social justice plays an important part, and it is these which we must identify if we are to examine the role which the image of social justice plays in the dynamics of society.

Before proceeding in full cry after these decisions in which the image of social justice is significant or even dominant, let me pause for a moment to look at the role which is played in decision-making by the perception of divergences between a perceived real situation and a perceived ideal situation. The concept of perceived divergence between real and ideal values also plays a dominant role in the explanation of the behavior of what have come to be called *cybernetic* systems, or control systems. A thermostatic system, for instance, has an ideal temperature at which it is set, say 70°. It has a thermometer which enables it to "perceive" the actual temperature. If the actual temperature falls below the ideal, the system sets in motion behavior to warm things up. If the perceived actual temperature rises above the ideal, the system sets in action behavior which will result in cooling things down. This is the principle of homeostasis which is of such great importance in understanding what Cannon called the "wisdom of the body." This principle can also be invoked to explain a great deal of human behavior at the cognitive or affective level. We keep our friendships in repair by much the same process by which we keep a constant temperature in our bodies or in the house: if a friendship is cooling below our ideal level, a letter, a telephone call, or a Christmas card may warm it up. If a friend is getting a little too affectionate and demanding, there are many ways of increasing the social distance which will cool him down.

The wisdom of the spirit, of course, consists in knowing where to set the ideal. A purely homeostatic mechanism is—within wide limitations—quite indifferent as to where the ideal is set. My home thermostat will maintain a steady temperature anywhere between fifty and eighty degrees. It is up to me to set it at the level which best reconciles the claims of health, vitality, and comfort. As we move toward social systems, the problem of where to set the ideal becomes of increasing importance. There is what may be called a homeostatic apparatus within the social system, which acts to reduce divergences between perceived actual and ideal values. In this homeostatic sense, social justice is an ideal; that is, it is something divergence from which is perceived and acts as a cue to behavior.

The perception of divergence between the perceived real value and the ideal value of any important psychological variable—that is, of any variable which is strongly related to utility or general satisfaction—may be labeled *discontent*. In this ·sense, discontent can be regarded as the prime mover of man to action provided that his image of cause and effect permits him to believe himself capable of such action as to reduce the divergence between the perceived real and the ideal. We may notice a point here, the importance of which will be clearer later. The divergence between the real and the ideal may be reduced by acting so as to manipulate the real. But it may also be reduced by adjusting the ideal. This is the way of renunciation—of wanting what you get, rather than getting what you want. It is traditionally associated with Eastern philosophies, and if adopted it is a powerful deterrent to rapid change.

The adjustment of the ideal is not, of course, necessarily "irrational." If activity results in a continued failure to reduce the gap between the perceived real and the ideal, a person may follow one of three courses. He may change his perception. This may be dangerous if the perception differs much from something which we can call reality, but, on the other hand, it is also comforting. A man may say that his wife really loves him in spite of that fact that she continually hits him over the head with the frying pan. Modern studies of perception indicate that what we think of as sense data are, in fact, so strongly guided by existing beliefs and by our value system that we cannot afford to dismiss as immediately invalid the alteration of perception in response to homeostatic failure. Only one cheer, however, for this solution; we do well to be suspicious of it and to give at least two cheers for the second alternative, which is the readjustment of the ideal. At its worst, this can be a retreat into apathy or into criminality. But somewhere along the line, as the bloom of youth is knocked off us by our contact with the world, we make this kind of adjustment. The third reaction, and the only one for which I am inclined to give three cheers, is that of finding a new course of behavior and of developing a more accurate image of cause and effect. Faced with homeostatic failure, the schizophrenic adjusts his perceptions, the weak man hauls down his ideals, and the hero puts in a new furnace and insulates the house. The wisdom of the spirit consists in the knowledge of the proper proportions of these three responses—the blind eye, the struck flag, and the renewed effort.

Now let us return to the concept of discontent and its relation to social justice. The crucial distinction here—both from the point of view of the definition of social justice, and also from the point of view of its impact on the general dynamics of society—is the distinction between what might be called personal discontent on the one hand and political discontent on the other. These are distinguished mainly by the reactions they arouse. Personal discontent is the individual's dissatisfaction with his place in society, created by his perception of a gap between his present condition within the framework of his society and the position which he feels he might attain through his own efforts. Personal discontent, therefore, drives the individual to seek a new situation within the existing framework. It does not drive him to seek to change the framework itself. If he is discontented with his income, he looks for a better job, he goes to night school, or he tries to marry a rich woman. If he is discontented with his marriage, he arranges for a divorce. If he dislikes the town where he lives, or if he cannot get along with his neighbors, he moves. Personal discontent is the muscle which moves Adam Smith's invisible hand. It has profound impact on the dynamics of society. It diminishes one occupation and increases another. It raises the population of one place and lowers that of another.

The political consequences of personal discontent may be prodigious, but they are indirect. The individual's political discontent has direct political consequences. Political discontent is discontent with the framework of the society in which a man operates. It may arise because of his inability to deal with personal discontents. He may have failed in his own efforts to improve his position: his new job is no better than the old, the new town and the new neighbors present all the old problems, his new wife turns out to be just as unsatisfactory as the old one. A purely rational individual, under these circumstances, might seek more fundamental means of assuaging personal discontent, such as religion or psychoanalysis. Failing this, however, or even after this, personal discontent may be redirected at the social framework. His failure to deal with his own discontent, he argues, cannot be the result of a personal deficiency or of ill-considered decisions. It must be the result of larger external forces—"the system." Political discontent does not always have to have disreputable origins, however; it may be, and frequently is, an expression of the noblest and the most altruistic motives. Political discontent is frequently found in persons whose personal satisfactions are of the highest, but who are observant and sensitive and who identify themselves with those who seem to be ill-treated or unhappy or unjustly served by the society—even though these others may not feel personal discontent with their treatment by society; yet even this form of political discontent may be said to arise from the individual's personal failure: his inability to do in a personal capacity what he would like for others. This failure, however, has a much more noble origin than the political discontent which arises out of merely personal failure to improve one's own position.

Whatever the sources of political discontent, its effects are frequently similar. It manifests itself in agitation for some kind of political

or social change. The word *agitation*, itself, derives from a very accurate analogy. The politically discontented individual acts, as it were,
to increase the Brownian movement of society, to stir up discontent
in others in the hope that the increased movement of large numbers of
individuals will eventually affect a change in the social vessel which
holds them. Political discontent, therefore, is expressed in organization,
meetings, propaganda, pamphlets, and—in its more extreme form—
armed rebellion. All wars, in fact, as distinct from piracy and free-
booting, must be regarded as expressions of political discontent. In
some ways, the political party, the election, the letters to the editor,
the pamphlets, the speeches, the processions, the sit-downs, the sit-ins,
and other forms of nonviolent resistance must be regarded as an organi-
zationally superior substitute for war. The characteristic of political
discontent is struggle. This is in marked contrast to the reaction to
personal discontent which is adjustment, to which such struggle as
there is is merely incidental.

The concept of social justice, because it is largely irrelevant to the
satisfaction of personal discontent, seems to be irrelevant to a very
large area of social life. The concept of social justice is quite fundamental, however, to political discontent, for it presumably represents
an ideal state of society from which the existing state is perceived as
a significant divergence. It is this divergence between the existing and
the ideal state of society which is perceived as the motivation for
homeostatic change. Even here, however, the ideal contains a good
deal more than the concept of justice. A good deal of thinking about
war and peace at the moment, for instance, reflects the view that, in
the present stage of military technology, it would be worthwhile paying a good deal in injustice for the establishment of a stable peace.
Although war has historically been one of the ways in which men
have attempted to correct what they perceive as injustices, at the present time it may be that war has become too expensive and too dangerous as a means of moving the world toward a more just order.
Similarly, there may be a conflict between the claims of social justice
and the desire for economic development. In certain societies, a higher
rate of economic development may be achieved by riding roughshod
over the more delicate issues of social justice. A similar competitive
relationship may exist between justice and freedom. Freedom and
justice are hard to measure, but it does seem that one may be expanded
at the expense of the other. The institutions of justice inevitably limit
much of the freedom of some, and some of the freedom of all. It may
be argued that this limitation of the freedom of some is in the interests
of greater freedom for all, but this conclusion is by no means neces-

sary. It can easily be shown that an over-meticulous concern for justice can easily interfere with peace, order, economic growth, and freedom. An obsession with "fair" shares may inhibit the growth of the total social product, may lead to costly conflict, or may severely limit the freedom of action of the individuals in the society.

It is clear from the above that political discontent has a good many dimensions, depending on the object of discontent. If there is discontent with the anarchy of violence and war which results from the present social system, political agitation will be directed toward the establishment of world government. Discontent with the rate of economic growth may lead to agitation for a self-conscious economic program for the creation of political institutions to promote growth. Discontent with restrictions on personal liberty or with the subordinate position of a particular people or race may lead to agitation for civil liberties, national liberation or civil rights. Discontent with the distribution of the privileges and burdens of society—the feeling that some are getting more than they deserve and some are getting less—may lead to agitation for progressive income and inheritance taxes, or even for expropriation of property. These last two forms of political discontent are the most closely allied to the concept of social justice. The concept of justice is profoundly two-dimensional. It encompasses, on the one hand, what might be called "disalienation," that is, the idea that nobody should be alienated from the society in which he lives. This is the aspect of justice which is reflected in the struggle for equality: the equality of individuals before the law, the equality of racial and religious groups in the culture as well as before the law and, in its extreme form, equality of income. The concept here is a familistic one—society is conceived as a great family from whose table not even the humblest of her members shall be excluded.

The second dimension of justice is the concept of *desert*. In a just society, each gets what he deserves, neither more nor less. It is this concept which gives rise to a productivity theory of distribution according to contribution, and leads to the view that he who does not contribute to the social product does not deserve any reward out of it. There is considerable tension between these two dimensions of justice. In general, they cannot both be satisfied. Many sit down at the table of society who do not deserve to be there and many eat from it who have not made any contribution. On the strict desert theory, the young may be admitted on the grounds that they will make a contribution in the future, and the old may be admitted on the grounds that they have made a contribution in the past. However, this leaves the question of the sick, the incompetent, and the mentally deficient. We face the dilemma, therefore, that if everyone gets his deserts, some may be driven from the table; and if everyone comes to the table, some may not get their deserts. In practice, this seems to be resolved by the establishment of a social minimum as reflected, for instance, in the poor law, in social security, and in various welfare services. The principle of desert may come into play above this social minimum. That is to say, society lays a modest table at which all can sup and a high table at which the deserving can feast. This general principle can be traced in almost all practical efforts to solve the problem.

The establishment of this principle, useful as it is, leaves a very great many problems unsolved. It is one thing to establish the principle of a social minimum; it is quite another thing to determine where this minimum shall be set. It may be set at the utmost limits of Malthusian rigor—a bare table with bread and water and no propagation. It may be set higher with more sympathy, but also, perhaps, with less long-run validity as in Speenhamland and in aid-to-dependent-children. Then, above whatever minimum has been set, the principle of to each according to his deserts may be permitted to prevail. Within these limitations of the principle, however, a wide range of controversy is possible. There is an almost universal consensus that an unrestricted market economy will give the rich more than they deserve. Hence, many countries impose progressive taxation designed, not with universal success, to diminish the divergence in income between the rich and the poor. The actual schedule of taxation in any country and the rate at which it progresses seem to depend largely on historical accident. There is no clearly ideal tax schedule, and there is a strong tendency for almost any schedule, once established, to persist. There may be political discontent with existing schedules, especially among the members within the upper brackets, but it seems to be very hard to translate this discontent into political action and into legislative results. The agitation to limit tax rates in the United States to 25 per cent of income, for instance, has achieved nothing. It is very hard to make the poor and the middle class who make up the majority feel a great deal of sympathy for the worries of the rich, and hence the rich in a democratic society have little political bargaining power.

Political discontent is, then, a powerful agent of social change. It is, indeed, the principal agent of what might be called "manifest" social change, in which the course of society is deliberately directed toward a self-conscious end. The dynamics of a society cannot be understood without reference to the prevailing images of a political future. As in the case of an individual, however, the images of the future may not be realized even though they are an important element in determining it. This is even more true in the case of social dynamics than it is in the dynamics of individual behavior. We do not go anywhere unless we have a ticket, and what is written on the ticket determines where we will go. But in society, even more than in the case of the individual, what is written on the ticket is not necessarily where we end up; the latent forces in the dynamics of society often confound even the explicit plans of the politically discontented. Thus, the Christian image of a heavenly kingdom has helped to organize a good many earthly societies which have not in themselves borne much resemblance to Zion. Similarly, the communist image of a classless society has, in fact, created totalitarian and highly stratified dictatorships. The Mormon vision of a community of latter-day saints led to the establishment of the State of Utah, which maintains a level of crime and divorce comparable to other less professedly virtuous communities.

That part of political discontent which is related to ideals of social justice is sometimes a very important agent of social change, and sometimes not. A very important problem in the theory of social dynamics is to determine those circumstances under which discontent takes a personal rather than a political form and those under which political discontent aspires after social justice rather than order, growth, or freedom. There are many puzzling problems here. It cannot be assumed, for instance, that just because people are poor they will be discontented, either personally or politically. History records the existence of many peoples whose misery and exploitation have been deplorably stable and who have not given any expression of personal or political discontent. One might venture on the proposition that there is very little discontent below a certain level of poverty simply because people do not have the energy to question their lot and merely drag out an existence from day to day on their meager resources. Above this level, it may take a large improvement in conditions to diminish discontent again, as a little improvement only raises the appetite for more. Another hypothesis is that any worsening of conditions will increase discontent even if people are fairly well off to start with. The individual comes to think that he merits what he is accustomed to; hence, any worsening of his condition is a serious threat to his self-esteem. A subordinate hypothesis may then be formulated: threats to our self-esteem are the principal source of discontent, either political or personal.

A third hypothesis is that discontent, once generated, can take either a personal or a political form, depending upon the opportunities and chances of success. In a rapidly advancing society in which individuals can, with a little effort, easily participate in the general wealth, most discontent will be personal and will express itself in efforts on the part of the individual to advance his position within the existing social framework. A society, on the other hand, which is stagnant or declining will be likely to generate political discontent, for the individual who attempts to solve his problems by purely personal means will be met with considerable lack of success. This will upset his self-esteem which can only be restored by attacking the social framework.

A fourth closely related hypothesis is that if the individuals of a society perceive that political change within it is easy, whether this is in fact so or not, the discontent will be likely to take a more personal form. Thus in democracies political discontent is likely to be mild, whereas in totalitarian or autocratic societies the very suppression of political activity leads to an intensification of political discontent.

Political discontent perhaps can be subdivided further into revolutionary discontent and constitutional discontent. Constitutional discontent expresses itself, as the name implies, within the constitution of the society: it may seek to effect a change in personnel or a change in party, but not a change in the essential political system. If discontent cannot be expressed constitutionally, it will be expressed in revolutionary ways. Revolutionary discontent despairs of adequate political change within the existing constitution of society and, therefore, sets out to change the constitution itself. The degree of intensity of political discontent is important also: a mild political discontent is likely to express itself constitutionally, whereas an intense political discontent is likely to express itself in revolutionary form. The more intense the discontent, the more likely is its expression to be violent.

The next problem is to determine the mode of political discontent: that is, the circumstances under which it is likely to be directed against anarchy and war, against poverty and the failure of economic growth, against restrictions on freedom or on dignity, or against social injustice. This clearly depends upon the nature of the image of the existing society and of the divergence between this image and the ideal image. Political discontent will be directed toward those elements in society which are felt to diverge most from the ideal. If the society is orderly and war is perceived only as a peripheral activity, the problem of order and anarchy will not receive much attention. Similarly, if the society seems to be progressing satisfactorily toward greater per capita income, there will not be much pressure for general economic reform. In a society which is both orderly and progressing but in which there are large divergencies between rich and poor, or in which there is discrimination between some class or group, political discontent will mainly take the form of a demand for social justice.

This gives rise to an interesting question: is social justice an ideal which becomes important only in societies which are already orderly and progressing, or is it prominent in the political discontent even of disorderly or stagnant societies? This cannot be answered without reference to the facts of history. One suspects that there is some tendency for a dominant order of this kind: that a strong political discontent directed at social injustice is only likely to arise in those societies which are relatively orderly and progressive, and that the demands for social justice may be low in disorderly and poor societies. A possible exception to this is in those societies which have developed, as it were, a habit of political action. In such societies, if the problems of order and progress are not well solved, political action will still divert itself into the quest for justice.

The relation between discontent and action is not, itself, an invariant one. When a society has a deep interest in politics and its human energy is not "diverted" into religion, art, domesticity, or economic advancement, a small amount of political discontent may produce a disproportionate amount of political action. Under these conditions, the quest for social justice may actually prove to be inimical to that very order and progress which permitted the quest. The difficulty here is that the ideal of social justice is less easily defined than other political ideals. It is all too easy to perceive disorder or economic stagnation, and it is—perhaps—easy to perceive gross injustice. The fine definition of justice, however, is extremely difficult and there is a wide range of social states over which controversy can range. Under these circumstances, the quest for social justice may actually endanger the very order and progress which permitted it. In the struggle about the final distribution of a cake, the cake itself may be thrown to the ground and lost. One sees this even within the family where the quest for personal justice among the children not infrequently results in a bitter and quarrelsome situation in which many of the values of family life are lost. Each, in trying to get his fair share, diminishes the total that is to be divided.

We may conclude by some historical illustrations of these principles. It can be argued that from about 1880 on in the countries of northwest Europe and in the United States, the quest for social justice became a very important element in political discontent and had a profound effect on the political activities of these societies. These societies were already rich and had been—for the most part—getting richer rapidly. These societies enjoyed a high measure of internal order within this period and, until very recently, war affected them only peripherally. Constitutional rights and individual freedoms were well-developed, and the great constitutional battles against autocratic government had been won. There existed, however, a strong habit of political action and advanced institutions for legislation. It is not surprising, therefore, that the political action, on the whole, took the form of a demand for social justice which, in turn, played a dominant role in the legislative activities of these societies. In the United States, which was advancing most rapidly, discontent still took a personal rather than a political form. The American labor movement, for instance, by contrast with European labor movements, was fundamentally an expression of personal discontent. The American union, especially the craft union of the American Federation of Labor, was not an instrument to change society or even the rules of society, but an instrument by which its members bargained for better incomes. As late as the Great Depression, the American Federation of Labor was still denouncing social security. Although the socialists had some influence in the union, they were never able to dominate it. In the European democracies, however, because the class structure was more rigid and the general rate of development not as high, the opportunities for individual advancement were fewer. It is not surprising, therefore, that the discontent took a more political form and that the labor movement in Europe gave rise to the social democratic parties of later years. Yet even in Europe, the discontent generally took a constitutional rather than a revolutionary form, because of the relative lack of alienation of the mass of the people from the institutions of society. It has been the most advanced countries in Europe, with the exception of France, which have retained the institution of the monarchy. And France, perhaps, is the exception that proves the rule, for her economic development, until very recently, has been erratic, localized, and unsatisfactory.

Another interesting case study in the pathology of social justice is agricultural policy. With economic development, the proportion of the population engaged in agriculture has continually diminished so that it is now a relatively small minority in all advanced countries. In spite of this, legislative activity devoted to promoting social justice for agriculture has continually increased, and large sums are spent to subsidize what is a relatively small part of the population. Psychoanalytic roots can, perhaps, be found for this behavior: many city dwellers have rural parents, grandparents, or great-grandparents; the move to the city may reflect a rejection of rural life and rural values, which is, in a sense, a rejection of the parent, the guilt for which has been compensated for by agricultural subsidies. Part of the explanation lies in a certain constitutional lag which has resulted in gross over-representation of agricultural populations in the legislatures—for example, in the American Senate. This is not sufficient to account for the phenomenon of agricultural subsidy, however, since nearly all these subsidies required the support of city voters. The rationale of agricultural policy can only be explained by an appeal to social justice. The farm interests have made much of the fact that per capita incomes in agriculture are only about half what they are in industrial pursuits. Support, therefore, is enlisted under the concept of parity, or of equality for agriculture. Such aid to agriculture, however, has generally taken the form of price supports. These, in fact, create more injustice than they rectify, for they inevitably subsidize the rich farmer more than the poor. The poor farmers are those who have little to sell; a better price does not much better their condition, but it benefits greatly those who have a lot to sell. Agricultural price policy, then, has been an attempt to legislate social justice, the effects of which are very likely to be perverse. Nevertheless, it is the appeal to social justice which must be invoked to explain the action.

Another example of an appeal to social justice with unintended consequences is the history of the minimum wage. Minimum wage legislation is usually argued on an appeal to the principle of a social minimum. Yet the short-run effects of a minimum wage are very likely to be the pushing of considerable numbers of people below the social minimum, for many of these who previously had employment below the new minimum wage will now be unemployed. The long-run effect of a minimum wage, however, may be a technical reorganization of the affected industries which would not otherwise have taken place, and which will eventually enable them to reabsorb workers at or above the minimum wage. What is designed to be an instrument of social justice turns out to be an instrument of economic development from which social justice, as a by-product, may eventually emerge.

The essentially subordinate status of social justice as a goal of rational political discontent is illustrated by the principle that any group will find it eventually unprofitable to redistribute income toward itself at the cost even of the smallest decline in the rate of economic development. For any group which succeeds in such a redistribution there will be some year in the future beyond which it will be worse off in an absolute sense because it affected the initial redistribution in its favor. The general conclusion seems to be that social justice is something that we ought to have but that we should not want too badly, or else our craving for it will dash it from our lips and, in our eagerness to snatch it, we shall spill it.

Because many problems which appear to be problems of distribution are, in fact, problems of relative growth, there exists the danger that their treatment as problems in distribution may destroy the growth which would solve them. This may be true in large measure even of the chief problem of the world today: its division into rich countries and poor. This is a problem which can be solved, not by redistributing the riches of the rich to the poor but by making the poor productive. The rich can, and should, play an important role in the task, but the more important role must be played by the poor countries themselves: they must reorganize their societies so as to permit rapid economic development. This may seem at times like a hard and ungenerous doctrine, but it is, unfortunately, all too true. In a very real sense, justice is something that only the rich can afford. Only as the poor become rich can social justice, in any of its meanings, be established. But this is not primarily a matter of present distribution, but a matter of eventual participation in the organization and productivity of a high-level society.

Lest I seem to have come out against social justice, let me add a word in its defense. There are processes in the development of a society which may be self-defeating because they violate the sense of social justice. A good example is the type of economic development in Cuba before the Castro revolution. Although it raised the per capita income of Cuba above that of any other Latin American country, it eventually destroyed itself because it violated the sense of social justice in so many people. The benefits of development were enjoyed by about twenty per cent of the people; the rest benefited little and in some cases even went backward. Discontent, which under more favorable circumstances might have found personal channels, under these conditions was channeled into purely political forms—both on the part of the peasant who felt cut off from opportunities for advancement in such a society, and on the part of his middle-class sympathizers. It remains to be seen whether the new and very different dynamic which has resulted from the revolution can, in fact, solve the problem of economic development together with the problem of social justice.

Economic development is not just a process of growth: it involves the radical reorganization of society itself. There is a stage, however, in any process of economic development at which only part of the society has been transformed. At this stage, since there are likely to be wide disparities of income between the transformed parts and the untransformed parts of the economy, development seems to have been purchased at the expense of social justice. This may be seen on a world scale today: in the eighteenth century, the per capita income in the richest country was probably not more than four or five times the per capita income of the poorest; now, the per capita income of the richest country is about forty times the per capita income of the poorest. This is not the result of exploitation but because of different rates of growth. When this disparity occurs within a society, it creates considerable strains within the social framework. The poor will inevitably become more discontented as they observe the increasing riches of the rich. If this discontent can express itself in personal terms and the process of development is such that the poor can better their condition through individual effort, political upheaval may be avoided. This was the pattern in Britain and the United States. It is also the pattern in Russia, where the Communists were able to persuade the working class to accept a sharp reduction of real income over a period of more than twenty years. This can happen only if the society can develop an ideology which prevents the poor from being alienated. If the poor are alienated, they will eventually overthrow the rich. This may bring the whole process of development to an end—as it seems to have done, for instance, in Mayan civilization. If the poor are led by the middle-class, however, the process of development could easily continue under new social forms.

These considerations underline the close relationship between the two concepts of social justice: disalienation and equality. Equality is a luxury of rich societies. If poor societies are to maintain any kind of peak achievement or civilization, they simply cannot afford it. Without sharp inequalities, we would not have had the Parthenon or the cathedrals or the great cultural achievements of any of the past civilizations. With the coming of the great revolution and what I have called post-civilization, however, equality becomes feasible as a social ideal. Equality, that is, is one of the fruits of development. On the other hand, if there is alienation, the inequality which inevitably develops in the process of development may arrest that development through political discontent. Social justice, therefore, is not a simple and a single ideal of society, but is an essential part of a great complex of social change for which some things may have to be sacrificed at times and which itself, in turn, may need at other times to be sacrificed for greater goods.

The Dimensions of
Economic Freedom[*]

Freedom is a troublesome concept and all the more important for
being troublesome. It is not something which can be measured easily
on a linear scale so that we can say, without equivocation, that one
person or one society is more or less free than another. It is a concept
which frequently has more emotional than intellectual content. We
all use it to mean what is fine, noble, and worthwhile about "our side."
It is significant, for instance, that *"Freiheit"* was one of Hitler's slogans;
that the Four Freedoms, which now, alas, seem almost to have passed
from public memory, were the watchwords of the Atlantic Charter;
that Engels' great phrase, "The leap from necessity into freedom,"
is a powerful weapon of Communist ideology; and that Portugal,
Spain, Haiti, and even Mississippi belong to the "free world." Amid
such a confusion of tongues it is almost, but not quite, pardonable to
be cynical. Cynicism, however, is never good enough. A confusion of
tongues is a challenge to an intellectual enterprise to clarify the sources
of the confusion and evaluate its consequences.

The confusion arises because freedom is a concept with more than
one dimension, and all its dimensions are important. A great deal of
unnecesssary political controversy and many false images of the world
arise out of the failure to recognize the existence of these various
dimensions. A person or society may be moving toward more freedom
on one dimension and less freedom on another. Under these circumstances it is not surprising if we concentrate on the dimension which
is favorable to us and neglect the dimension which is not. Hence we
get into seemingly irreconcilable arguments about the meaning of
these movements, with each party perceiving himself as becoming
more free and the other party as becoming less. In this paper I shall

[*] *Midway*, 18 (Spring 1964): 70–95. Edwards: *The Nation's Economic
Objectives*. Rice University Semi-Centennial Series.

This paper was originally presented at Rice University as a part of a
series of lectures on The Nation's Economic Objectives on February 28,
1963.

distinguish three major dimensions of freedom which I shall symbolize by the names power, law, and understanding. These three dimensions almost certainly do not exhaust the concept; they do, however, seem to represent the three *major* dimensions, and the failure to distinguish among them seems to be the principal source of controversy.

The first and most obvious dimension of freedom is power, that is, the generalized ability to do what we want. Power in turn has a number of dimensions, depending on the social system in which it is embedded. I have elsewhere distinguished three major organizers of society, corresponding to three major subsystems within the larger social system, which I have called exchange, threats, and love. To each of these there corresponds a dimension of power. In terms of the exchange system, power is purchasing power and is equivalent to wealth or riches. The richer a person or a society is, the more commodities can be commanded, the more can be bought of that which is offered for sale, and the more can be produced that has exchangeable value.

The second dimension of power relates to the threat system. Power here signifies the capability of doing harm and the capability of preventing another from doing harm to one's self. This is a complex and unstable system with some very peculiar properties, very little explored by social scientists. Violence is an important, though not the only, aspect of this system, and the institutions of national defense are of course its main organizational embodiment. Whereas in the exchange system we increase our power by increasing our ability to do things which others regard as good for them, that is, by being productive, in the threat system we increase our power by producing things which enable us to do to others what they regard as evil. For this very reason, exchange systems have a much better chance of being positive-sum games in which the total of everybody's welfare constantly increases, and threat systems tend to pass over into negative-sum games.

The third dimension of power relates it to what might be called the "integrative system." This is the kind of power which is given by status, respect, love, affection, and all those things which bind us to each other. The power of the teacher over his students, who acknowledge his superior knowledge and ability to teach; the charismatic power of a political or religious leader over his followers; the power of a beloved parent or a respected friend—these are examples of this dimension. Power in this sense is also an important organizer of society, the study of which has again been much neglected. Integrative systems, like exchange systems, are likely to develop into positive-sum games in which everybody is better off. In general we may venture the hypothesis that threat systems, as embodied, for instance, in slavery, oppression, and conquest, have a low horizon of development; exchange systems, a much higher one; and the integrative systems, the highest of all.

In all these three systems, freedom or power must be measured by the distance from the party concerned of the boundary which separates what is possible to him from what is impossible. This I have called the "possibility boundary." Each individual, organization, or society stands, as it were, at any moment of time at a point representing the existing state of the world. There are a large number of other conceivable points representing other states of the world, and we can divide the set of conceivable states into two subsets, the possible and the impossible. The impossibility of the impossible may be for a number of different reasons. There are states of the world, for instance, which are technologically impossible to reach at the present time. I can be in Detroit tomorrow, but I cannot be on the moon. The exchange system imposes limitations on me depending on what I can afford. It would be technologically possible for me to be sunning myself in Hawaii tomorrow, but I cannot afford either the time or the money for this agreeable excursion. There are limitations likewise which are imposed by the threat system. It is technologically possible for me to refuse to pay my income tax next month, but I am constrained from advancing toward this delightful state of the world in part, at least, because of the threat system which is involved in the law and its sanctions. I would very much like to go to China, and I would be willing to afford both the money and the time to do this, but the law prevents me. The integrative system likewise imposes a boundary depending on my status and on my position in the whole web of personal and organizational relationships. For some reason which is a little mysterious to me, I seem to have the power, once suitable preliminaries have been arranged, to get up and make a speech in a perfectly strange city, and a few people, at any rate, will come and listen to me. This is a power not possessed by everybody, and it depends clearly on the position of the individual in the integrative system.

As the main subject of this paper is economic freedom rather than freedom in general, we should perhaps give particular attention to that aspect of power which is most concerned with economics, that is, wealth, or its converse, poverty. In the absence of any good measurements of power or of freedom, any propositions regarding which are the *most* severe limitations on freedom are debatable, but it can at least be argued with some cogency that the most severe limitation on freedom for the mass of mankind is sheer poverty. In spite of two centuries of rapid economic development in some parts of the world, most human beings still do not have the freedom to travel much beyond the confines of their native village. They do not have the freedom to have full stomachs and healthy bodies; they do not have the freedom to provide their children with education; and the most severe limitations which are imposed on them are imposed by the sheer scarcity of commodities. For the very poor, the economic limitation is so severe and constricts them in so small a living space that other possible restrictions on freedom, such as those arising out of political dictatorship, are like distant mountain ranges beyond the close, high wall of poverty which shuts them in. It is only as economic power is increased from this extremely low level at which so much of the world still lives that other aspects of power become important. The relations here are complex. It may be, for instance, that a change in a political relationship and an increase in political freedom may be necessary before a process can be set in motion which will eventually lift the burden of poverty. The poor themselves, however, have very little say in whether this happens or not.

The second dimension of freedom concerns itself not so much with power, that is, with the distance of the boundary which divides the possible from the impossible, as with the nature or quality of the boundary itself. A slave and a free laborer may be equally poor and equally impotent, and the boundary of possibility may be drawn tightly around them by their sheer poverty. They may both be unable to enjoy full stomachs, physical ease, wide sources of information, and travel. In one case, however, the boundary is perceived as the will of another, that is, the master, whereas in the other case the boundary is an impersonal one, imposed by the market.

I have identified this aspect of freedom with "law" with some hesitation, because the concept of law itself is certainly wider than the notion of the kind of boundary which forms the limits of power. The problem of law also includes more than the problem of freedom. It includes, for instance, justice, which is an independent and equally important object of social organization. Thus in the sense in which I am using the word it is perfectly possible to have an unjust law, but it still remains a law. The extreme opposite of law in this sense, perhaps, is "whim," which is irrational and unpredictable behavior, especially toward another.

The difficulties of measurement and even of conceptual clarity in this dimension are great, and it is hard to tell whether a man or a society has more or less freedom in this regard. We are faced here with a multidimensional network of interlacing relationships, and in a brief essay we cannot do more than point to some of the major problems. There is, for instance, the dimension of certainty or uncertainty about the position of the boundary which limits our power. Sometimes we do things which we think we have the power to do, and we turn out to be disappointed. One of the difficulties here is implied in the very notion of a boundary: as long as we stay well within the boundary it is very hard to find out where it is. The effort to find out where a boundary lies involves probing operations which may be costly and which may even result in an actual constriction of the boundary. Our image of the nature and quality of the boundary therefore is almost inevitably derived from hearsay, that is, from written or verbal information rather than from actual experience. Most of us stop, if not within the boundary of the law, at least within the boundary where we think the law will catch up with us. We all, almost without exception, break traffic regulations up to the point where we think it may get us into trouble. Frequently, a few detections and penalties may be necessary before we learn where that boundary lies.

Another quality of the boundary of freedom which is of great importance is the quality of legitimacy. This is a very puzzling concept which nevertheless is obviously of great importance in establishing social organizations and the course of social dynamics. A boundary is legitimate when it is accepted as just and proper by a person who is limited by it. We can regard it, perhaps, as a threat-submission system in which the submission is not merely made out of fear of the consequences of not submitting but is made because the system as a whole is acceptable and is considered in the interests of the person submitting. A good example of a system of this kind is taxation. Most of us submit to be taxed, not merely because certain penalties will be imposed if we refuse, but also because we recognize that taxation in some degree is necessary for our own welfare. If taxation were completely voluntary, a lot of people would escape it. I do not mind, therefore, being forced to pay taxes myself as long as everybody else is forced to pay them likewise. Here freedom—and a specifically economic freedom in the sense of the freedom to enjoy a larger income—is limited by the tax system, presumably, however, in the interests of a larger freedom, that is, most of us feel that we might have less income, if there were no tax system at all, than the net income we enjoy under a tax system. At this point the problem of freedom seems to be inseparable from that of justice, for only limitations of individual freedom which are seen as just are likely to enhance this freedom in the long run.

Many of these problems fall into a category which might be called problems of conflict resolution. These are problems which arise when the power of one person or organization limits the power of another. Conflicts of this type all arise out of scarcity in some sense, where, if A succeeds in pushing his boundary of freedom away from him, this at the same time pushes B's boundary closer to B. A great deal of the political and organizational apparatus of society is concerned with situations of this kind. The institution of property, for instance, is a socially legitimated boundary system which divides a field of scarce goods into areas of freedom around each particular owner. Within limits, I can do what I like with my own. Property rights, of course, are never absolute and they are always created by society. The process of creating and limiting them, however, must also be legitimated, and this is one of the main functions of law. A good example of this kind of conflict resolution is a stop light at an intersection. The use of the intersection is scarce in the sense that two parties cannot occupy it at the same time. If there are no means of regulation, the exercise of the freedom of all is likely to result in the freedom of none—the parties will be dead. The traffic light creates property; it gives the right of way part of the time to travelers on one thoroughfare and part of the time to travelers on the other. It is inalienable property and not usually subject to exchange in the market, but it is property nevertheless, and when the fire truck comes by it may even be alienated. It is property, furthermore, which is established by some kind of legitimate process which is recognized as legitimate by all parties. Legitimate process is *due* process, which suggests, incidentally, why this concept is so important to civil liberties and to political freedom.

The constitution of a society is a set of rules for deciding conflicts. These rules may be either written or unwritten, and there are indeed always a good many unwritten rules which constitute, as it were, the tacit part of the social contract. Majority rule, for instance, is one such constitutional compact; in practice, however, it is always modified by unwritten restraints on the arbitrary power of the majority, for otherwise the social contract tends to break down. In the international sphere we still have no adequate social contract, and the development of a world social contract, whether written or tacit, is the highest-priority task of our time. Without this there is likely to be no freedom for anybody.

The "law" aspect of freedom, as applied to the particular arena of economic freedom, presents some problems of peculiar interest. In classical economic theory, the concept of perfect competition itself can claim to optimize the nature of the boundary which is imposed on individuals by economic constraints. In the first place, under perfect competition the boundary is not subject to the arbitrary whim of any person. Under perfect competition the seller faces many buyers; the buyer, many sellers; and if he cannot make a bargain with one he can make a bargain with another. Perfect competition is thus the state of affairs the furthest removed from slavery, in which the slave has no choice of master. The very existence of a labor market is an important guarantee of personal economic freedom and is a powerful check on the arbitrary power of organizations. In perfect competition, the economic power of the individual is limited by what seem to be impersonal forces, namely the systems of relative prices which face him. It is true, of course, that these impersonal forces are the result of the aggregation of a large number of personal ones, but in the aggregation, at least, the arbitrary quality of personal forces is lost, and the individual is faced with a boundary which may perhaps be affected by the whims of fashion but is *not* affected by the whim of any one person. Under perfect competition, furthermore, economic conflict scarcely arises, simply because the range of bargaining is so small. Economic conflict arises between two parties over the terms of a bargain: where, for instance, a commodity is bought and sold for money, the seller would like to have a high price; the buyer, a low price. Under perfect competition, however, there is practically no occasion for conflict of this kind. If a seller tries to raise his price above the market, nobody will buy from him; if a buyer tries to lower his price below the market, nobody will sell to him. If, in addition, people are highly mobile between different occupations, there is practically no change in the state of the society which is capable of making one group of people permanently better off at the expense of another group. If a commodity suffers a loss of demand, or if it is taxed and becomes unprofitable to produce, those who produce it will simply quit their occupation and go and find another one, up to the point at which those who are left receive normal returns.

As we move away from perfect competition toward monopoly and—alas!—reality, the situation, of course, changes. Under monopoly, the quality of the boundary of freedom changes severely for the worse. The monopolist is felt to exercise a personal or organizational power over those who have to buy from him, for if there are no other sellers there is no way to escape the relationship. As we move toward bilateral monopoly, the situation gets even worse. Here economic conflict becomes intense and obvious; bargaining is difficult and costly and often breaks down; and each party has a sense of being limited by the will of the other, which is seldom regarded as legitimate. The problem of how to develop institutions by which the bargaining process can be legitimated in the case of monopoly power may be regarded as one of the major unsolved economic problems of our society. In the case of the unilateral increase in steel prices, for instance, there seemed to be no recourse but the presidential anger. In the case of a failure of collective bargaining in the labor market, as in the newspaper strike in New York City, there does not even seem to be this recourse. Once we get away from perfect competition, the whole process of legitimation of the relative-price structure is in total confusion. The arbitrary and confused nature, for instance, of the whole antitrust enterprise is a case in point.

The problem of legitimation becomes even more acute as we move from the exchange economy into what I have called the "grants" economy. A slowly increasing part of our economic life is governed by essentially unilateral transfers rather than by exchanges, which are bilateral transfers. In an exchange, something goes from A to B and something else from B to A. It is not always easy to tell a grant from an exchange; interest payments, for instance, have a good deal of the character of a grant in the short run but may be exchange in the long run. Tax payments have a good deal more of the character of a grant, although we can conceive ourselves as getting something rather tenuous for them. Subsidies, whether to industries or to individuals, and philanthropic donations clearly have the character of grants, though even here we have tricky cases. The support of the aged and also of the young can be regarded as part of a long-run exchange between those in middle life and those at the extremities. In youth and in old age we are recipients of grants, that is, we get more than we give; in middle life we tend to be makers of grants—we give more than we get. Part of this may be thought of as paying back what we received when we were young; part of it is paying out in the expectation of receiving grants when we are old. Even when we have eliminated all elements of long-run exchange, however, the grants system still looks pretty large. Here, unfortunately, we have practically no institutions of legitimation—indeed, practically no theory of what is legitimate, apart from some vague notions of merit. Philanthropy, whether public or private, seems to be a part of the economy where the rules are even less clear than they are in the case of antitrust legislation and prosecutions. The problem is hidden by the fact that the receipt of a grant always looks like an extension of the freedom of the recipient, whereas those who do not receive them are not conscious of any diminution of their freedom. In fact, however, insofar as resources are scarce, the giving of grants diverts resources from the nonreceivers to the receivers and hence represents a real economic conflict of which (and perhaps this is fortunate) we are not fully aware.

The third great dimension of freedom is freedom from error, both intellectual and moral. A man may have a lot of power, and the boundary which limits his freedom may enclose a wide field. This boundary, furthermore, may be subject to the full blessings of law and legitimacy and free from dependence on the will of another or from uncertainty and arbitrariness. This man, however, can still be the slave of his passions and his stupidities. The more power he has and the wider the boundary of his freedom, the more quickly he may be able to damn himself. The mere quality of the boundary itself and all the majesty of law assembled will not save him. This is a dimension of freedom which is not, I think, encompassed in the other two, and yet which can be neglected at our great peril, for freedom misused will soon be destroyed.

Here again we face a problem of formidable size and complexity. We cannot discuss freedom from error without knowing something about the nature of truth. Pilate may not have been jesting, and he might not even have got the answer had he stayed, but his question, "What is truth?" has lost little of its difficulty. Nevertheless there is something both appealing and meaningful in the idea that "Ye shall know the truth, and the truth shall make you free." Freedom in this sense means the ability to fulfil an image of the future. If my image of the world contains my being at a certain place on a certain date in the future, and if when that date arrives, I find myself where I expected to be, this is a fairly convincing demonstration that the relevant part of my image of the world was true. A difficulty arises, of course, in that all images of the future have a degree of probability attached to them, and the mere fact that a particular expectation is fulfilled says nothing about the correctness of that probability. My being at a particular place at a particular time may, in fact, have been very improbable, but if I am there, in fact, there is no way of finding out how improbable it was. The test, therefore, of both truth and freedom in this sense is the amount of disappointment in the long run. If I am constantly disappointed, it is clear that there is something wrong with my image of the world; what I think is truth must in fact be error, and in consequence my actual forecasts are constantly falsified by this ignorance.

Freedom in the first sense of power is, of course, highly dependent upon knowledge of the truth. That knowledge is power is no mere copybook platitude, but perhaps the first law of social dynamics. The technology which so enormously increases our freedom in the physical sense is a direct and obvious result of increased knowledge of the nature of matter, energy, and space. One may hope also that in human relations and social systems an increase in knowledge will lead to a social, political, and economic technology which will preserve us from some of the disasters of the past.

In regard to economic freedom, the major problem here is the relation of the prevailing image of the economic system, especially among important decision-makers, to its actual development. It is perfectly possible, of course, to do the right thing for the wrong reasons, and in economics this is not treason at all but just sheer good luck. Our own agricultural policy, for instance, which was based on what seems to me to have been a wholly mistaken view of the nature of economic justice and of the effects of altering the price system, in fact has turned out to be a powerful stimulus to technological development, not only in agriculture, but in the whole economy. It is quite likely that if we had known better we would have done worse. Ignorance is bliss, however, only in the short run and in stochastic processes. In the long run, ignorance can hurt us and only knowledge can save us. What Engels meant, I think, by the "leap from necessity into freedom" was that when man achieves an understanding of the dynamics of his own society, he can then develop an image of the future for that society as a whole into which it has the power to progress. Man is no longer then the object of blind social or natural forces which he cannot control, and he can move forward into a future of his own making. This is a noble idea and should not be rejected out of hand. In our day, indeed, it is accepted by all—except, perhaps, by the most unreconstructed obscurantists. It is one thing, however, to say that we *can* know the truth and quite another thing to know it. The difficulty here is that it is the convincing image which is powerful, and the convincing is not always true. A good many people have come along, among them even Marx and Hitler, and have claimed that *their* service was perfect freedom. Man has never lacked for false prophets. Furthermore, in the absence of a process of cumulative social learning it is very hard to learn to tell the false prophets from the true. Merely because it is difficult, however, the problem cannot be pushed aside. In a great many of these matters we cannot simply suspend judgment; we must act upon *some* view of the universe. The hope here, as I have suggested, lies in a careful, cumulative process of long-run information collection, processing, and dissemination which can do for social learning what the scientific method has done for our knowledge of the physical universe. This goal may seem a long way off, but there are signs that we are moving toward it.

The economic aspect of this third dimension of freedom relates, of course, to the growth of economic knowledge itself. This is seen, for instance, in relation to two of the major economic problems of our day, economic development and economic fluctuations. That extraordinary process of economic development which began to accelerate with such force in the eighteenth century, in the full tide of which we find ourselves today, was certainly not initiated by any conscious plan or any clear knowledge of the dynamics of economic systems. Its origins lie deep in latent and unconscious processes which can, perhaps, be understood in retrospect but which certainly were not and could not be understood at the time. Who would have guessed, for instance, that the turnip and the potato would have engendered so great a revolution? The failure of economic development in many parts of the world, however, indicates that it is not a necessary process and that the West may simply have been lucky. We are now, therefore, desperately trying to understand the nature of this process in order that we may prescribe what needs to be done in those parts of the world that, to judge by results, have not yet done it. The full understanding of the process may not therefore be necessary to "lucky" economic development but may be necessary to make it certain and independent of luck.

Economic fluctuations represent an area where, in the Western world at least, an increase in economic knowledge has had a profound effect on the dynamics of the system. It would have been almost inconceivable, for instance, for Herbert Hoover to have proposed a substantial tax cut as a remedy for his depression. To do so requires not only a sophisticated economic theory—it requires an information-processing apparatus in the shape of econometric models and national income statistics which we simply did not possess thirty years ago. One of the critical problems at the moment, indeed, is that the image of the economy which is possessed by virtually all professional economists extends only a little way beyond their ranks; many of the people and perhaps even a majority of congressmen are operating with an image of the economic system which is so far removed from reality that we are in grave danger of being enslaved to our own ignorance and of failing to make our system operate successfully because those who have to make the important decisions do not possess the truth about it. On the other hand, we have to recognize that it is easy for economists to be wrong; that the truth about an economic system is very hard to obtain, especially in a system as complex as ours; and that there must be room for knowing when we don't know as well as when we do.

Beyond these matters of what might be called economic technology, there are more fundamental questions of the critique of values or objectives themselves, which not even the economists can escape, even though they frequently like to disclaim responsibility in this area. We do not have to go all the way toward believing in objective values and natural law to see that a critique of ends may be necessary even for quite positivistic social dynamics. Nazi Germany was fairly successful in solving the problem of depression and might even have done fairly well with economic development, but it used its freedom for such outrageous ends that it was destroyed. We cannot escape the fact, therefore, that there are ends which can destroy us, and it is important to identify them. If we use wealth for futile idleness, for meaningless luxury, for corrupt gratifications, and for the expression of hatred and prejudice, then the richer we are the sooner we will be damned. Besides the knowledge of means, therefore, there must be a very real knowledge of ends, and if we do not have true ends we will be enslaved by false ones. In this sense, too, the truth makes us free; but in this sense also it is hard to come by.

By way almost of an epilogue, it may be of interest to test the theory of the dimensions of freedom which I have outlined above in terms of the current ideological struggle between the Communists and the "free world," to see if we can throw any light on where the argument really lies and on what the conflict is about. This exercise is all the more important because both ideologies claim to be champions of human freedom, and the differences between them, important as they are, are at times surprisingly subtle. The image which the Communist has of himself is that of a liberator of mankind from age-old error and poverty, even if in that process man must be temporarily subordinated to a dictatorship. In the mind of the West, these promises are false and have been disproved by painful experience, and ideologically, therefore, the West envisages itself as the defender of political freedom, individual rights to privacy and non-conformity, and economic development which is mainly private and based on these virtues. The struggle is deeply felt and represents, in many cases, honest differences on both sides. Evangelical fervor, however, can easily turn into xenophobic fury when it is frustrated, and in a world of nuclear weapons this presents a constant and present danger. Where great and noble words like "freedom" and "democracy" are used in different senses by both sides, there is danger of misunderstanding and, worse, mounting mutual frustration which can end only in violence. It may be something more than a mere intellectual exercise, therefore, to apply the concept of freedom as I have analyzed it to this outstanding problem of our day.

I have equated the first dimension of freedom with power, and economic freedom in this sense is wealth. It is now becoming apparent that economic development from poverty to wealth is not a property either of socialism or of capitalism as such, but of a process of cumulative social learning of the kind which increases the productivity of labor. This cumulative process of social learning depends more than anything else on the proportion of resources which are devoted to it and on the efficiency of their use. It has become clear in recent years that it is not the mere accumulation of physical capital which brings about economic development, but a restructuring of the form of that capital in ways which represent greater and greater quantities of information. The learning process in society as a whole in all its institutions, not only those of formal education, is therefore crucial to the whole movement. In this regard the argument between socialism and capitalism is largely irrelevant. If we think of capitalist societies as guided mainly by the market and the price system, and socialist societies as guided mainly by the budget and the economic plan, we see that while both the market and the budget are, under certain circumstances, agents of the social learning process, neither of them by itself is sufficient. Market-oriented societies are old enough so that we have a number of examples of unsuccessful market development as well as of successful market development, and the difference here, one suspects, lies largely in the nature of the non-market institutions. Totalitarian socialism is so young that we have not yet had time to experience any clear examples of socialist failure, mainly because existing socialist countries have encouraged the educational process on which economic development rests. I suspect, however, that we shall find cases of unsuccessful socialist development, perhaps even in China, and we shall see that from this point of view the argument between socialism and capitalism is in large part irrelevant. The United States certainly would never have been a success if it had not been for the large non-market element in its social system. On the other hand it seems pretty clear that the prejudice against the market in socialist countries is a real handicap to them, and that those socialist countries which can most successfully overcome it, such as Poland and Yugoslavia, are the most likely to make rapid development.

Freedom in its second dimension is measured by the rule of law,

the development of legitimacy, and the successful resolution of conflicts. In this sense democratic capitalism gets very good marks and
totalitarian socialism very bad marks, though totalitarian market societies, too many of which are included in the so-called free world, fare
pretty badly too. Political liberty and the absence of spiritual monopoly are very precious aspects of freedom, and ones in which the
socialist countries do poorly. It is a bad sign when one of the principal
exports of a society is refugees. This is a sign of gross domestic failure
to provide personal liberty, the rule of law, and successful conflict
resolution. The socialist societies of East Germany and Cuba are particularly to be indicted on these counts. It is the great virtue of a
market-oriented society that it lends itself to the rule of law, that it
operates more successfully under conditions of political liberty and
impartial justice, and that discrimination and the denial of civil rights
are a severe economic handicap—as the southern states have found to
their cost. In market-oriented societies, furthermore, there is likely
to be a wide diffusion of economic power. Up to now at any rate, we
have discovered no administrative devices which can solve this problem in a socialist state, where all the economic activity in the society
is concentrated in a single firm, which is the state; where the concentration of economic power in the matter of decision-making reaches its
height; and where mistakes on the part of a few powerful individuals
can cause universal suffering. In the absence of a true labor market,
the almost inevitable limitations on the right of the individual to
change jobs can easily be a more fundamental limitation on individual
freedom than the deprivation of political liberty. When we add to
this the denial of the right of the individual to start enterprises of his
own, or to hire labor, or to create organizations outside the monopoly
of the one-firm state, simply because of a theology of surplus value,
we can see the socialist state as imposing limitations on individual
freedom in which the boundary is of very low quality, often arbitrary
and essentially meaningless.

On the other hand, we must not underestimate the ability of the
socialist state to acquire legitimacy in the minds of its citizens. With
the exception of East Germany and Czechoslovakia, there is no widespread alienation or denial of legitimacy in the socialist camp, even
among those, like the Christians, who are discriminated against. It
seems to take an enormous amount of discrimination to create alienation, as the experience of the Negro in the United States, the Christian
in the socialist states, the outcastes of India, and the Eta of Japan
seems to indicate. Legitimation, however, is a variable that is very

hard to evaluate. The Tsar of Russia seemed unshakably legitimate in 1914, in spite of widespread dissent. The Emperor's legitimacy in Japan survived an even more shattering defeat and occupation.

In the third dimension of freedom, in which freedom is equated with "truth" or a correct view of the world, there is obviously plenty of room for controversy. One can concede this much to Marxism: that the idea of social self-consciousness, that is, the idea that society as well as an individual can have a realistic image of its own future into which it can progress, is an idea of far-reaching importance for the whole future of mankind. In a sense, like a great many things in Marxism, it goes back to Adam Smith, whose *Wealth of Nations* is largely a study of the "progress of society" and how to get it. To say that a society *can* have such an image, however, is not necessarily to give it a true one. The Marxist image, in particular, is a case so special that for most societies it is grotesquely untrue. It involves an absurdly oversimplified notion of class structure, a fallacious view of the dynamics of the distribution of income, and a quite insufficient appreciation of the ability of capitalist society to develop itself along evolutionary lines while still retaining its essentially market-oriented character. The fact that Marx's own predictions have been largely falsified is well known. Communism has come, not in the countries of advanced capitalism, but in countries of very early capitalism which have a strong feudal and "folk" residue. Its success, insofar as it has been successful, has not been the result of appeal to class conflict, which has been almost universally disastrous, but in its ability to keep real wages low or even declining; to exploit the present generation ruthlessly, presumably for the benefit of the future; and its determination to devote large resources to education and investment in people. Communist development, however, has been achieved at a high social cost not only in terms of class war, refugees, the extermination of whole groups in society, and social disorganization but also in terms of the atrophy of much artistic and intellectual life, in the development of a harsh, barren, provincial puritanism, full of false values and heavy sentimentality, without even the grace notes of religion. The Communist's image of the world is quite reminiscent of that of the Prohibitionist, with its oversimplified and unduly moralistic approach to complex social problems. It is, of course, changing, and mostly for the better. One hopes for the rise of a liberal generation, as a result of so much investment in higher education, who will revolt against sterile austerities and moralistic platitudes. In the present generation, however, the oversimplified and distorted view of the social system which the decision-makers in these societies possess has involved them in severe social costs and grave errors.

By contrast, capitalist society frequently has no general public image of the future at all. The strength of a market economy lies often in the fact that there is, indeed, an "invisible hand," and that, as Adam Smith remarked, the market itself exhibits a tendency toward health which even the greatest absurdities of governmental doctoring cannot quite overthrow. On the other hand, capitalist society is also subject to certain diseases which the mere operation of the market mechanism itself cannot cure. It does not necessarily distribute income or even the fruits of progress in such a way as to prevent the alienation of large numbers of its people, as we saw in Cuba. Without any governmental stabilization, the market mechanism is subject to essentially meaningless fluctuations which can cause unnecessary loss and distress. It is not clear also that the market-oriented society will necessarily devote enough of its resources to social overhead and the investment in human capital to guarantee a sufficiently rapid rate of development. For all these reasons, knowledge of society itself is needed. Right-wing capitalists frequently have an image of society which is as grotesquely unrealistic as that of the Marxists and which can have equally disastrous consequences. There are, indeed, striking similarities between the right and the left. They are both impatient and moralistic, eager for short cuts, and unwilling to take the long, hard road that leads to truth. The conservative whose image of his own society is untrue, no matter how much he loves it, will not be able to conserve it, just as the revolutionary whose image is untrue will not be able to reform it. In both socialist and capitalist societies, therefore, deeper understanding is the key to freedom in the third sense. Freedom, if I may be pardoned for parodying Holy Writ, is power, law, and understanding; and the greatest of these is understanding.

In all these various dimensions then, is there any way in which it makes sense to say that there can be a "policy" about freedom? For some people the very idea of a policy for freedom may seem contradictory, for to them freedom means the absence of policy. It will be clear from the above that I do not hold this view and that though some freedom grows wild in the great jungle of social species, it flourishes best when it is intelligently tended. In each of the three dimensions which I have outlined above, therefore, I would argue that a policy for freedom is possible. It is possible to have an image of the future in the furtherance of which present decisions are made, and in that future, freedom in any or all of its senses may grow. Policy in this sense is not a monopoly of government, for decisions of private persons also may be taken in the light of an image of a future of increasing freedom. Government also, however, may be a servant of freedom as well as its enemy, and one of the great objects of political development is precisely to learn how political institutions may be devised and used in the service of freedom. But if political power and, still more, military power are often illusory and self-defeating, and if the law which is imposed from above often seems to destroy more freedom than it creates, the reasons must surely lie in our deficiencies of understanding. It is only as we come to understand the social system and the long-run dynamics of power that we can learn to use even coercion in the service of freedom, once that coercion is legitimatized and constrained. This once again points to the dimension of understanding as the greatest of the three, and the one without which the others will be in vain.

The Economics of the Coming Spaceship Earth*

We are now in the middle of a long process of transition in the nature of the image which man has of himself and his environment. Primitive men, and to a large extent also men of the early civilizations, imagined themselves to be living on a virtually illimitable plane. There was almost always somewhere beyond the known limits of human habitation, and over a very large part of the time that man has been on earth, there has been something like a frontier. That is, there was always some place else to go when things got too difficult, either by reason of the deterioration of the natural environment or a deterioration of the social structure in places where people happened to live. The image of the frontier is probably one of the oldest images of mankind, and it is not surprising that we find it hard to get rid of.

Gradually, however, man has been accustoming himself to the notion of the spherical earth and a closed sphere of human activity. A few unusual spirits among the ancient Greeks perceived that the earth was a sphere. It was only with the circumnavigations and the geographical explorations of the fifteenth and sixteenth centuries, however, that the fact that the earth was a sphere became at all widely known and accepted. Even in the nineteenth century, the commonest map was Mercator's projection, which visualizes the earth as an illimitable cylinder, essentially a plane wrapped around the globe, and it was not until the Second World War and the development of the air age that the global nature of the planet really entered the popular imagination. Even now we are very far from having made the moral,

* In: *Environmental Quality in a Growing Economy, Essays from the Sixth RFF Forum,* Henry Jarrett, ed. (Baltimore, Md.: Johns Hopkins Press for Resources for the Future, Inc., 1966), pp. 3–14.

This paper was presented at the Sixth Resources for the Future Forum on Environmental Quality in a Growing Economy in Washington, D.C. on March 8, 1966.

political, and psychological adjustments which are implied in this transition from the illimitable plane to the closed sphere.

Economists in particular, for the most part, have failed to come to grips with the ultimate consequences of the transition from the open to the closed earth. One hesitates to use the terms "open" and "closed" in this connection, as they have been used with so many different shades of meaning. Nevertheless, it is hard to find equivalents. The open system, indeed, has some similarities to the open system of von Bertalanffy,[1] in that it implies that some kind of a structure is maintained in the midst of a throughput from inputs to outputs. In a closed system, the outputs of all parts of the system are linked to the inputs of other parts. There are no inputs from outside and no outputs to the outside; indeed, there is no outside at all. Closed systems, in fact, are very rare in human experience, in fact almost by definition unknowable, for if there are genuinely closed systems around us, we have no way of getting information into them or out of them; and hence if they are really closed, we would be quite unaware of their existence. We can only find out about a closed system if we participate in it. Some isolated primitive societies may have approximated to this, but even these had to take inputs from the environment and give outputs to it. All living organisms, including man himself, are open systems. They have to receive inputs in the shape of air, food, water, and give off outputs in the form of effluvia and excrement. Deprivation of input of air, even for a few minutes, is fatal. Deprivation of the ability to obtain any input or to dispose of any output is fatal in a relatively short time. All human societies have likewise been open systems. They receive inputs from the earth, the atmosphere, and the waters, and they give outputs into these reservoirs; they also produce inputs internally in the shape of babies and outputs in the shape of corpses. Given a capacity to draw upon inputs and to get rid of outputs, an open system of this kind can persist indefinitely.

There are some systems—such as the biological phenotype, for instance the human body—which cannot maintain themselves indefinitely by inputs and outputs because of the phenomenon of aging. This process is very little understood. It occurs, evidently, because there are some outputs which cannot be replaced by any known input. There is not the same necessity for aging in organizations and in societies, although an analogous phenomenon may take place. The structure and composition of an organization or society, however, can

---

[1] Ludwig von Bertalanffy, *Problems of Life* (New York: John Wiley and Sons, 1952).

be maintained by inputs of fresh personnel from birth and education as the existing personnel ages and eventually dies. Here we have an interesting example of a system which seems to maintain itself by the self-generation of inputs, and in this sense is moving towards closure. The input of people (that is, babies) is also an output of people (that is, parents).

Systems may be open or closed in respect to a number of classes of inputs and outputs. Three important classes are matter, energy, and information. The present world economy is open in regard to all three. We can think of the world economy or "econosphere" as a subset of the "world set," which is the set of all objects of possible discourse in the world. We then think of the state of the econopshere at any one moment as being the total capital stock, that is, the set of all objects, people, organizations, and so on, which are interesting from the point of view of the system of exchange. This total stock of capital is clearly an open system in the sense that it has inputs and outputs, inputs being production which adds to the capital stock, outputs being consumption which subtracts from it. From a material point of view, we see objects passing from the noneconomic into the economic set in the process of production, and we similarly see products passing out of the economic set as their value becomes zero. Thus we see the econosphere as a material process involving the discovery and mining of fossil fuels, ores, etc., and at the other end a process by which the effluents of the system are passed out into noneconomic reservoirs— for instance, the atmosphere and the oceans—which are not appropriated and do not enter into the exchange system.

From the point of view of the energy system, the econosphere involves inputs of available energy in the form, say, of water power, fossil fuels, or sunlight, which are necessary in order to create the material throughput and to move matter from the noneconomic set into the economic set or even out of it again; and energy itself is given off by the system in a less available form, mostly in the form of heat. These inputs of available energy must come either from the sun (the energy supplied by other stars being assumed to be negligible) or it may come from the earth itself, either through its internal heat or through its energy of rotation or other motions, which generate, for instance, the energy of the tides. Agriculture, a few solar machines, and water power use the current available energy income. In advanced societies this is supplemented very extensively by the use of fossil fuels, which represent as it were a capital stock of stored-up sunshine. Because of this capital stock of energy, we have been able to maintain an energy input into the system, particularly over the last two centuries, much larger than we would have been able to do with existing techniques if we had had to rely on the current input of available energy from the sun or the earth itself. This supplementary input, however, is by its very nature exhaustible.

The inputs and outputs of information are more subtle and harder to trace, but also represent an open system, related to, but not wholly dependent on, the transformations of matter and energy. By far the larger amount of information and knowledge is self-generated by the human society, though a certain amount of information comes into the sociosphere in the form of light from the universe outside. The information that comes from the universe has certainly affected man's image of himself and of his environment, as we can easily visualize if we suppose that we lived on a planet with a total cloud-cover that kept out all information from the exterior universe. It is only in very recent times, of course, that the information coming in from the universe has been captured and coded into the form of a complex image of what the universe is like outside the earth; but even in primitive times, man's perception of the heavenly bodies has always profoundly affected his image of earth and of himself. It is the information generated within the planet, however, and particularly that generated by man himself, which forms by far the larger part of the information system. We can think of the stock of knowledge, or as Teilhard de Chardin called it, the "nöosphere," and consider this as an open system, losing knowledge through aging and death and gaining it through birth and education and the ordinary experience of life.

From the human point of view, knowledge or information is by far the most important of the three systems. Matter only acquires significance and only enters the sociosphere or the econosphere insofar as it becomes an object of human knowledge. We can think of capital, indeed, as frozen knowledge or knowledge imposed on the material world in the form of improbable arrangements. A machine, for instance, originated in the mind of man, and both its construction and its use involve information processes imposed on the material world by man himself. The cumulation of knowledge, that is, the excess of its production over its consumption, is the key to human development of all kinds, especially to economic development. We can see this preeminence of knowledge very clearly in the experiences of countries where the material capital has been destroyed by a war, as in Japan and Germany. The knowledge of the people was not destroyed, and it did not take long, therefore, certainly not more than ten years, for most of the material capital to be reestablished again. In a country such as Indonesia, however, where the knowledge did not exist, the material capital did not come into being either. By "knowledge" here I mean, of course, the whole cognitive structure, which includes valuations and motivations as well as images of the factual world.

The concept of entropy, used in a somewhat loose sense, can be applied to all three of these open systems. In the case of material systems, we can distinguish between entropic processes, which take concentrated materials and diffuse them through the oceans or over the earth's surface or into the atmosphere, and anti-entropic processes, which take diffuse materials and concentrate them. Material entropy can be taken as a measure of the uniformity of the distribution of elements and, more uncertainly, compounds and other structures on the earth's surface. There is, fortunately, no law of increasing material entropy, as there is in the corresponding case of energy, as it is quite possible to concentrate diffused materials if energy inputs are allowed. Thus the processes for fixation of nitrogen from the air, processes for the extraction of magnesium or other elements from the sea, and processes for the desalinization of sea water are anti-entropic in the material sense, though the reduction of material entropy has to be paid for by inputs of energy and also inputs of information, or at least a stock of information in the system. In regard to matter, therefore, a closed system is conceivable, that is, a system in which there is neither increase nor decrease in material entropy. In such a system all outputs from consumption would constantly be recycled to become inputs for production, as for instance, nitrogen in the nitrogen cycle of the natural ecosystem.

In regard to the energy system there is, unfortunately, no escape from the grim Second Law of Thermodynamics; and if there were no energy inputs into the earth, any evolutionary or developmental process would be impossible. The large energy inputs which we have obtained from fossil fuels are strictly temporary. Even the most optimistic predictions would expect the easily available supply of fossil fuels to be exhausted in a mere matter of centuries at present rates of use. If the rest of the world were to rise to American standards of power consumption, and still more if world population continues to increase, the exhaustion of fossil fuels would be even more rapid. The development of nuclear energy has improved this picture, but has not fundamentally altered it, at least in present technologies, for fissionable material is still relatively scarce. If we should achieve the economic use of energy through fusion, of course, a much larger source of energy materials would be available, which would expand the time horizons of supplementary energy input into an open social system by perhaps tens to hundreds of thousands of years. Failing this, however, the time is not very far distant, historically speaking, when man will once more have to retreat to his current energy input from the sun, even though this could be used much more effectively than in the past with increased knowledge. Up to now, certainly, we have not got very far with the technology of using current solar energy, but the possibility of substantial improvements in the future is certainly high. It may be, indeed, that the biological revolution which is just beginning will produce a solution to this problem, as we develop artificial organisms which are capable of much more efficient transformation of solar energy into easily available forms than any that we now have. As Richard Meier has suggested, we may run our machines in the future with methane-producing algae.[2]

The question of whether there is anything corresponding to entropy in the information system is a puzzling one, though of great interest. There are certainly many examples of social systems and cultures which have lost knowledge, especially in transition from one generation to the next, and in which the culture has therefore degenerated. One only has to look at the folk culture of Appalachian migrants to American cities to see a culture which started out as a fairly rich European folk culture in Elizabethan times and which seems to have lost both skills, adaptability, folk tales, songs, and almost everything that goes up to make richness and complexity in a culture, in the course of about ten generations. The American Indians on reservations provide another example of such degradation of the information and knowledge system. On the other hand, over a great part of human history, the growth of knowledge in the earth as a whole seems to have been almost continuous, even though there have been times of relatively slow growth and times of rapid growth. As it is knowledge of certain kinds that produces the growth of knowledge in general, we have here a very subtle and complicated system, and it is hard to put one's finger on the particular elements in a culture which make knowledge grow more or less rapidly, or even which make it decline. One of the great puzzles in this connection, for instance, is why the take-off into science, which represents an "acceleration," or an increase in the rate of growth of knowledge in European society in the sixteenth century, did not take place in China, which at that time (about 1600) was unquestionably ahead of Europe, and one would think even more ready for the breakthrough. This is perhaps the most crucial question in the theory of social development,

---

[2] Richard L. Meier, *Science and Economic Development* (New York: John Wiley and Sons, 1956).

yet we must confess that it is very little understood. Perhaps the most significant factor in this connection is the existence of "slack" in the culture, which permits a divergence from established patterns and activity which is not merely devoted to reproducing the existing society but is devoted to changing it. China was perhaps too well-organized and had too little slack in its society to produce the kind of acceleration which we find in the somewhat poorer and less well-organized but more diverse societies of Europe.

The closed earth of the future requires economic principles which are somewhat different from those of the open earth of the past. For the sake of picturesqueness, I am tempted to call the open economy the "cowboy economy," the cowboy being symbolic of the illimitable plains and also associated with reckless, exploitative, romantic, and violent behavior, which is characteristic of open societies. The closed economy of the future might similarly be called the "spaceman" economy, in which the earth has become a single spaceship, without unlimited reservoirs of anything, either for extraction or for pollution, and in which, therefore, man must find his place in a cyclical ecological system which is capable of continuous reproduction of material form even though it cannot escape having inputs of energy. The difference between the two types of economy becomes most apparent in the attitude towards consumption. In the cowboy economy, consumption is regarded as a good thing and production likewise; and the success of the economy is measured by the amount of the throughput from the "factors of production," a part of which, at any rate, is extracted from the reservoirs of raw materials and noneconomic objects, and another part of which is output into the reservoirs of pollution. If there are infinite reservoirs from which material can be obtained and into which effluvia can be deposited, then the throughput is at least a plausible measure of the success of the economy. The gross national product is a rough measure of this total throughput. It should be possible, however, to distinguish that part of the GNP which is derived from exhaustible and that which is derived from reproducible resources, as well as that part of consumption which represents effluvia and that which represents input into the productive system again. Nobody, as far as I know, has ever attempted to break down the GNP in this way, although it would be an interesting and extremely important exercise, which is unfortunately beyond the scope of this paper.

By contrast, in the spaceman economy, throughput is by no means a desideratum, and is indeed to be regarded as something to be minimized rather than maximized. The essential measure of the success of the economy is not production and consumption at all, but the nature, extent, quality, and complexity of the total capital stock, including in this the state of the human bodies and minds included in the system. In the spaceman economy, what we are primarily concerned with is stock maintenance, and any technological change which results in the maintenance of a given total stock with a lessened throughput (that is, less production and consumption) is clearly a gain. This idea that both production and consumption are bad things rather than good things is very strange to economists, who have been obsessed with the income-flow concepts to the exclusion, almost, of capital-stock concepts.

There are actually some very tricky and unsolved problems involved in the questions as to whether human welfare or well-being is to be regarded as a stock or a flow. Something of both these elements seems actually to be involved in it, and as far as I know there have been practically no studies directed towards identifying these two dimensions of human satisfaction. Is it, for instance, eating that is a good thing, or is it being well fed? Does economic welfare involve having nice clothes, fine houses, good equipment, and so on, or is it to be measured by the depreciation and the wearing out of these things? I am inclined myself to regard the stock concept as most fundamental, that is, to think of being well fed as more important than eating, and to think even of so-called services as essentially involving the restoration of a depleting psychic capital. Thus I have argued that we go to a concert in order to restore a psychic condition which might be called "just having gone to a concert," which, once established, tends to depreciate. When it depreciates beyond a certain point, we go to another concert in order to restore it. If it depreciates rapidly, we go to a lot of concerts; if it depreciates slowly, we go to few. On this view, similarly, we eat primarily to restore bodily homeostasis, that is, to maintain a condition of being well fed, and so on. On this view, there is nothing desirable in consumption at all. The less consumption we can maintain a given state with, the better off we are. If we had clothes that did not wear out, houses that did not depreciate, and even if we could maintain our bodily condition without eating, we would clearly be much better off.

It is this last consideration, perhaps, which makes one pause. Would we, for instance, really want an operation that would enable us to restore all our bodily tissues by intravenous feeding while we slept? Is there not, that is to say, a certain virtue in throughput itself, in activity itself, in production and consumption itself, in raising food and in eating it? It would certainly be rash to exclude this possibility. Further interesting problems are raised by the demand for variety.

We certainly do not want a constant state to be maintained; we want fluctuations in the state. Otherwise there would be no demand for variety in food, for variety in scene, as in travel, for variety in social contact, and so on. The demand for variety can, of course, be costly, and sometimes it seems to be too costly to be tolerated or at least legitimated, as in the case of marital partners, where the maintenance of a homeostatic state in the family is usually regarded as much more desirable than the variety and excessive throughput of the libertine. There are problems here which the economics profession has neglected with astonishing singlemindedness. My own attempts to call attention to some of them, for instance, in two articles,[3] as far as I can judge, produced no response whatever; and economists continue to think and act as if production, consumption, throughput, and the GNP were the sufficient and adequate measure of economic success.

It may be said, of course, why worry about all this when the space-man economy is still a good way off (at least beyond the lifetimes of any now living), so let us eat, drink, spend, extract and pollute, and be as merry as we can, and let posterity worry about the spaceship earth. It is always a little hard to find a convincing answer to the man who says, "What has posterity ever done for me?" and the conservationist has always had to fall back on rather vague ethical principles postulating identity of the individual with some human community or society which extends not only back into the past but forward into the future. Unless the individual identifies with some community of this kind, conservation is obviously "irrational." Why should we not maximize the welfare of this generation at the cost of posterity? "*Après nous, le déluge*" has been the motto of not insignificant numbers of human societies. The only answer to this, as far as I can see, is to point out that the welfare of the individual depends on the extent to which he can identify himself with others, and that the most satisfactory individual identity is that which identifies not only with a community in space but also with a community extending over time from the past into the future. If this kind of identity is recognized as desirable, then posterity has a voice, even if it does not have a vote; and in a sense, if its voice can influence votes, it has votes too. This whole problem is linked up with the much larger one of the determinants of the morale, legitimacy, and "nerve" of a society, and there is a great deal of historical evidence to suggest that a society which

---

[3] K. E. Boulding, "The Consumption Concept in Economic Theory," *American Economic Review*, 35:2 (May 1945), pp. 1–14; and "Income or Welfare?," *Review of Economic Studies*, 17 (1949–50), pp. 77–86.

loses its identity with posterity and which loses its positive image of the future loses also its capacity to deal with present problems, and soon falls apart.[4]

Even if we concede that posterity is relevant to our present problems, we still face the question of time-discounting and the closely related question of uncertainty-discounting. It is a well-known phenomenon that individuals discount the future, even in their own lives. The very existence of a positive rate of interest may be taken as at least strong supporting evidence of this hypothesis. If we discount our own future, it is certainly not unreasonable to discount posterity's future even more, even if we do give posterity a vote. If we discount this at 5 per cent per annum, posterity's vote or dollar halves every fourteen years as we look into the future, and after even a mere hundred years it is pretty small—only about 1½ cents on the dollar. If we add another 5 per cent for uncertainty, even the vote of our grandchildren reduces almost to insignificance. We can argue, of course, that the ethical thing to do is not to discount the future at all, that time-discounting is mainly the result of myopia and perspective, and hence is an illusion which the moral man should not tolerate. It is a very popular illusion, however, and one that must certainly be taken into consideration in the formulation of policies. It explains, perhaps, why conservationist policies almost have to be sold under some other excuse which seems more urgent, and why, indeed, necessities which are visualized as urgent, such as defense, always seem to hold priority over those which involve the future.

All these considerations add some credence to the point of view which says that we should not worry about the spaceman economy at all, and that we should just go on increasing the GNP and indeed the gross world product, or GWP, in the expectation that the problems of the future can be left to the future, that when scarcities arise, whether this is of raw materials or of pollutable reservoirs, the needs of the then present will determine the solutions of the then present, and there is no use giving ourselves ulcers by worrying about problems that we really do not have to solve. There is even high ethical authority for this point of view in the New Testament, which advocates that we should take no thought for tomorrow and let the dead bury their dead. There has always been something rather refreshing in the view that we should live like the birds, and perhaps posterity is for the birds in more senses than one; so perhaps we should all call

---

[4] Fred L. Polak, *The Image of the Future*, Vols. I and II, translated by Elise Boulding (New York: Sythoff, Leyden and Oceana, 1961).

it a day and go out and pollute something cheerfully. As an old taker of thought for the morrow, however, I cannot quite accept this solution; and I would argue, furthermore, that tomorrow is not only very close, but in many respects it is already here. The shadow of the future spaceship, indeed, is already falling over our spendthrift merriment. Oddly enough, it seems to be in pollution rather than in exhaustion that the problem is first becoming salient. Los Angeles has run out of air, Lake Erie has become a cesspool, the oceans are getting full of lead and DDT, and the atmosphere may become man's major problem in another generation, at the rate at which we are filling it up with gunk. It is, of course, true that at least on a microscale, things have been worse at times in the past. The cities of today, with all their foul air and polluted waterways, are probably not as bad as the filthy cities of the pretechnical age. Nevertheless, that fouling of the nest which has been typical of man's activity in the past on a local scale now seems to be extending to the whole world society; and one certainly cannot view with equanimity the present rate of pollution of any of the natural reservoirs, whether the atmosphere, the lakes, or even the oceans.

I would argue strongly also that our obsession with production and consumption to the exclusion of the "state" aspects of human welfare distorts the process of technological change in a most undesirable way. We are all familiar, of course, with the wastes involved in planned obsolescence, in competitive advertising, and in poor quality of consumer goods. These problems may not be so important as the "view with alarm" school indicates, and indeed the evidence at many points is conflicting. New materials especially seem to edge towards the side of improved durability, such as, for instance, neolite soles for footwear, nylon socks, wash and wear shirts, and so on. The case of household equipment and automobiles is a little less clear. Housing and building construction generally almost certainly has declined in durability since the Middle Ages, but this decline also reflects a change in tastes towards flexibility and fashion and a need for novelty, so that it is not easy to assess. What is clear is that no serious attempt has been made to assess the impact over the whole of economic life of changes in durability, that is, in the ratio of capital in the widest possible sense to income. I suspect that we have underestimated, even in our spendthrift society, the gains from increased durability, and that this might very well be one of the places where the price system needs correction through government-sponsored research and development. The problems which the spaceship earth is going to present, therefore, are not all in the future by any means, and a strong case can be made for paying much more attention to them in the present than we now do.

It may be complained that the considerations I have been putting forth relate only to the very long run, and they do not much concern our immediate problems. There may be some justice in this criticism, and my main excuse is that other writers have dealt adequately with the more immediate problems of deterioration in the quality of the environment. It is true, for instance, that many of the immediate problems of pollution of the atmosphere or of bodies of water arise because of the failure of the price system, and many of them could be solved by corrective taxation. If people had to pay the losses due to the nuisances which they create, a good deal more resources would go into the prevention of nuisances. These arguments involving external economies and diseconomies are familiar to economists, and there is no need to recapitulate them. The law of torts is quite inadequate to provide for the correction of the price system which is required, simply because where damages are widespread and their incidence on any particular person is small, the ordinary remedies of the civil law are quite inadequate and inappropriate. There needs, therefore, to be special legislation to cover these cases, and though such legislation seems hard to get in practice, mainly because of the widespread and small personal incidence of the injuries, the technical problems involved are not insuperable. If we were to adopt in principle a law for tax penalties for social damages, with an apparatus for making assessments under it, a very large proportion of current pollution and deterioration of the environment would be prevented. There are tricky problems of equity involved, particularly where old established nuisances create a kind of "right by purchase" to perpetuate themselves, but these are problems again which a few rather arbitrary decisions can bring to some kind of solution.

The problems which I have been raising in this paper are of larger scale and perhaps much harder to solve than the more practical and immediate problems of the above paragraph. Our success in dealing with the larger problems, however, is not unrelated to the development of skill in the solution of the more immediate and perhaps less difficult problems. One can hope, therefore, that as a succession of mounting crises, especially in pollution, arouse public opinion and mobilize support for the solution of the immediate problems, a learning process will be set in motion which will eventually lead to an appreciation of and perhaps solutions for the larger ones. My neglect of the immediate problems, therefore, is in no way intended to deny their importance, for unless we at least make a beginning on a process for solving the immediate problems we will not have much chance of solving the larger ones. On the other hand, it may also be true that a long-run vision, as it were, of the deep crisis which faces mankind may predispose people to taking more interest in the immediate problems and to devote more effort for their solution. This may sound like a rather modest optimism, but perhaps a modest optimism is better than no optimism at all.

The Learning and Reality-Testing
Process in the International System*

The Aztecs apparently believed that the corn on which their civilization depended would not grow unless there were human sacrifices. What seems to us an absurd belief caused thousands of people to be sacrificed each year. The arguments by which the Aztecs rationalized this image of the world have largely been lost, thanks to the zeal of the Spanish conquerors. One can, however, venture upon an imaginative reconstruction. The fact that the corn did grow was probably considered solid evidence for such a view; and in those years when the harvest was bad, it was doubtless argued that the gods were angry because the sacrifices had been insufficient. A little greater military effort would result, a few more hearts would be torn from their quivering bodies, and the following year it was highly probable that the harvest would be better and the image consequently confirmed. Not only empirical evidence would support the doctrine, however; the great truth that it represented could easily be held to be self-evident. The seed must die if the corn is to grow. We all know, furthermore, that the spectacle of violent death arouses the seed in man and is likely to produce an increase in the population. What could be more resonable, therefore, than to assume that these two phenomena are connected?

If this is a parody, it is too close to the truth to be wholly comfortable. Arguments of this kind have often been used to justify human sacrifice and the image of the world that demands it, whether on the part of a religion or on the part of a state. The sponsors of the Inquisition thought that by roasting some people alive they would save many souls from roasting after death. The proposition that South Vietnam is a domino that has to be propped up by the dropping of napalm, the

---

* *Journal of International Affairs* 30, 1 (1967): 1–15.
This paper was commissioned for the special issue of the journal in which it appeared.

burning of villages, the torture of prisoners, and the sacrifice of American blood is a proposition that appeals to us much more strongly than these others; but it is being tested in much the same way as the Aztecs and the inquisitors tested their views of the world: by appeals to analogy, to self-evidence, and to the principle that if at first you don't succeed try more of the same until you do.

Image and Reality

The problem of what constitutes realism in our image of the world has bothered philosophers from the very beginnings of human thought, and it is certainly far from being resolved. Indeed, Hume may well have demonstrated that it cannot be resolved, simply because images can only be compared with other images and never with reality. Nevertheless, common sense leads us to reject Humean skepticism in practice; we must live and act for the most part as if our images of the world were true. Moreover, there are processes for the detection and elimination of error; so that even though truth constantly eludes us, by the progressive and systematic elimination of error, that is, false images, we may hope that we may gradually approximate it.

The elimination of error is accomplished mainly by feedback. From our image of the world we derive an expectation, that is, an image of the future. As time goes on, the future becomes present and then past. It is then possible to compare our image of the future with our image of the same period when it has become the past. In January we recall our image of December as we had it in November, and we compare this with our image of December as we have it in January. If the images do not correspond, we are disappointed and hence act to adjust one image or the other. There are actually three adjustments that can be made. We can adjust our image of the past and say that it was mistaken, that what apparently happened did not really happen and that we have been misinformed. We can adjust our past image of the future; that is, we can say that the image of December that we had in November was wrong. We can do this for two reasons, for our image of the future is derived by inference from our general view of the world. We can therefore say, on the one hand, that the inference was wrong and that our view of the world did not really imply that December should have turned out the way we expected; or, if we cannot deny the validity of the inference, then we must revise our general image of the world. The elimination of error can take place at all three of these levels.

The elimination of error, however, is only one of the results that disappointment can produce. Error exists primarily in our general image of the world. Disappointment, unfortunately, does not always force a revision in this image, for it can cause us to deny either the image of the past or the inference that gave rise to the image of the future. If a genuine learning process—the continual elimination of error in our image of the world, as well as the enlargement of this image—is to take place, there must be safeguards against rejecting inferences or rejecting the image of the past.

There are two levels of human learning-processes at which these conditions for the progressive elimination of error are met. One is the process of folk learning in everyday life, in which we learn about the immediate world around us and the physical, biological, and social systems that constitute our direct and immediate environment. Here feedback tends to be rapid; the images of the immediate past are especially hard to reject; and, because we are operating with fairly simple systems, the inferences that we draw from our general view of the world are likewise hard to reject. Consequently, disappointment causes us to make revisions in our general image of the world, and if these revisions result in further disappointments they will be further revised until disappointment is reduced to a tolerable level. People who are incapable of responding in this way to the feedbacks of ordinary life eventually find themselves in mental hospitals. Indeed, what we ordinarily think of as mental disease is the inability to perform reality-testing—the progressive elimination of error—on the folk-learning level. If a person's image of the world is entirely self-justified and self-evident, he will soon get into serious trouble. Suppose, for instance, that he is a paranoid and thinks that everybody hates him. All his experience will confirm this image no matter what the experience is. Experience that fails to confirm the image will be dismissed as due to either false inferences or mistaken images of the past. His fundamental image of the world is unshakable by any event that seems to contradict it. Such a person is incapable of learning, and it is this incapacity that really constitutes mental disease.

The other field where error is progressively eliminated and a genuine learning process takes place is in the subculture of science. Contrary to common belief, the method of science does not differ essentially from the method of folk learning. Both proceed through disappointment. (Indeed, it is only through failure that we ever really learn anything new, for success always tends to confirm our existing images.) Both methods are safeguarded against denials of the image of the past, that is, of experience, and against the denial of inferences; hence in both cases experience that does not jibe with an image prompts modifications in the image. The only difference between folk learning and scientific learning is in the degree of complexity of the systems that are involved in each image of the world. Science deals with complex systems and folk learning with simple systems; but the methods by which errors are eliminated are essentially the same. Because of the complexity of the systems with which science deals, however, it must use refined instruments and precise means of measurement in the development of its image of the past. It must likewise use highly refined methods of inference, employing mathematical and logical methods in order to derive its expectations of the future from its image of the world. It is in the refinement of perception and inference, however, not in the essential nature of the learning process, that science distinguishes itself from ordinary folk-learning.

We may perhaps illustrate the difference with reference to our image of space. The folk image of the world is that of a flat earth encased in the dome of the sky. For the ordinary business of life this image is quite adequate, and as long as we confine our movements to our immediate neighborhood it gets us into no trouble. Over a range of ten miles the curvature of the earth is quite irrelevant to the activities of ordinary life; and although the hills and valleys of the surface are much more relevant, we can learn about them through the ordinary processes of folk learning. For an astronaut, however, it would be quite disastrous to take an image derived from folk experience and to generalize it to the world as a whole. An astronaut requires the scientific image of a spherical—indeed, pear-shaped—earth. He must have very refined instruments and means of measurement. He must, at the very least, live in a Newtonian world and be capable of Newtonian inference, and as speeds increase he may even have to make Einsteinian adjustments. The folk image here would lead to immediate and total disaster. Nevertheless, this highly refined image of space has been obtained in ways that differ only in degree of sophistication from the methods by which we derive our image of how to get from our home to the post office.

The Literary Image and the International System

Between the world of folk learning and the folk images derived from it, and the world of scientific learning and the scientific images derived from it, there lies another world of images that I have elsewhere described,[1] perhaps unkindly, as the world of literary images. It is in this world that reality-testing is least effective and that the elimination

---

[1] Kenneth E. Boulding, *The Image* (Ann Arbor: University of Michigan Press, 1956).

of error either does not take place at all or is enormously costly. It is precisely in this world, however, that we find the images of the international system by which its decision-makers are largely governed, and it is for this reason that the international system is by far the most pathological and costly segment of the total social system, or sociosphere, as it is sometimes called. If we look at the various elements of the social system that are ordinarily regarded as pathological, such as crime, mental and physical disease, and economic stagnation, the international system probably costs about as much as all these put together, with the possible exception of economic stagnation, which is itself in part a function of the nature of the international system.

The direct cost of the international system must now amount to something like 150 billion dollars a year. This would include the total spent by all the nations on their military establishments, information systems, foreign offices, diplomatic corps, and so on. In addition, some estimate of the present value of possible future destruction should be included. Any figure placed on this is at best a wild guess. To be pessimistic, let us suppose that the destruction of a third world war would amount to half the present physical capital of the world, or about two thousand billion dollars, and that the chance of this happening is about five per cent in any one year; in this case we should add a kind of depreciation or discounting factor to existing world wealth of about 100 billion dollars a year. This would represent, as it were, an insurance premium for war destruction. A more optimistic assumption of, say, a one per cent chance of a major world war would reduce this to 20 billion annually. It is interesting to note, incidentally, that the size of the current expenditure on the war industry is almost certainly much larger than any reasonable insurance premium for war destruction would be. This points up a general principle that the cost of the war industry for any country in terms of resources withdrawn from the civilian economy is much larger than any insurance premium that might be conceived for a policy covering destruction by enemy forces. This is often true even in time of war. A study of the impact of the war industry on the Japanese economy[2] suggests that even during the Second World War the cost of the Japanese war industry to the Japanese economy was of the same order of magnitude as the destruction by the American war machine. One's friends, in other words, generally do more damage than one's enemies.

---

[2] Kenneth E. Boulding (with Alan Gleason), "War as an Investment: The Strange Case of Japan," *Peace Research Society (International) Papers*, Vol. III, 1965, pp. 1–17.

If we suppose that the gross world product is roughly 1,500 billion dollars, the international system and the war industry account for about ten per cent of this. It would be extremely surprising if all the other pathological elements in the social system taken together account for more than this. Crime and disease are likely to account for no more than five per cent of it, or 75 billion dollars. Even if we include the potential loss resulting from the failure of economic development, and if we suppose that a projected annual growth rate of two per cent is not realized, this would only amount to a loss of 30 billion dollars a year, as a measure of what might be called the pathology of the world economy. Even if we raised this projection to an optimistic four per cent, the loss would only be 60 billion, far below the cost of the international system.

One may object, of course, that it is unfair to regard the cost of the international system as if it were not offset by benefits, even if it is very hard to put a dollar value on them. We get the benefits of nationality: tangible ones like protection when we go abroad, and intangible ones like the sense of identity that thrills to the flag, that expands beyond the narrow limits of family and locality, and that responds gladly to the call for self-sacrifice. The sense of satisfaction that comes from being American or German or British or whatever is certainly an important benefit, however hard it is to evaluate. It must be recognized, however, that such advantages of nationality are virtually the only advantages of the nation-state system. There are no economic payoffs to the present system; indeed, in addition to the loss of resources we should also add the cost of tariffs and trade restrictions, and of the almost universally deleterious effects on the rate of development caused by high military expenditures. There was a time, perhaps, when the international system paid off for its principle beneficiaries, the great powers, in terms of the economic exploitation of their colonial empires. Even if the international system produced little gain for the world as a whole, it could be argued that it redistributed the world product in favor of those who played the international game successfully and became great powers. Today even this argument has little validity. Empire in the last 100 years has turned out to be a burden rather than an asset, and in terms of the rate of economic growth, being a great power has not paid off. The British and French growth rates, for instance, from 1860 on were considerably less than those of many less ambitious countries, such as Sweden or even Japan. The German and Japanese attempts to become great powers were enormously costly; but their ultimate failure provides an even more striking insight into the realities of the present international system.

After total military defeat and a complete loss of their great-power status, they have both achieved absolutely unprecedented rates of economic growth, far exceeding the growth rates of the victors.

This is indeed a strange world, in which nothing fails like success and nothing succeeds like defeat, in which great powers find that their greatness impoverishes them, and in which the way to get rich is to stay home and mind one's own business well and to participate as little as possible in the international system. Of course there are also historical examples of countries for whom defeat has been disastrous, though such examples are rather scarce since Carthage, or perhaps Byzantium. It is also possible to find examples of countries that stayed home and minded their own business badly. Such examples, however, do not affect the fundamental proposition that at least since 1860, when the impact of the scientific revolution on economic life really began to be felt, we have been living in a world that is qualitatively different from that of the past, a world in which, as I have said elsewhere, one can extract ten dollars from nature for every dollar one can exploit out of man. The scientific revolution, therefore, has completely eliminated any economic payoffs that might have been available through the international system in the past. And while diminishing the system's returns, the scientific revolution has at the same time enormously increased the cost of the system. In order to justify the continuation of this costly and precarious system, we have to put an enormous value on the nation-state as such and on the national identity it confers on the individual. It should at least be asked whether the value of these things is commensurate with the risks and costs of maintaining the system.

The Pathological State of the International System

What, then, are the sources of this pathological state of the international system? A number of answers can be given. Most significantly, a system of unilateral national defense, which still characterizes the international system in spite of the small beginnings of world political organization, is a "prisoner's dilemma" system:[3] the dynamics of the system produce an equilibrium in which everybody is much worse off than in some alternative state of the system. In the two-country version of this system, let us suppose that each country has two choices: disarm or arm. They will clearly be better off economically and more secure

---

[3] Anatol Rapoport and Albert M. Chammah, *Prisoner's Dilemma: A Study in Conflict and Cooperation* (Ann Arbor: University of Michigan Press, 1965).

politically if they both disarm. If both are disarmed, however, it pays one to arm—at least it may in terms of his image of the system. And if one is armed, the other will have a powerful incentive to follow suit. Both will probably end up by being armed, in which case both will be worse off than they would have been had they remained disarmed.

Whether there is an equilibrium in the world war-industry depends largely on the reactions of the parties concerned. The fundamental parameter here is the "reactivity coefficient," that is, the extent to which one country will increase its arms expenditures for each additional dollar that it perceives being spent on arms in another country. I have shown in another paper[4] that in a two-country system the product of the reactivity coefficients must be less than one if there is to be an equilibrium; otherwise the war industry will expand explosively until the system breaks down as the result of war or of some sort of parametric change. It can also be shown that the more parties there are in the system, the smaller the reactivity coefficient must be if an equilibrium is to be attained. It must certainly average less than one. As a reactivity coefficient of one might be regarded as normal, it is clear that a system of this kind must be abnormally unreactive if it is to achieve an equilibrium. It is not surprising, therefore, in the light of existing reactivity coefficients, which are certainly close to one if not above it, that the world war-industry maintains an uneasy and continually upward-groping equilibrium at about 140 billion dollars per year. Furthermore, this equilibrium, even if it exists, is inherently precarious in that a very slight change in the reactivity coefficients even on the part of a single country can destroy the equilibrium altogether.

The reactivity coefficients are themselves functions of the value systems of the decision-makers and of their general image of the international system, or perhaps of their images of other people's reactivity. And all these in turn are related to the gathering and processing of the information on which the decision-makers depend. The pathology of the international system, therefore, is closely related to the method by which it generates and processes information and the way in which these information inputs influence the decision-makers' images of the world. The question as to what is meant by the "reality" of these images in the international system is a very difficult one. In the first place, insofar as the system itself is determined by the decisions of a relatively small number of decision-makers it inevitably contains a considerable

---

[4] Kenneth E. Boulding, "The Parameters of Politics," *University of Illinois Bulletin* (July 15, 1966), pp. 1–21.

random element. The image of the system, therefore, should always be an image of probabilities rather than certainties. There is no very good way, however, of finding out what the probabilities of the system are. We do not have enough cases to compute frequencies like the life tables of insurance companies, and whenever one hears the expression "a calculated risk" in international politics one tends to interpret this as meaning "I really don't have the slightest notion." The epistemological problem itself, in the case of international systems, is very difficult; and one certainly cannot come up with any perfect solution for the problem of producing truth in the image of the system, for the system itself consists in considerable part of the images about it.

Even if the truth in an absolute sense may elude us, this still does not prevent us from discussing health, or at least disease, and there are certain diseases of the information system (and the images it produces) in the international system that can be diagnosed. The basic problem, as I have suggested earlier, is that adequate images of the international system cannot be derived from folk learning, because the simple feedbacks of the folk-learning process are quite inadequate to deal with the enormous complexities of the international system. At the present time, however, the role of science is extremely limited, indeed, almost nonexistent. We do not apply scientific techniques of information gathering and processing, even those available in the social sciences, to the image-creating processes of the international system. Social science, indeed, is regarded with considerable suspicion by most of the professional practitioners in the international system, perhaps rightly so, for it represents a certain threat to their status and power. On the whole, therefore, the images of the international system in the minds of its decision-makers are derived by a process that I have described as "literary"—a melange of narrative history, memories of past events, stories and conversations, etc., plus an enormous amount of usually ill-digested and carelessly collected current information. When we add to this the fact that the system produces strong hates, loves, loyalties, disloyalties, and so on, it would be surprising if any images were formed that even remotely resembled the most loosely defined realities of the case.

Almost every principle we have learned about scientific information gathering, processing, and reality-testing is violated by the processes of the international system. Indeed, the conflict of values between the subculture of science and the subculture of the international system may well turn out to be one of the most fundamental conflicts of our age. In science secrecy is abhorrent and veracity is the highest virtue. In science there is only one mortal sin: telling a deliberate lie. In the international system, on the other hand, secrecy is paramount and veracity is subordinated to the national interest. The national interest can indeed be said to legitimate almost every conceivable form of evil: there is not one of the seven deadly sins that is not made into a virtue by the international system. Another fundamental characteristic of the scientific community is that it is basically a community of equals, for the very good reason that hierarchy always corrupts communication. A dialogue can only exist between equals. In a hierarchy there is an inescapable tendency toward pleasing the superior, and hence confirming his own ideas. Hierarchy in organizations, therefore, produces a condition akin to paranoia in individuals. The information-gathering apparatus always tends to confirm the existing image of the top decision-makers, no matter what it is. This organizational "mental illness" is nowhere better illustrated than in the international system, which is composed of numerous foreign-office and military-establishment hierarchies that thrive on self-justifying images.

Finally, in the scientific community power is supposed to have a low value and truth the highest value, whereas in the international system the reverse is the case. It is not surprising that under these circumstances the international system is so spectacularly pathological in an organizational sense. Indeed, if one were designing an organization to produce pathological results, one could hardly do better than an information system dependent mainly on spies and diplomats. This is not to say, of course, that the individuals who occupy these roles in the international system are themselves necessarily crazy, although they do suffer from certain occupational diseases. On the whole, the people who run the international system are well above average in intelligence and education and even in personal morality, for they would probably not be content to serve in a system so absurd if they did not possess high moral ideals. Economic man does not go into the international system. He can live a better life outside it. It is the moral, patriotic, and self-sacrificing individuals who are most likely to be the active participants in the international system. It is the organization, not the individuals, which is pathological, by reason of the corruption of both the information and the values that have produced it.

Can the System Be Cured?

The next question, therefore, is whether we can learn to change the organization in ways that will make the whole system less pathological.

There seem to be two general answers to this question. One is given by the advocates of world government, who feel that the defects of the present international system cannot be remedied and that therefore the only solution is to abolish it by transferring the locus of sovereignty from independent states to a world government. It is argued that this is a logical extension of the ongoing process in which smaller states have been absorbed or federated into larger ones, and that we have now reached the point where the existing international system is so dangerous and so costly that the sacrifice of national sovereignty sacrifices nothing but the dangers and costs. Only world government, it is argued, can prevent war or establish anything that even remotely resembles justice.

A somewhat less drastic view holds that stable peace is possible within the framework of an international system, given certain conditions, and that therefore world government in the strict sense is unnecessary. It is argued, in effect, that the pathological character of the international system which is so striking today is not necessary, but is rather a function of certain parameters and characteristics of the system, and that a nonpathological, healthy international system is conceivable and possible. Such a rehabilitated system, it is felt, might be more desirable in many ways than a unified world government.

These two approaches may not be as contradictory as they seem at first sight, though they do represent, in effect, two different solutions to the problem of the prisoner's dilemma, which, as we have seen, is at the root of the pathology of the international system. One solution to the prisoner's-dilemma problem is to change the payoffs of the game through the intervention of some third party. This is in effect what law, especially in its penal aspect, is supposed to do. The prisoner's dilemma in a sense governs all forms of the social contract, where each party has the choice of being either "good" or "bad." If they are all good, they will all be better off; and yet if they are all good it may pay one of them to be bad, in which case it pays all of them to be bad and they all end up worse off. The function of law and of government, in its role as the creator and sustainer of law, is that of altering the payoffs for the individual decision-maker so that it will not pay him to be bad even if everybody else is good. The business of government, then, is to define what is "bad" and to see that this kind of behavior is appropriately penalized so that the social contract is not broken.

The other approach to the problem of the prisoner's dilemma is the development of farsightedness on the part of the players themselves. This involves a learning process, and as Anatol Rapoport's experiments have suggested,[5] many people do learn after a while that "bad behavior" does not pay off in the long run. Hence they refrain from trying to gain temporary advantages that unilateral bad behavior might give them.

In the long-run development of the international system, both these processes may be observed. On the one hand, we have seen the development of supranational political institutions of slowly increasing capacity: the Concert of Europe, the League of Nations, and the United Nations. Each catastrophe apparently teaches mankind to set up institutions that might have prevented it, though they usually do not prevent the next catastrophe. Just as the generals are always supposed to be prepared to fight the last war, so the international institutions are designed to prevent it. The slow learning process nevertheless goes on, and the institutions themselves can be regarded as repositories of political skill and knowledge. Indeed, for the meagre resources that we devote to the international order, we get a remarkable return. This becomes apparent when we consider that the combined budget for all the international agencies is less than that of the Ford Foundation.

Along with this process of developing world political institutions, we have also seen the development of areas of stable peace within the international system even without supranational institutions. The two best examples are probably North America and Scandinavia, though the socialist camp may be another example and perhaps by this time all of Europe, although it is a bit early to say. Stable peace, at any rate, is a recognizable phase of the international system, which tends to pass into this phase when a certain level of maturity in national behavior has been reached. One might even suppose, perhaps a bit optimistically, that relations between the United States and the Soviet Union might develop as they have between the United States and Canada or among the Scandinavian countries.

The growth of stable peace requires a learning process on the part of the national decision-makers, a learning process that includes the accumulation of tradition and role images which are passed on from role occupant to role occupant. The process involves a change in values as well as in actual images of the system, and these are closely related in a very intricate and complex manner. The nation-state can no longer be treated as a sacred institution; there must be a deflation of the emotions and values that attach to it, a decline, if you

---

[5] Anatol Rapoport, *op. cit.*

will, in the passion with which people love their countries and an acceptance of the nation-state and the nation-state system as essentially mundane institutions designed solely for public convenience.

One great problem that the world is likely to face in this connection is that the maturation process of the nation-state takes place at different rates, so that at any one time some are much more mature than others. This, however, may give the immature ones an advantage, since they will be able to elicit more passionate devotion to the national cause from their citizens. This is perhaps one of the most persuasive reasons why the mature states, who have outgrown the adolescent disease of nationalism, should be all the more concerned to set up world political institutions that have some hope of exercising restraint on the less mature states. What might be called the "mature-conflict-behavior solution" of the prisoner's dilemma depends on both parties being mature. If only one party is mature, then a third-party alteration of the payoffs is the only solution, which in this case means world government.

The development of the social sciences and especially of a genuine social science of the international system, which is only in its infancy, is likely to have a substantial effect on the progress of the international system toward maturity. War is a crude, extremely expensive but often effective form of reality-testing, which has the added disadvantage of changing the reality to be tested. The improvement of the information system and the prevailing images of the international system that would follow from the development of a genuine social science of the international system would almost certainly have the effect of diminishing the probability of what might be called unintended war, that is, war that results from a lack of realism in the estimate of the consequences of decisions. Thus it is highly probable that the war of 1914 would not have occurred if the international system had possessed a more objective, carefully sampled, and adequately processed information system, which could have given the makers of a number of disastrous decisions a different image of the system. A more realistic image might have prevented these decisions, even without any change in ultimate values.

An improvement in the information system, however, would not leave ultimate values unchanged. The development, for instance, of a certain measure or index of success is likely to direct attention toward that aspect of the system which the index measures and to cause a high value to be placed on it. Thus the development of a way to measure the rate of economic growth has profoundly affected the valuation that many political decision-makers now place upon economic policy.

Similarly, a measure of, shall we say, the general level of hostility in the international system, which would be quite within the present capability of the social sciences, might have a very profound effect not only on the image of the world held by the international decision-makers but also on the values they apply to it.

One word of hesitation and warning is worth making here, along the lines of Alexander Pope's admonition about a little learning. The image of the international system even in the best informed minds is subject to a large amount of uncertainty, and the decisions that are made in it should reflect the real uncertainties of the system. In a system of great uncertainty, he who hesitates is frequently saved. There is a danger that the techniques of the social sciences might be used to give an illusion of certainty where none exists. There is some evidence that war-gaming has had this effect, which could easily be disastrous. There is danger also that value systems are moved too easily in the direction of what is measurable and apparently known. Decision-making in systems as complex as the international system inevitably requires the operation of the unconscious as well as the conscious mind. The wisdom in decision-making that comes from wide experience and an almost unconscious appreciation of reality is not as good as explicit knowledge. Nevertheless when knowledge lingers, as it inevitably must, wisdom will have to do; and an attitude of mind that rejects wisdom in favor of imperfect knowledge may easily be disastrous. In this connection, the present tendency to try to develop rational modes of behavior in decision-making must be looked upon with a great deal of suspicion as well as some enthusiasm. Nevertheless, to reject knowledge where it exists in favor of a doubtful wisdom is no wisdom at all. The development of improved methods of collecting and processing information from the international system by such techniques as sample surveys, content analysis, correlation and factor analysis of complex systems, and the whole expansion of information processing and indexing that the computer makes possible is almost bound to have a maturing effect on the national images, both in regard to realism of content and humaneness of values.

The one possible cause for optimism about the international system is that there exists what might be called a "macro-learning" process, which seems to be cumulative in much the same way as science. It is only within the last 200 years, for instance, that we have achieved something that could be called a security community or stable peace in segments of the international system. During that period, we can trace something that looks like a progression from stable war into unstable war into unstable peace and finally into stable peace. As experience accumulates and as the memory of disastrous feedbacks affects present images of the system, these more mature images become a kind of folk wisdom that is transmitted from generation to generation, however precariously; and with the rise of genuinely scientific images of the international system we may expect this cumulative learning process to accelerate. It is reasonable to hope, therefore, that we may be fairly close to that key watershed in which the international system passes from a condition of unstable peace, albeit with enclaves of stable peace, into one in which stable peace becomes a property of the general system, which still however may have enclaves of unstable peace within it. At the moment, it must be admitted, the enclaves of stable peace appear as figures upon a ground of unstable peace. However, a little expansion of the figures to include, let us say, all of Europe, the United States, the Soviet Union, and Japan, and the ground will become the figure and the figure the ground. Quantitatively this change may be very small; yet it will be a watershed, and the system will never be the same again. One may then expect the enclaves of unstable peace to diminish as the learning process continues, until finally the vision of a world in stable peace, which has haunted mankind so elusively for so long, will finally be realized. When it is realized it will be the result of a long process of learning, in which cheap methods of learning such as science and perhaps even accumulated folk wisdom are substituted for the expensive methods of learning such as war.